CRITICAL ACCLAIM

"An honest and wholehearted attempt to fulfill a task that is incumbent upon us all, whatever our faith: to get beneath the layers of self-righteousness and defensiveness that have accumulated over the centuries, to learn from the complexities of history, and to make our traditions speak with compassion and respect to our dangerously polarized world."

> — *Karen Armstrong,* New York Times *bestselling author of* A History of God: The 4,000-Year Quest of Judaism, Christianity and Islam

"Reading Liepert's book left me feeling rejuvenated.... Liepert remains hopeful that we can change, that we can live together in peace, that instead of being the problem, our religions might become the solution — if we're willing to listen to what they actually say.... I highly recommend this book."

> — *Sheila Musaji, founder and editor of* The American Muslim

"A fascinating read.... His reflections on the teachings and interrelationship of the Abrahamic traditions provide fresh and valuable insights for religious leaders, students, and all who are interested in interreligious understanding."

> — *John L. Esposito, author of* The Future of Islam *and Professor of Religion and International Affairs at Georgetown University*

"Dr. David Liepert is a brilliant new North American Muslim voice. He has put much work into his tireless efforts, building bridges between our faiths and civilizations. I know his commitment to dialogue, respect, and understanding among different faiths, and I hope this work will be another step towards that vision."

> — *Dr. Imam Hamid Slimi, Chairman of the Canadian Council of Imams*

"One danger of interfaith dialogue is that differences in theology or dogma can be so smoothed over or diluted that the integrity of each religion is sacrificed for the sake of an ecumenical consensus. Dr. David Liepert's Muslim, Christian, and Jew takes a very different path. As much a fascinating spiritual autobiography as a plea for interfaith understanding, Liepert (who has been engaged in interfaith dialogue for many years) confronts rather than waters down differences in a textual criticism of the three Abrahamic religions. This often takes the form of an internal dialogue, particularly when dealing with his own conversion from an evangelical Christianity to what might be described as an evangelical Islam.

"The binding thread to this book is a recurrent and impassioned plea for the practitioners of Islam, Christianity, and Judaism to transcend their undeniable differences and relatively recent past histories on the basis of that 'Common Word' shared by all three religions — love of God and love of neighbor — and to apply this core conviction existentially and not just affirm it."

— *S. Abdallah Schleifer, Reviewer for the Oxford* Journal of Islamic Studies, *Distinguished Professor of Journalism at the American University in Cairo, former Cairo bureau chief for NBC News*

MUSLIM, CHRISTIAN, *AND* JEW

Finding a Path to Peace
Our Faiths Can Share

DR. DAVID LIEPERT

FAITH OF LIFE PUBLISHING

For information, address:

Faith of Life Publishing
P.O. Box #399
Station Etobicoke B
Toronto, Ontario
Canada M9W 5L3
E-mail: publisher@faithoflifepublishing.com

For foreign and translation rights, contact Nigel J. Yorwerth.
E-mail: nigel@publishingcoaches.com

ISBN: 978-0-9813882-0-5

10 9 8 7 6 5 4 3 2 1

Cover design: Nita Ybarra
Interior design: Alan Barnett

Grateful acknowledgements to Nigel J. Yorwerth, Patricia Spadaro, and the expert team at Yorwerth Associates/PublishingCoaches.com for their invaluable advice and guidance every step of the way.

CONTENTS

PREFACE

This will likely be different from any other book on religion you've ever read. Virtually every other religious book portrays the act of *believing*—the decision a believer makes to accept that his or her own religion's particular assumptions and explanations are true—as if it is a good thing. Frankly, I think believing is dangerous.

Everyone believes something. Even those of us who don't believe *in* anything at all still believe that we're right. No matter *what* we believe, we each cherish our own perspectives, but since most assume that anyone who disagrees with us has to be at least to some extent wrong, some feel obliged to deride the rest. As a result, when people with different religions interact, an anxious and judgmental air often enters into our encounters, which can inflame even the most minor disagreement. Religious diversity makes it easy to condemn those whose beliefs deviate from ours as irreconcilably "different," and all too often, the next thing you know, we're killing each other.

Here, I've sought more of a consensus. It's been attempted before, with questionable success, but I have the advantage of a new approach. Most books that try to bridge the gaps between our different religions are brought up short by one problematic fact: every religion we've got seems designed to prevent its members from thinking that they're too similar to the members of the others or that they'll be able to get along too well with the rest. But I use that supposed obstacle as my starting point.

Given the state of the world, it might surprise you to learn that the Quran actually tells Muslims we're only allowed to argue about religion if we think it's going to stop people from hurting each other. As a Muslim myself, I'm supposed to take that injunction seriously. However, with four children growing up I've decided I have to do my bit to limit the crossfire they could be caught in when they enter the world on their own. My bout with cancer three years ago also reminded me that I'm not going to be able to keep them safe by myself forever. Since I *am* allowed to argue with people when they're hurting each other, I've chosen to address this book primarily to followers of Islam, Christianity, and Judaism, because so much damage is being done in the names of those faiths, but I hope it's useful to anyone who reads it, whatever his or her faith or lack thereof.

The thrust of my argument is simple: All of us think that our religion is "good" and that those in apparent (and often politically motivated) opposition to it are "bad." But the real truth is that all of our religions are equally guilty of being used to promote violence, and—thanks to centuries of political manipulation that have distorted the way we read our holy books—all of us are equally guilty of not following what our religions really say. In all honesty, are any of us as good as we think we are?

That's the challenge I confront in Part I, "The Problem with Religion." I look at the growing body count—the grim tally of Christians, Muslims, and Jews through the centuries killing each other in the name of God— and the paradox it presents: If our religions are really helping us be better people, shouldn't they be making us do good things for each other instead? It's enough to make us ask what purpose belief is serving and what our religions are for in the first place. Do our different faiths only doom us to fighting with each other, or are they meant for something more?

To find the right answers, you have to ask the right questions. Part II, "Beginning with Christianity," charts my journey of questioning from the very start. Growing up as a Christian, I believed that the path to heaven was believing the right things about God, the way the Bible taught them. But every religion claims to be leading its followers along the true path, following its own books and revelations, and this troubled me, until I realized that when you look at what the books actually say, they're really not that different. Armed with this conviction, I set out to make my Muslim friends into Christians, using the books as backup. Then, when I read both the Bible and the Quran carefully, instead of helping me prove I was right, they took the other side—and showed me that being "right" or "wrong" wasn't all that important to one's experience of God after all. As I probed the history of the differences between Islam, Christianity, and Judaism— from cultural shifts to scriptural revisionism—I came to understand the pressures that had forced these faiths so far apart, and I began to hope that they could find their way back together.

Christianity taught me that different religions can serve God in different ways, and being different doesn't make them wrong. Islam taught me that different people can serve God in different ways, too, and that doesn't make them wrong either. In Part III, "Into Islam," I explore how Islam has gone from being a religion capable of sustaining a vibrant multicultural and multireligious civilization to the source of intolerance and conflict we have today. Muhammad predicted this, saying that we would fight over religion and politics until we forgot what was important. Well, we've been fighting over the Quran for the last thousand years. We've been so busy fighting over who's right about what it says that we've forgotten to read it, and fighting over the path has driven us so far from it that many of us don't even recognize it anymore. But under the guidance of their holy books, the earliest Muslims lived with vibrant diversity; those books can show today's Muslims how to live with other people, too.

And that includes Jews. Judaism wasn't created just to set Jews apart from the rest of us, and Islam wasn't revealed to condemn Jews or Judaism. The Covenant of justice and brotherhood speaks to all the children of Abraham; when the Torah calls for love, charity, kindness, and fulfilling our promises to God, it uses a Hebrew word that's almost identical to the Arabic term in the Quran. Part IV, "Working with Judaism," takes a close look at the path this faith has followed, from the first days of the Covenant to the conflict in the Middle East—driven by forces less religious than political—and posits a solution: if *we* made politics, and we believe that *God* made *us*, shouldn't our faith lead our politics instead of the other way around?

The Torah showed me that God wants us to learn to get along, and all our religions are trying to tell us how. We just have to listen—and to do that, we need a fresh approach to faith. Part V, "Faith: The Solution," explores belief and human nature in a new light to explain how Freud's theories of the subconscious and the quantum physics' model of the subatomic universe provide some of the best proof we have that God exists. In Part V, I also offer a way to restore religion to its rightful role in our lives and our world and conclude that we're all a lot closer to where we should be than we think.

I'm convinced that every religion I've studied has value for those who choose to follow it with care. At the same time, each of our faiths has dark places we often choose to avoid. As we journey through them together, I'll ask that you stay with me until we're done. Once you see where I'm going, I think you'll understand the reasons for the path I took to get there.

AUTHOR'S NOTE

Muslim, Christian, and Jew covers a lot of ground, and I've worked hard to give a balanced and respectful presentation of every system of belief that I touch upon. I sincerely hope that no one who reads this book will find offense in it. One matter I struggled with was which pronoun to use for the Creator. Even though I wrote the first draft using a nice, nonsexist "They," I learned most readers found that too confusing, so I settled on "He," despite that pronoun's obvious inadequacies.

Unless otherwise stated, standard Bible quotations are from the Holy Bible, New International Version, reprinted with the kind permission of Zondervan Publishing, and the apocryphal quotations are from *The New Oxford Annotated Apocrypha*, with thanks to Oxford University Press. I used Abdullah Yusuf Ali's translation of *The Meaning of the Holy Quran*, but found my Hadiths and Sunnah (the words and acts of the Prophet Muhammad) in a number of places. The material enclosed in parentheses within the set-off quotations from the Quran are the additions of Abdullah Yusuf Ali, and the parenthetical material in the quotations from the other Muslim texts are the additions of their respective translators. Islam has a strong oral tradition, and I am indebted to Imam Hamid Slimi in Toronto and Imam Jamal Hamoud, Alaa Elsayed, and Dr. Reda Bedeir in Calgary for their help. I have carefully confirmed the validity of each translation with at least two sources.

PART I

THE PROBLEM
WITH RELIGION

CHAPTER 1

....

THE PURPOSE
OF RELIGION

Given a choice, you know we'd all prefer to go to heaven when we die. Heaven is why most people who believe in God belong to their religions: we all hope to God they'll help us get there. That hope is something virtually every believer shares. Whether you believe in God or not, I expect we can all agree that if heaven exists, it's reserved for people who deserve it. Believers will all agree that the ones who deserve it have made the right choices in their lives. In fact, most of our religions don't even disagree about what most of those choices are. The deal that they offer us is quite a simple one: in return for belonging to them, they tell us what we're supposed to do to become the sort of people that our God wants us to be, and then they help us make those choices instead of the alternatives. As a bonus, most of them even throw in leaders to guide us and a community where we can belong. It's all supposed to work together, making us more deserving of our heavenly reward.

If that's all true, then it follows that believers who belong to "good" religions should be people of obvious goodness, and the most committed among us should be the best ones of all. Every religion claims it's good, and most of us obviously think our own is wonderful, but if *that* were true, don't you think we'd be seeing some positive results by now? We're not: around the world, arguments and conflicts rage just as they always have. Our planet remains an awfully dangerous place for the most part, religion seems responsible for much of the bloodshed, and it may even be getting worse. Even though most believers blame the trouble on all the people who are following religions that are different from their own, it seems that every one of our faiths ends up being blamed by someone.

Why do we all care so much what other people believe? If our own faith is only supposed to help us make it into heaven, then other people's beliefs should hardly matter to us at all. However, few religious leaders seem content with quietly looking after the posthumous prospects of their own followers anymore. Islam, Judaism, and Christianity in particular are often invoked to justify or even encourage the active preemption of other faiths. Each claims to be the finest guide extant on how to live a good and proper life. Each claims to be God's gift not only to its own members, but to the rest of the world as well. Despite that, whenever our religions find themselves in conflict all our faith seems more like a curse than a blessing, both to us and to the rest of the world. That's unfortunate, because Muslims, Christians, and Jews in particular really should be able to get along.

I'm Muslim, and I have a friend and colleague who's an Orthodox Jew. We once took a quiz that claimed to be able to predict someone's religion from his or her answers to a series of forty questions. Both of us scored between 99 and 100 percent Muslim and 99 and 100 percent Jewish simultaneously! Although it might be hard to believe, the teachings of Judaism and Islam about our relationship to our Creator and to the rest of creation are hard to tell apart. Christianity is not much different; its only significant departures from the other two are its insistence that God has three distinct personalities and the importance it ascribes to believing this. But all three religions stress the importance of honoring our relationship with God. All three teach us that our actions matter and that what we do influences the way we experience faith and grace. All three say that choosing to do what's right, pleasing God, exercising faith, and accepting God's gracious acceptance of us in return will grant us our heavenly reward.

We do have our differences. Jews don't believe that Jesus is the Messiah, or Muhammad a prophet. Christians think that Jesus is both Messiah and God. Muslims believe that God is God, Jesus was (and is) the Jewish Messiah, and Muhammad was the last prophet to be given a revelation in the words of the Holy Quran. Most people act as though those differences overwhelm any similarities and sometimes even any hope for peaceful coexistence. Muslims, Christians, and Jews share the same Creator, many prophets, and much of their history, yet many of us seem convinced that the members of the other two religions are either misguided or evil. If we believe that, then we'll inevitably end up not getting along, but none of us think we're the bad ones. We're all sure that we're the believers following the only religion that's on the right track, and we anticipate the eventual demise of any alternatives. We've been waiting for thousands of years for that to happen. Now we seem to be getting impatient—and maybe even trying to help things along.

Judaism has a precedent for what to do when different religions think that they're on the same path. When Christianity was just beginning, a wise old rabbi named Gamaliel said:

> "Men of Israel, consider carefully what you intend to do to these men. Some time ago Theudas appeared, claiming to be somebody, and about four hundred men rallied to him. He was killed, all his followers were dispersed, and it all came to nothing. After him, Judas the Galilean appeared in the days of the census and led a band of people in revolt. He too was killed, all his followers were dispersed, and it all came to nothing. Therefore, in the present case I advise you: Leave these men alone! Let them go! For if their purpose or activity is of human origin, it will fail. But if it is from God, you will not be able to stop these men; you will only find yourselves fighting against God!"

You can find the quote in Acts 5:34–39 in the Christian Bible. The principle Gamaliel presented is really quite simple. According to him, believers should trust God to look after everyone's place in the big picture. The idea is basic to Judaism and the God it describes, and obviously, the people who included this comment in the Bible appreciated Gamaliel's perspective. Even Islam's Holy Quran agrees that every one of us has a place in God's plan. Al Baqara 2:62 proclaims:

> Those who believe in the Quran, and those who follow the Jewish Scriptures, and the Christians and the Sabians—any who believe in Allah and the Last Day, and work righteousness, shall have their reward with their Lord, and on them shall be no fear, nor shall they grieve.

Gamaliel predicted that religions without divine support would simply pass away, but there's little question that Judaism, Christianity, and Islam are all here to stay. Islam and Christianity both have over a billion adherents worldwide; they're the two largest religions in the world! Islam in its current form has been practiced for over a thousand years, and Christianity has been around for almost twice that long. Judaism has survived for even longer, and even though it's much smaller than the other two religions, its influence and power are greater than its size would suggest. Based on the comments recorded in our holy books (and the fact that we're all still here), it looks like God's pretty comfortable with all three religions. However, we still spend a lot of time fighting with each other. If we were the only victims, that would be tragedy enough; but as time goes by and our capabilities for inflicting injury increase, our battles hurt everyone else more and more. Before they go on much further, I think it's time to ask ourselves whether fighting is really what God wants us to do.

Most religions attract followers by offering to do the same three things. Their primary function—the one that's most dependent on the existence of a deity—is to help us become what God wants us to be. They tell us what it will take to make God happy, explain to us why we should try, provide background to explain some of our questions, and then (occasionally) give us specific instructions to follow, leaders to listen to, and a community where we can belong. A good religion leaves us with an internally consistent way to live. While all those "ways" have a fair bit of variation between them, each well-designed religion makes sure that its expectations, explanations, background, instructions, rules, and rewards follow a logical progression within itself.

The second promise religions make is that their internally consistent way of living will be objectively good. It's true that each religion encourages or forbids a few things that don't matter as much to other religions. Dietary restrictions, marriage customs, and rules for how we deal with each other financially are common and understandable areas for variation. Different cultures have different needs, and religions have always had to be sensitive to that. There are far more important matters that everyone agrees are either right or wrong. For example, both murder and oppression are almost universally condemned.

Since God is the Ultimate Good, most religions claim that their way is good in an ultimate sense, too. In fact, good is so important that most religions replace the idea of regular good with an absolute sort of goodness that's supposed to be far better. In English, it's called "righteousness," but instead of helping us become the best we can be, righteousness seems to be what's getting us all into trouble with each other. While we all agree that subjective goodness (we think we're good) is a step in the right direction, and objective goodness (everyone else thinks we're good) is even better, we're all convinced that righteousness is the best good of all. It's supposed to be what happens when you're doing exactly what God wants, so God thinks you're good, too. Religions all have their own pathway there—an inside track for committed followers. Some of us choose to follow that path—even though it's often not easy, popular, or much fun—because we believe that if you're righteous, there's no question that you deserve the greatest reward of all. Righteousness trumps either subjective or objective goodness. If you're righteous, you're good no matter what anyone else thinks.

Tragically, if we look at history, we learn that those of us who are the most convinced we're righteous often don't look particularly good to anyone. The self-righteous mayhem being committed by believing Muslims, Christians, and Jews today graphically illustrates the true extent of the problem. Muslims call Islam the religion of peace, and we all claim that we're only trying to make the world a better place. By now, most people have learned that *jihad* really means "striving" and has nothing to do with terrorism. If only someone would tell the terrorists. Christians also maintain that they are only trying to make the world a fairer, better place and that they live meekly, mildly, and lovingly, like Jesus said. However, many of them have interpreted that to mean they should make the world a better place for *them*, while the rest of us accept it meekly and mildly. Most of us are left wondering if that's what Jesus really had in mind. Finally, despite the fact that most believing Jews honestly think that they're bringing the goodness of God to the Middle East, that sentiment rings true only if you believe that God wants to be good to just a few of us, who should be protected from the rest with tanks, walls, artillery, and a standing force at arms.

If any of us were actually as good as we think we are, the world would be very different from the way it looks now. Muslims would be recognized around the world as peacemakers and sought out as neighbors. Property values would soar when a Muslim moved into the neighborhood! The Christian nations of the world would be renowned for their generosity, patience, and restraint, and Israel would be a land of peace and security for everyone. Instead, Islam has become the religion of war, terrorism, hatred, and revenge; Christianity has turned into both the source of and the justification for most of the economic inequity in the world; and Zionism has created a state in Israel whose security comes only at the cost of the suffering and death of thousands of innocent Jewish and non-Jewish souls alike.

It's true that we all have our saints as well as our sinners, and it's unfair to judge any religion by either extreme. There are also many self-proclaimed "followers" in all these faiths whose actions make it obvious that they have no fear of God at all. We can't blame everything on them, though, because apparently committed believers—members who think they represent the mainstream of their faiths and have the full support of their fellows—are doing most of the damage. We can deny our own culpability and responsibility as much as we like, but if we want to ensure that all our self-defense and reassurance isn't just self-satisfied, self-serving self-deception, we should look more closely at how often bad things happen—and how often Christians, Muslims, and Jews turn out to be the ones doing them.

- **Everybody who's got a religion thinks that it's the (only) right one.**
- **All believers think that their religion is helping them to be good.**
- **In all honesty, are any of us as good as we think we are?**

························

CHAPTER 2

THE GROWING
BODY COUNT

When you look at the world today, it's obvious that there's something wrong, either with our religions or with us. The body count we're generating is a sad sign of just how bad things are—for everyone. The precise numbers are lost in the depths of time, but the World Christian Encyclopedia estimates that over two hundred million people have lost their lives to religion in the last two thousand years, the majority of them to someone claiming to follow one of our three sets of religious instructions. In our defense, we've mostly killed each other—at least up to now. Christians have done away with some seventy million unfortunate souls who either weren't Christian or were the wrong sort in the wrong place at the wrong time. Muslims have killed about the same number, almost all of them other Muslims, in our battles over who's supposed to be in charge. The only ones who haven't collected as much blood per capita on their hands in the last two millennia have been the Jews—and honestly, that's probably been due to lack of opportunity. The Bible does tell of some significant slaying in the ancient Kingdom of Israel, and recently Israel's security has justified an awful lot of preemptive strikes against Arabs in Lebanon, Palestine, and elsewhere. I guess it could be worse: statistically, we've been consistently killing about one hundred thousand people a year through the centuries, despite the fact that the world's population has been going up. If there hadn't been any improvements in human nature, you'd expect the number of deaths to climb in step with the rising world population. Perhaps that means we're getting better after all.

People kill each other for a lot of reasons: politics and money, sex, hate, greed and envy, even simple misunderstanding. However, when someone who believes in God kills a person, he does so aware of the act's potential impact on his eternal fate. Whatever our religion, we know that murder is one of those things that God pays attention to. If you're a person who fears the judgment of God, there are only two contexts for killing, other than self-defense: self-interest and service. If you know it's wrong but can't help doing it, you commit murder despite your religion, because your motivation outweighs any moral considerations, and you can only hope for God's mercy. Sometimes, though, believers will decide to kill someone because they think God wants them to. When that happens, the moral considerations actually become part of the motivation, and the killers look forward to getting God's greatest reward!

A lot of people, regardless of their religious background, wonder why Muslims, Christians, and Jews are all so angry at each other. The answer is simple: we all have members who are guilty of murdering for the sake of their faith, while hypocritically pretending to be nothing more than innocent victims. It's been going on for centuries and continues because many of us think our religions allow, support, or even encourage it. Finally, only a blessed few of us are doing much of anything to make it stop.

If you're interested in checking my figures, a gentleman named Matthew White has collated both news and government records of the death toll we've generated and made the information available over the Internet. He has even gone to the trouble of recording his references. According to those sources, during the last three awful decades Muslims have killed half a million other Muslims in Iraq, Iran, Somalia, and the Sudan; ten thousand Christians worldwide; and over two thousand Israeli Jews. There's no question we're a rough bunch, but those same news reports and government estimates have also quietly chronicled how, since 1980, Israeli Jews or their agents have killed somewhere between forty and eighty thousand Muslim and Christian Arabs in Palestine, Gaza, and Lebanon (estimates of casualties vary widely because of the difficulty of attributing responsibility during the concurrent Lebanese Civil War). Likewise, armies of men and women from the Christian nations of the West—most of whom probably consider themselves good Christians—have done away with over five hundred thousand Muslims in Azerbaijan, Bosnia, Chechnya, Iraq, and Afghanistan. When Western editorials and commentators call for moderate Muslims to condemn Muslim terrorists, the vast majority of us agree. But we would be able to respect your advice more if you hadn't killed almost fifty times more of us than we have of you.

Few of us have much difficulty accepting our own sides' explanations for why violence is sometimes a necessary evil. Most of us seem reassured by the belief that we're better than the other guys, but the numbers on the news prove that we're pretty much all the same. Muslims and Christians, with half a million victims over the last thirty years and over a billion members worldwide, have a believer-to-body-count ratio of approximately 2000 to 1. Proportionately, even though there are only thirteen million Jews in the world, so many Arabs have been killed in the name of Zionism in the last thirty years that Judaism's statistics might even be a little worse. Experts and pundits can quibble over the exact numbers (and whether some of the victims deserved it), but the fact remains that the number of deaths for which members of our religions are responsible is proportionate to the sizes of our congregations. No matter how thinly you spread the blood on our hands, you can still see the stain. There's a recurring theme throughout the reporting and rhetoric here in the West that implies that only Muslims are backward enough to think God approves of our violence, but the old truism "There are no atheists in foxholes" has never been truer than it is today. Every soldier inevitably makes his or her own peace with God. At one time or another we've all needed to put some of our sons and daughters into the field of battle, and we've all got some children there today. To encourage them, even though we all worship a God who commands us "Thou shalt not kill," our religions have all made some kinds of killing into a virtue. For all our sakes, I hope that if God does end up being real, He'll at least appreciate the irony.

Jesus was quite clear about what he expected from his followers in his Sermon on the Mount. There, he said that Christians were supposed to be meek, humble, and merciful peacemakers who were just and generous, obeyed the laws of Judaism and its prophets, and even held themselves to a higher standard whereby their motivations could be examined as closely as their deeds. He said that they should be honest and kind, and he explicitly warned that the love of money would prevent many of them from serving the love of God.

Muslims strive to follow the religion of Islam, a word whose root means both "peace" and "submission." The Quran promises that if we're good, bad things will happen only to purify us or teach us humility. A word that describes a righteous person, *as-Salihin*, means "good," "honest," "upright," and "sound," with the connotation of a peacemaker. We're explicitly told not to kill people, especially not for revenge. Righteous Muslims are supposed to be humble and patient, vigilant and grateful for the lessons life brings us. We're supposed to serve God, do our best to care for the rest of God's creation, and guard all life. Put it all together and we should be good to have around.

Few of us have become the sort of people that our religions promised they would help us be. Instead, many of us have become the polar opposites of what our holy books commend, and all our leaders have done little but blind us to our faults along the way. Despite Jesus' warning that the love of money *would* (not *could* or *might*) prevent them from serving God, the world's richest Christians have gone to war to protect their wealthy way of life. The leaders of the United States and Britain have both used their Christianity to justify destroying Iraq and Afghanistan—two of the poorest nations on the planet. At the same time, instead of serving as God's stewards, many Muslims have chosen to condone terrorists' killing of innocent men, women, and children in anger, retaliation, and revenge. In many Muslim nations—which a thousand years ago were beacons of human rights and freedom—leaders who seem interested only in their own power rule as despots.

What has happened to Judaism may be the greatest tragedy of all. All our holy books tell us that the Jews are God's chosen people. Exploring what they were actually chosen for might have at least distracted us from killing each other for a while. It's not a secret. Genesis, the first book in both the Christian Bible and the Jewish Torah, disclosed God's purpose to everyone in chapter 18, verses 17 through 19:

> Then the Lord said, "Shall I hide from Abraham what I am about to do? Abraham will surely become a great and powerful nation, and all nations on earth will be blessed through him. For I have chosen him so that he will direct his children and his household after him to keep the way of the Lord by doing what is right and just, so that the Lord will bring about for Abraham what he has promised him."

The book of Genesis promises that we are all going to be blessed by God through the Jews. Clearly, a real child of Abraham is supposed to be a blessing not just for himself or herself, but for everyone else, too.

There's blessed little blessing coming out of any of us these days. It should be blatantly obvious that none of us are even close to the paths that we were meant to follow. Regardless, the vast majority of us continue to go to our churches, mosques, and synagogues; pray to our one God; and tell ourselves that we're only trying to live our lives the best we can. Few of us are comfortable with what's going on, but even fewer of us are prepared to consider doing something about it. If we honestly believe in God, we had better reconsider. Even though most of us aren't murderers, in God's eyes we are likely all complicit. We have our holy books, but few of us read them very carefully or critically. Most of us are content to listen to what we're *told* they say. We have the examples given to us by our prophets, but we've learned how to treat their words and deeds like incantations and rituals and to interpret them in ways that permit us to do what we want to do, instead of what they say we should do. We all believe that we're more different than we are similar, and we all seem to accept that those differences justify homicide. Worst of all, because of what we do and what we believe, our children are at risk of death or worse. In all our religions, our children sometimes become the opposite of what they should be. Instead of following the instructions of God, some will make choices that are eternally condemned by both God and man.

That's the great paradox of modern religions: instead of making their most committed followers the best people in the world, religions today often seem to make them the worst. The best evidence for that is the sorry fact that our most committed believers commit the worst atrocities. Hypocritical backsliders aren't the ones who kill for their beliefs, nor the ones willing to risk their lives in wars, invasions, pogroms, or acts of revenge and retribution. We've all got one thing in common: whether we're suicide bombers killing innocent Israeli children, holy warriors fighting either for or against Islam, soldiers defending our countries' interests or economies, or merely coreligionists watching it all from the safety of our homes, we all think we're right. Jewish settlers driving Palestinians away from their ancestral olive trees and those same Palestinians throwing rocks, stones, or hand grenades in return both think they're doing what God wants them to do. Very few of us are willing to consider that we might all be in the wrong.

Those of us who believe in God and faith teach our children that religion will make them good people. We tell them that for religion to do that well, they have to believe in and belong to that system. Those of us who don't believe in God or faith tell our children the opposite thing for exactly the same reason! Today, it's looking more and more like the latter group is right. None of us, and none of our religions, have any reason to be proud. In all honesty, I sometimes wonder how I can even dream of teaching any religion to my kids at all. Why should any of us teach our children that they have to believe that the things we tell them are true, particularly when it seems so clear that what we teach them can make them so very bad?

The source of all our conflicts can't be the fact that we all think we're right; that's just human nature. It's likely not even that we think everybody else is wrong, although it would certainly be more useful if we took the time to talk honestly and openly about why. The problem seems to be that because we're sure we're right, we all assume that we have to impose our vision on the people we think are wrong and actively prevent them from doing the same thing to us. That's where the conflict begins: when we move from the act of thinking we're right to the act of thinking that being right justifies doing things that we know are bad.

There's always been a profoundly bitter irony to all our battling. From the very first, our worst wars have always been between "us" and "them," but every conflict we've endured proves that both sides are really the same. People everywhere require the same resources to survive, and we all ascribe value to intangible commodities like freedom, justice, and honor. Ideological excuses aside, virtually every war religious followers have ever fought has been for the control of land or resources that both sides have craved equally, driven by the conviction that they were too different from each other to share.

If faith could give believers something more in common, it could mitigate those horribly destructive misperceptions and help move everyone from "them" to "us." Failing that, if the moral codes our religions profess to teach us could at least be trusted to moderate our behavior toward each other, that might cut down on the amount of harm we do when we're acting out of fear. Instead, all our religions seem better suited to inflame our differences and justify our prejudices, no matter how similar we might actually be. Some of us believe in different Gods, but that shouldn't be a problem with Judaism, Christianity, or Islam. We all worship the Omniscient, Omnipresent, and Omnipotent Creator of the universe; not a lot of deities fit that description. Alternatively, we might think that only one of our holy books is right; the notion that one of our prophets was either evil, misguided, or an imaginative liar has been quite popular. However we choose to explain why we don't get along, the fact is that despite our public recognition of the honest commitment each of us makes to what we believe, few of us are really capable of respecting another's beliefs; most of us believe that we aren't even allowed to. The root of the problem is that so many of us think that our beliefs make us enemies who can never be friends. "We" believe that "they" can never be "us."

Despite everything we share, many if not most Christians believe that Muslims are condemned by their rejection of Jesus' Godhood and that Jews, by rejecting Jesus as their Messiah, have made themselves the cannon fodder of the apocalypse. Many Muslims, on the other hand, think that the Jews have lost the right to claim Israel for their own, condemned by their ongoing failure to live up to their Covenant responsibilities, and that by making Jesus a god, many Christians have condemned themselves as well. Finally, most of today's Jews believe that (for a variety of historical, political, racial, or religious reasons) Jews and Judaism must be allowed to dominate in the Holy Land. Based on what's being said and done here and in the Middle East, a lot of them seem to believe that people who don't share that vision deserve to be condemned, too.

In the end, the justifications for our conflicts with each other come down to some simple assumptions: We assume that our religions are right and that our Omniscient, Omnipresent, and Omnipotent Creator has made a mistake in allowing the others to exist. We conclude that as a result the world has gone horribly wrong and it's our job to fix it. I'll admit that those assumptions sound rational and make each of us more internally cohesive, but they really, really (really) beg a few questions: What if we're the ones who've made the mistake, not God? It seems to me that assuming God has made a botch of things is inherently disrespectful. That sort of thing is just not compatible with the sort of God that Muslims, Christians, and Jews are supposed to know that God is. What if, instead, we're all supposed to be different, supposed to do our different jobs, and supposed to independently contribute to the plan that God has made? What if our different beliefs don't really justify our malleable sense of morality? What if "we" are all "us"?

- **Christians, Muslims, and Jews are all killing each other.**

- **Our religions tell us that sometimes it's okay to kill people when we think they're wrong because we think we're right.**

- **If they're really helping us be better people, shouldn't our religions be making us do good things for each other instead?**

CHAPTER 3

....

WHY BELIEF?

Once upon a time just before the turn of the last century, there were actually a few years that went by without a single major war being fought anywhere in the world. That wouldn't have seemed like much to get excited about at the time, but to many of us alive today, our planet would have seemed like a paradise. Back then we all lived very similar lives in vastly different ways, but few of us noticed. Most of us were separated from each other by geography and distance, and we went about our lives in relative isolation. Regardless, our communities were structured around the purposes they fulfilled; our roles were defined by common needs like food, shelter, and survival; and, with no atrocities to justify, our religions all helped us through the rough spots.

Religions have always had an important place in our communities. They help some of us feel more connected to our various deities, but they've also been one of the most important ways that we connect to each other as well. Shared religion is one of the bonds that hold people together. Belonging to them confirms our right to belong to our community too. Unfortunately, when religion is used to define a community, it's generally at the expense of making one group's members seem distinct from everyone else. Having different religions has always held people apart. That didn't cause perpetual problems in the past only because openly practicing different religions in the same community is a relatively new occurrence. History and experience will both confirm that when it's happened, religion has become a source of conflict. That's likely because part of belonging to a religion entails believing that it's better than any of the alternatives.

Time passed, the world changed, and the moment of peace slipped away. The whole planet has become one community, and evidence of our vast diversity can be found on our own doorsteps. When the modern age of easy communication, travel, and mobility first dawned in the second half of the last century, many of us were optimistic about what might happen when we all started to interact with a broader range of people more often. Regardless of our level of optimism, I think we all sincerely hoped that we'd experience a great drawing together based on all the things we share—starting with our humanity. A television commercial even implied that all people in the world would have a giant celebration when we all discovered that we love Coca-Cola! Instead, we've learned—often the hard way—that the only thing we have in common is the feeling that none of us are treated quite as well as we should be. Virtually every person, group, and nation among us has a tale to tell about the way they're being victimized, threatened, or oppressed. Today, almost every one of us stands accused of something. Many live in anxious anticipation of some sort of violent preemption, retaliation, or revenge. Instead of becoming one big, happy human family, we've apparently chosen to become a contentious bunch of cantankerous people living on a steadily shrinking globe. Instead of coming together, we've gradually divided into an increasing number of groups, gangs, and ideologies, defined with progressively greater precision and detail: east vs. west, old vs. new, fundamentalist vs. conservative vs. liberal vs. radical. There are now so many different ways to categorize people—whether the distinctions are political, economic, religious, or philosophical—that it is almost inevitable that any two individuals meeting for the first time will find some reason why they can't get along. Our shrinking world has only placed us all within easy reach of each other with our differences and our grievances; moreover, our improved communication has only made it easier for us to air them.

There's still a chance for religion to become a unifying force, as virtually every faith says the same general thing about humanity: that from a divine perspective, we have the same expectations, the same basic standards, and the same rewards. Regrettably, most religions reserve those rewards for their own members, and believers often say nasty things about the rest of the population to explain why. Some of us behave so badly that a growing percentage of people don't want to believe in anything anymore. It's become virtually impossible to find any sort of consensus in religion—or even the basis for a civil conversation. I sit on an interfaith dialogue committee in

Calgary (one of the first that includes Catholic and Protestant Christians, as well as Sunni, Shia, Ismaili, and Ahmadiyyah Muslims), and most of our time is spent trying to figure out how to talk to each other and whether we should even try. Despite the honest effort many of us are finally putting into building bridges, disagreements about theology and belief continue to be used around the world to justify some of the worst carnage we inflict. I hope the time is coming when we all start trying to find some common ground. It's been a rough few decades for everyone, and if we don't start soon, we might find ourselves beyond saving. The more damage we do to each other, the more entrenched we get behind our walls and the less basis we have for reconciliation. The more hurt we absorb, the more we all just want revenge.

But even though commonalities are getting harder to find, and looking for them is becoming progressively less popular, religious belief may still be a good place to begin. The tendency we have to believe—even if it's just in ourselves—continues to be one of the few things that we all have in common. There are even some obvious aspects of religion that we can all agree on. We know that some people believe in God and some don't. We know that believers frequently don't believe the same things. For instance, we're not able to agree about how many gods there actually are, what we should call them, what they want, or even whether they want anything at all. Perhaps most important, in all our tales of miraculous survival—be they in the face of tsunamis or earthquakes, plagues or famines—we've seen that God seems to answer prayers by whatever name "He" or "She" or "It" is called, regardless of what the ones who are praying have done, said, or given. Frankly, some of our gods even seem to be there when they're not called upon by any name at all.

The idea that God might sometimes just *do* things can make everyone a little uncomfortable: we all know that things happen for a reason, and we'd like to believe that those reasons are things that we can understand and perhaps control. Of the two sorts of people—believer and nonbeliever—those of us who don't believe in God may actually be more comfortable with the inexplicable than those who do. People living without faith can generally accept that they just don't know enough about what's going on, come up with a good rationalization, and continue with their worldview relatively unchanged. It's the believers who have more of a problem.

Believers prefer it when we ask God for things first and the response comes afterward, showing an obvious cause-and-effect relationship. We like to think that means we're doing something right and that God's giving us special attention. The feeling of control it gives is reassuring. In fact, it's the main selling point of most of our current religions. They all claim to know what it is that our gods want and how you should give it to them. They then promise to make their followers more likely to get what they want in return. Keeping track of what's worked is important because if we don't know what we're doing right, then we can't be sure that we can keep on doing it. Religions are quite competitive about it; promising to help us do what God wants (and to get what we want in return) better than the others is what makes them more attractive to the rest of us. Most believers agree that what God wants from us most is something called faith, but few of us are sure what faith actually is. Most believe that it's important and that it has two parts: what we do and why we do it. We know that it consists of our actions, how we justify them, and the consequences we expect. By that definition, even those of us without a religion have faith! Every one of us does what we do for a reason, and we all think that those reasons are good enough to justify what we do. Almost all of us even agree about what sorts of things are ultimately "good" and which are ultimately "bad." You might think that would make finding consensus relatively easy. Regrettably, few if any of our religions accept such a broad definition of faith. Most religions stress belief (why we do what we do) over action (the doing itself). If nothing else, it makes us easier to tell apart.

Few believers are comfortable with egalitarian reflections on how God, random chance, or even simple blind fate treat us all the same; we think it signals weak religious commitment. The truth is, the distinctions between us are important for many reasons. Most of us like belonging to a group, even when that means excluding those who don't. We're comfortable living in communities in which we know where and why we belong. We're used to that. We also like it when we can understand and control the criteria of inclusion and exclusion; it makes it less likely that we'd ever find ourselves unexpectedly on the outside looking in. We even seem to prefer having (a few) people around who disagree with us—perhaps because having outsiders on hand to exclude strengthens our connection to the people with whom we want to belong (just like when we were children, playing in a playground).

Whether we're comfortable with each other or not, if we all just quietly did what our religions tell us to do, there's little doubt that we could all get along. Instead, we've turned the practice of religion into an exercise in "competitive believing" that's become strikingly similar to Olympic diving. When believers compete, we show off how many flashy doctrinal backflips, twists, and turns we're capable of between our own "leap of faith" and the big, splashy finish we all expect to come to at the end. We like to pretend that believing is difficult and that choosing to believe shows some sort of profound commitment. It's also convenient and inexpensive to join a religion that promotes belief over virtues like generosity—which might be why people in our wealthiest nations esteem belief so much. It sounds dramatic without seeming cheap. But the fact is that everybody believes something. Believing is simple and easy to do, and most of us enjoy it so much that we cultivate it even when there's no reason to. In North America, we share with our children Santa Claus, the Tooth Fairy, the Easter Bunny, and a host of other fictitious creations, in part to allow us to vicariously reexperience the pleasurable sensation of believing. It's obvious that we're good at it, and it's obvious that it's fun. In every culture in every part of the world, people create beliefs to amuse themselves and their children. Everyone believes something: even those of us who don't think we believe anything at all still *believe* that we're right.

We often confuse faith with belief and sometimes even equate them, even though we know that faith and belief can't be the same thing—if only because we know so well what believing is. Faith is another matter entirely. No one agrees what it is, many don't want it, and those who do want it often worry whether they're doing it well at all! The only matter we seem to agree on is that there's something special about the faith of children; they're certainly more prepared to believe in things they can't see than most grown-ups are. Some of us have been able to hang onto that childish openness better than others. Some of us think that's why certain adults can still believe in God and others can't, but that may be true only to a point. Children's openness makes them willing to believe just about anything we tell them. Believing grown ups, on the other hand, tend to be much more specific, careful, and exclusive about what those beliefs actually are. Those of us who believe in God think that those who don't believe as we do are in danger of serious consequences. Those who don't believe in God at all think that those who do are either stupid or just pretending. I hope we all know in our hearts that almost everyone's just trying to do what's right and believe what's true.

I remember my parents told me that going to church made God happy with me. They told me that God cared about what I did and why I did it, and that my Sunday school teachers would help me get it right. I'm sure it's the same everywhere: believers teach their children that their religion will help them do the right things for the right reasons. We teach them that religion will serve and guide them, and then the practice of religion absorbs their time, their energy, and sometimes their entire lives. Instead of it serving them, they sometimes end up serving it. We try to justify all the effort by telling them that religion is there to help them become what God wants them to be. Those of us who still believe in God and religion use our children's faith and trust in us to direct them into religion because we believe that's a good thing to do. Those of us who don't believe in God do the opposite for the same reason.

It's clear that something has gone horribly wrong with the idea that belonging to a religion is good for you. Because of the risks inherent in religious belief, many nonbelievers do exactly the opposite of what believers do with their own children. They point them away from religion for the same reason that we point our children toward it: we all think we're doing the right thing. Many people honestly feel they have sufficient cause to despise even the idea of religion. Although every religious community has its inspirational men and women, we also share a common history of atrocity, abuse, oppression, and suffering. Some believers have achieved incredible moments of greatness, but most of us have left a lot to be desired. Neither religion nor belief in religion seems to have worked out very well for any of us so far.

- **Our religions used to help us get along.**

- **Today, religion has become our main excuse for fighting.**

- **Many of us seem convinced that we shouldn't even try to get along anymore.**

....

CHAPTER 4

WHY RELIGION AT ALL?

My little daughter (I have two—one older, one younger—otherwise pretty much the same) started to cry one night when my wife and I were putting her to bed. She'd been upset since coming home from school. Initially she didn't want to talk about what was bothering her, but eventually she said that her classmates had been talking about heaven and hell, and she had found out that hell was for bad people. My beautiful, sweet, kind, generous, and obsessively loving little girl immediately remembered every bad thing she had ever done in her years of life (all nine of them) and concluded that she was bound for Hades! It got me wondering why we put up with religion at all.

I think I'm justified in saying that everybody would like to go to heaven when he or she dies. Even those who don't believe in God or an afterlife would probably admit that they wish all the stories were true, if only so they'd have something to look forward to. If a place like heaven exists, people all agree that it's a reward for responding to the good found in each of us. Likewise, we all agree that if there's a hell, then it's ultimately got to be a punishment for giving in to the bad. The arguments our religions have (that we all get drawn into) aren't so much about the absolute concepts of good and bad or punishment and reward as they are about the definitions of those terms, the standards of judgment, and how those standards are applied.

So what should I have told my daughter? I think the most reassuring response would have been that there is no God and she needn't fear any absolute judge of right and wrong. Sometimes I wish that were what I could say! Many of us think that would be the right response. Is God even there? Some think so, but many don't, and there's no way to be sure. God, if He exists, seems to like it that way, despite the fact that the idea of an invisible, all-knowing, and all-encompassing Creator who both notices and cares about everything we do is terrifying for anyone—especially for a little girl. If I could have honestly reassured my daughter that there wasn't any reward or punishment she needed to be concerned with outside of what she already knew, it would have made her life a lot easier; it would have shrunk her universe back down to a more acceptable size. Kids (and their parents) are much more comfortable with Santa Claus as the purveyor of moral lessons. Santa either rewards the good children with presents or withholds that reward from the bad ones, and in doing so provides an inducement to good behavior that's much less threatening than the wrath of a punitive God is.

If it turns out that there isn't any God, then I'll have to agree with all those pro-Santa parents out there. If the whole idea of a God who made us, and of an eventual Judgment Day when we will all be measured and consigned to some unimaginable and permanent fate, is just a figment of our collective imaginings, then both the hope of heaven and the fear of hell are unnecessary and cruel. If our lives really are finite, then the consequences of what we do should be finite as well. The use of such terrifying threats and such compelling promises to control our children is wrong if they are only lies. The great thing about action and consequence in a universe without God is that the events of our lives are never completely outside of our control.

On the other hand, most people who believe that God created the universe would advise strongly against me telling my little girl that He doesn't exist. Whatever else they think is true, the vast majority of religious people are convinced that God is real. Most of them also believe that God is a supervising deity who cares about what we do and that there are serious consequences to our actions beyond our understanding or control. I think they'd all recommend that even if you don't actually believe in God, it's still wise to act as if you do because of the downside of being wrong. They have a point. If God is real, then the consequences of thinking He isn't are likely a lot worse than the consequences of the opposite proposition! The problem is that most believers then expect you to accept their particular set of explanations, rules, and doctrines to the exclusion of everyone else's. Furthermore, the act of accepting those same explanations, rules, and doctrines often seems to make us a lot more difficult to get along with.

One has to ask, though, even if there is a God and a final judgment, do our children really need religion to make it into heaven? Even without religion, they seem to be closer to making it there than many of the rest of us. Even though they often don't understand much about religion, they all seem to know that they should be good. No matter how they've been raised, children seem pretty comfortable with the idea that "Someone" made everything and everyone and that that "Someone" cares what they do, even if no one has yet been able to give them a convincing explanation as to why. Children accept that being good is a matter of choice, and they know that there have to be rules. Even if those rules aren't the same for everyone, they know that things like expectations and rewards tend to balance out. Kids seem to instinctively understand the concept of fairness. They know that if they choose to be good, they'll be rewarded, and if they don't, they'll be punished. Kids have firsthand experience of those same matters from their parents, teachers, and other grown-ups. They know that we're there to teach and guide them toward those rewards with our punishments and to make sure that things even out in the end. They just put God into the same category as grown-ups and conclude that He does the same things in a bigger way.

I still have vivid memories of my own childhood faith. In fact, I can't remember a time when I didn't believe in God. The word *immanence* is sometimes used to describe an awareness of God's presence. It's generally spoken of as an uncommon experience, but immanence was a part of my daily life long before I knew the word. My mother tells me that as a preschool child, I frequently reported visits from something I called the Blue Giant, a glowing, friendly entity who came by at night to see how I was feeling. According to her, I told her that he was my guardian angel.

One evening as a teenager, I was riding my bicycle along a path between two fences when I heard a voice in both my ears say "Duck!" I did, immediately and without thinking. When I stopped to investigate, I could see no one for hundreds of feet around me, but I did find a fine piano wire strung between two fence posts across the path that I'd been riding, it would have cut off my head had I not immediately and unthinkingly obeyed the command. Another time the same voice made me back up in traffic just before an eighteen-wheeler drove over the front of my car. I always obeyed this voice and its infrequent commands without question— sometimes to my own frustration. When I was about sixteen, a married woman was making an obvious attempt to seduce me. I got up and walked away, wanting to return but completely unable to control my legs!

I know I'm not unique; as interesting as my life has been, I've never had any reason to think that I'm all that different from anyone else.

Everyone knows someone who's got the same sorts of stories. I've never felt particularly equipped to understand anything about these experiences, nor have I thought that trying to explain them would change anything about them or about me. But I've always been interested in why people believe what they do. Most people think that different doctrines are a product of different experiences, but I've never been very comfortable with that explanation. I once conducted an experiment with a close friend who lives as a committed atheist. He really, really (really) doesn't believe in God. He even gets angry when the subject is raised. One day, I challenged him to start asking God for things and to keep track of the outcome. I was impressed when he agreed; it was quite a leap of faith! His life swiftly filled with what I would think of as miracles: weather changed, electronic devices began to function properly, and stoplights became subordinate to his will. He concluded that one of us was psychic; I concluded that despite our wildly different beliefs, God was listening to both of us and had answered both our prayers. Our lives and worlds were changed by what happened, but neither of us changed at all. The events we experienced were explained and categorized within the religious milieus in which we respectively lived. They became incorporated into our individual doctrines and theologies, completely subordinate to the explanations furnished by our belief systems rather than the other way around.

Like everyone else, I've lived, learned, and walked my own path. I've had the opportunity to get to know people from different religions, and I've studied many others. I've always been refreshed by the incredible similarities found in all our spiritual experiences, regardless of the religion. I've also been frightened by the depth and the breadth of disagreement and conflict that can be generated in the explanations and interpretations that religions furnish to us. Each of us believes that our religion is the right one; in fact, that may be the only belief we all have in common. The only thing that I know for certain is that my relationship with God has always been the same, regardless of how my beliefs have changed. Unless God plays favorites, that should hold true for everyone. If God really did create everything, then He obviously made us all different. Our ability to understand things, and our motivation to try, vary even at different times in our own lives. Our explanations for our relationship with our Creator must be less important than that relationship itself, unless God truly has made some of us to be saved and some of us to be damned. Do any of us think God actually prefers wealthy, self-absorbed, middle-aged intellectuals like me?

Worrying about things like faith and belief is easy for wealthy, privileged people who are living safe and protected lives and have time on their hands—but it's not easy for everyone. Historically, few of us have had much choice about either our religion or our beliefs; they've mostly been a consequence of where we've grown up. Every religion excludes and includes people based on what they think we believe, and people exclude themselves based on whether they feel that they can believe anything at all. I've never been sure that our fixation on belief is appropriate. There are many places in the world where the struggle to exist eats up every moment of every day. People there don't have the time to participate in complex theologies or to wonder whether they're right about religion or not. When we're considering big questions like why we're here, most of us take the word of people around us whom we respect: kids believe whatever their parents tell them to. If I told my son that God wanted him to rub blue mud on his belly, I'm sure he would, religiously. If that were the wrong thing to do, would God blame him or me?

If the things we believe (the "facts" that make up the nuts and bolts of our religions) are really so important, then the devil should be the best of us all! Religions that believe in him all agree that he's been around a long time. We have different names for him and slightly different explanations for what he's been up to, but we all know that he does more than just believe; because of who he is and regardless of what he believes (if anything), Satan has acquired direct knowledge and experience of the true nature of reality. Any one of us who's sure that our religion is right about everything will have to admit that if that's the case, then Satan has to know with absolute certainty everything that we can only believe to be true. And I think we all have to admit that knowing for certain everything that we can only hope to be true hasn't done him a lot of good so far.

Are beliefs of any sort, and particularly our belief in religion, really that important? Are they really all that's necessary to help us please God? I know people who don't believe that there's a God who cares about what they do, but they live their lives as if there were because they think it's the right way to behave. I know many more who are uncertain whether they were "created for a reason," but who still live their lives as if they were, because they hope it's true. On the other hand, I know of people who believe in God and yet choose to live horrible, selfish, and destructive lives, convinced that they'll still end up in paradise because of either what they know or Who they know. Despite the fact that many Christians are convinced they're going to heaven because they think they know Jesus, some of the best people I know say that they can't believe in anything anymore because of all the horror that has been done in his name. The same holds true for Muslims and Allah, and Jews and HASHEM. It seems that some people become nonbelievers simply because they revere the idea of God so much that the conflicting religions and self-serving cruelty of the rest of us have driven them away from believing in believing at all.

From the day we're born until the day we die, in every country, on every continent, we all have two things in common: we all make choices, and we all have reasons for the things we do. Although our actions and explanations are often different, they share one characteristic: we do what we do for reasons that seem right to us. Some of us choose to be motivated by selfish goals and our own pleasure, while others of us find motivation in the belief that what we do is right.

Our beliefs are different as well. Even those of us who share a religion can't possibly believe in everything it teaches in exactly the same way. Some don't believe in God at all. Some believe in one; others believe in many. Despite those differences, for many of us the motivation to act remains directed toward some sort of objective "good" outside of ourselves. For others, whether we're believers or not, our primary motivation is our own pleasure, power, and control. Are any of us really comfortable when our various religions tell us that a person who believes in God because of the reward that he or she expects is better than the person who doesn't? Can a selfish believer really be better than someone who is kind to others, despite expecting no reward at all? Or is the selfish believer better than someone who wishes that there really was a God, but who's afraid to believe because of what he or she has seen belief make other people do? Are grasping, heaven-obsessed, hell-fearing believers really going to be rewarded more than those people who believe in good so strongly that the only thing that they can still believe about God is that a good God can't possibly be real?

There's obviously a big problem with our religions, or at least with what we've made of them. We tell our kids that religion will help make them better people, but the way the system stresses believing and belonging weakens its impact. By giving people a pathway to paradise that bypasses goodness, kindness, and love, religions sometimes make believers even worse than they were before they believed. When that happens, religions themselves become the best support for the belief that so many of us today have developed—that religions have either gone bad or always have been.

Is it possible to reconcile the hope (and the hype) of religion with the hypocrisy? Is it possible to bridge the gap between promise and practice? Is it even worth the bother? Your responses to those questions depend on what you believe, but then your responses and your reasons for giving them prove that deciding whether to believe in the hope, potential, and power of religion is a function of belief, too. Whatever the correct answer is, we all believe we're right and refuse to believe we're wrong. We also tend to blame all the problems on the people who disagree with us. And that means we have a lot more in common than we think, so that's probably as good a place as any to start looking for answers.

- **Children grow up knowing that they should be good.**

- **Parents tell their children that a religion will help them be better people.**

- **Today, many of us are acting as if believing in a religion and belonging to a faith can replace trying to be better people.**

To find the right answers, you have to ask the right questions.

The question I had to ask was:

Do our different faiths only doom us to fighting with each other, or are they meant for something more?

PART II

BEGINNING WITH
CHRISTIANITY

CHAPTER 5

....

EARLY EXPLORATIONS

I think I probably learned about God the same way as everyone else: my parents raised me as a Christian because that was how they'd been brought up, Mom as an evangelical Christian in the Four Square Gospel Alliance and Dad as a Lutheran. Despite a few doctrinal differences, they agreed they would teach their children that Christianity was the one and only way because that's what their parents had told them. Sharing the good news of the Gospel of Jesus is still the main purpose of every branch of Christianity; Jesus' Great Commission at the end of the Gospel of Matthew commands Christians to make believers of everyone! My parents explained that Jesus was actually God in human form. They told me he had been tortured and had died on the cross to pay the penalty that God-in-heaven demanded before He could forgive me for my sins. In essence, my parents promised that in return for believing what they said and undergoing rituals like baptism and communion, I'd receive the grace of forgiveness and an assured place in heaven. They even promised that I'd gradually become a better person, as God's Holy Spirit (the final aspect of the three-part God-Who-Made-Everything) changed me from the inside out.

I still miss Christianity. It was a pretty good deal! In fact, the deal's so good that it's helped spread Christianity for the last two thousand years. According to Christians, the New Covenant of their religion is a contract between God and the rest of humanity that Jesus brokered while he was here. It's what makes Christianity different from every other religion, and the only reason Jesus could set it up on our behalf was that he was both God and man at the same time. As part of the eternal Trinity, he could negotiate, sign for, and make the human sacrifice necessary to activate the pact, all simultaneously. My parents assured me that this was what the Bible taught and that the words of the Bible were true because the Bible was the literal Word of God. They also assured me that Christianity was completely based on what the Bible said. According to my parents, my responsibility as a Christian would be going to church; believing in God, Jesus, and the rest of Christianity; and trying to do what was right—knowing I wouldn't succeed but knowing that it didn't matter. If I was a Christian, they told me that I could live the rest of my days secure in the knowledge that God would love me no matter what I did, as long as I believed and did my best. They told me all this before I was even ten years old. I was sold!

Raised in the family and community that I belonged to, my becoming Christian was probably inevitable. The only people I could find who actually believed in God were Christians! Although I knew lots of nonbelievers who recommended that I follow their lead, their explanations of why I shouldn't believe never really made any sense to me. I didn't understand how someone's beliefs could influence whether or not God existed. Whether God was real or not had to be independent of what anybody happened to believe at the time. I felt like I'd known God forever, and I knew that I wanted to be on His good side. To do that, I knew what I needed most were appropriate instructions. I was just a kid, and since people who claimed to know God even better than I did surrounded me, I listened to them.

I first started to struggle with Christianity as a teenager when I began to examine its promises a little more closely. I had figured out what sins were and was grateful that I was forgiven because of God's goodness rather than my own. Since I knew how much fun sin could be, and just how little goodness I was capable of sometimes, I found it all very reassuring. I was convinced that my failings weren't even really my fault. My Christian teachers said that because of something called "original sin," I hadn't been made to be perfect. Only God could make me better than I was.

In a way, I even believed that God was responsible for my imperfections. Original sin—which I understood explained the urge to do what was wrong even though I knew what was right—was something God had saddled me with simply because I had been born. Since my faults before God-my-Judge were a consequence of my existence, preordained by God-my-Creator, it seemed only fair that God-my-Savior was responsible for their correction. More than anything else, I was grateful; that made Christianity quite easy to practice. When I was choosing between pleasure and righteousness, I didn't have to worry too much about the consequences if I happened to slip up from time to time. What was important was that I could unconditionally count on God's forgiveness because of my belief and my baptism. It gave me a certain measure of control over the eventual fate of my soul, independent of my behavior—something my religious instructors called my "assurance of salvation."

No one really had much to say about repentance. Worrying too much about sin and righteousness was actually deemphasized, labeled "Works Christianity," and even condemned as a pathway leading to the inevitable rejection of God's willingness to sacrifice Himself in my place! Wanting to be too good was being ungrateful. Although that sentiment made practicing my faith more convenient and simple, it also made it uncomfortable for me to read the Gospels; there Jesus (who was, as I understood it, the One who had been sacrificed, and therefore arguably the One who would know the most about it) seemed to stress repentance and obedience very strongly. I sometimes found myself in situations where my own behavior, as well as that of my friends and teachers, stood in stark contrast to the behavior of the men and women of the Bible. I realized one day that there was little real impetus for us to obey the moral code expressed in the Bible, even though we all professed to follow what it said. We all believed that our drive to transgress was inborn and that our salvation was a result of God's direct intervention in our lives. Since that meant that our beliefs assured our forgiveness and made any punishment impossible, most of us lived the prayer "O God, make me perfect, but not yet!" so that we could continue to live as we wanted rather than as we knew we should.

It seemed that few people I knew took God very seriously. Since we could always count on God's mercy, we had no reason to do what we knew was right, unless we really wanted to. I was frequently present at tearful scenes of repentance that were preceded by joyful rebellion and followed by more of the same. I tried to enjoy that sort of life for myself, but I wasn't very good at it. Whenever I actually sat down and read the Bible, I found Jesus condemning that sort of hypocrisy. Since what I really wanted was certainty about my fate under God's judgment, the apparent contradiction between what Jesus said and what we, the followers of Jesus, practiced made me a little anxious about my eventual fate. I decided that I had to examine the fundamentals of my faith more carefully.

One thing that had always troubled me about the Lutheran Church was that even though the Bible was supposed to be the basis of everything we believed, a lot of the lessons came from other sources. In addition, the Bible verse that was the starting point for a class was often a long way from the conclusion that we finally arrived at. Noticing this gave me the uncomfortable feeling that we Lutherans were relying too heavily on the opinions of our teachers and their favorite philosophers and not enough on the opinion of God. I eventually left to find a group that focused on Scripture straight from the Bible and who had a healthy distrust for intellectual manipulations. I went to the Baptists, because they claimed that everything they believed was 100 percent based on the Bible. Almost everything they said was what I had heard before, with one important difference: they taught that obedience to God's law was important. I found that much more compatible with what Jesus had said in the Gospels.

As a Baptist, I was expected to live a righteous life with God's help, but day-to-day righteousness was still a gift from God. Thus, I was able to avoid "Works Christianity," but I still didn't have to be good all the time. In fact, even my attempts at goodness were a sure sign of God's spirit working inside me. I thought that was great! It was very reassuring to know that I would do well with God's help rather than fail miserably in spite of it. Even better, it meant that simply by making good choices, I proved that God liked me.

Although I'd switched churches and thought that I'd made some significant changes to my beliefs as well, they were really still the same. I remained convinced that having faith meant that I had an assured place in heaven because I believed that Jesus-as-God had died to pay the price for my sins. I also believed that Christianity was simultaneously a gift from God that promised eternal life in heaven and a special club that set those of us who believed it apart from others who didn't. Believing I belonged to that club was still the most important thing I had. Even though I thought I'd been examining the fundamentals of my faith, they hadn't changed. Since I thought that my faith in God was the same as believing everything I'd been taught, in my deepest heart I was afraid that uncertainty would be seen as a sign of weakness. I knew that strong faith was good and weak faith led to hellfire. That meant questions could become damnation if they went too far. But as long as I never crossed that line, God would still have to accept me into heaven when I died.

It had happened so gradually that I didn't even notice how all my thinking and believing had turned me into the worst sort of hypocrite. I was convinced that I lived by faith like I was supposed to, but my faith was in what I believed about God, not in God Himself. Instead of trusting God, I trusted in what I believed to save me from Him. In Bible study, whenever we talked about Abraham and other pre-Christian people of the Old Testament who had been "saved by their faith," I always assumed that it meant that they'd all been given an opportunity to acknowledge Christian doctrine, the divinity of Jesus, and the universal nature of his sacrifice before their own judgment time came. Even while I was going through my first theological crisis (the one that led me to the Baptists), I never questioned the validity of the basic things that I had been taught in my Christian studies about God. This was mostly because I was afraid that looking at my beliefs too closely might make everything I was hoping for go away.

I knew that faith was a gift from God, but I had convinced myself that faith was also believing in Christianity, even though I knew that people just like me had developed most of the more complicated bits on their own. I had even decided that my religion and its molders were in some fashion interdependent; that the human factor introduced with the intellectual development of Christianity was somehow inevitable and a further sign of God's plan. It was all just rationalization. The truth was that I had to believe that faith was the acceptance of Christian doctrine; doing so guaranteed that everything would go the way I wanted it to when I died.

One day I noticed that I didn't fear God anymore and even started to wonder if I'd ever feared him at all. In fact, I believed that God was my friend! In all my Sunday schooling, I had been taught that God had come to earth as Jesus and had sacrificed himself so that I would not have to suffer for the bad things I'd done. I wasn't even responsible for the hard work of obedience because I knew that God would look after that with the help of the Holy Spirit. Until He did, as long as I meant well and believed the right things, I could do pretty much whatever else I felt like; I believed that the Holy Spirit would keep me from feeling like doing what I shouldn't, and even if I did do something wrong, I'd be forgiven. I didn't know what I could possibly be afraid of. I had even developed a rationalization by which I avoided sin and tried to do what was right because I pitied Jesus. I imagined that every wrong thing that I did added to Jesus' suffering on the cross, so I tried to avoid sinning to limit his pain. Eventually, instead of fearing God, I had finally come to the place where I thought that I could feel sorry for Him.

My attitude troubled me a little, not because my arrogance was astonishing, but because I thought I was pretty smart. I knew that King Solomon had said that fear of God was the beginning of wisdom. I knew that wisdom was even better than just being bright. Even though I told myself that I didn't fear God because I'd "passed beyond fear into real knowledge," I wanted to be wise, too. Knowing that it had worked for Solomon, I asked for wisdom from God. I actually kind of expected that God would find a way to tell me that I was already right about everything—and maybe make me rich as well. Instead, my marriage of nine years fell apart when my wife left me for my best friend, the hospital where I practiced was put in danger of closing, all but one friend decided my soon-to-be ex-wife was better off with the other guy, and a tree fell on my car.

I'll admit these events caught me by surprise. The first thing I learned in the midst of all my catastrophe was to laugh at myself and the arrogance of my assumption that I had known anything at all about being wise. I hadn't seen any of it coming. I struggled to figure out exactly what was going on, but it was obvious that everything that had happened was connected to my request for enlightenment. It also seemed obvious that the one thing absolutely everyone in heaven and on earth agreed about was that I needed more than a little work. Strangely, I didn't doubt that God was still working in my life, and I didn't feel cursed—just chastened. I had asked, after all.

I didn't know what to do next, but then an opportunity to serve God pretty much dropped into my lap. I had always known Muslims, and I'd even taken some short classes in comparative world religions in the course of my early religious instruction. I was quite convinced that I knew everything significant about Islam. I believed that Muslims were wrong, but I gave their faith little thought. Now, suddenly, I noticed that Muslims surrounded me. New friends, colleagues, and respected mentors whose faith I had paid little attention to all turned out to follow Islam. I was astonished by their kindness, their devotion to their God, and their attention to their holy book—even though I thought that the book was false. I was particularly impressed by the fact that they all prayed five times a day.

I decided that if I really cared about those people, I would have to change my Muslim friends into Christians. Since I was sure that faith and doctrine were the same, it followed that fixing their beliefs would save their souls from hell. It honestly sounded like a simple thing to do. I knew that Muslims revered Jesus as a prophet and agreed with Christians that the Bible had been divinely inspired. I also knew that the words of the Bible were the basis for my Christian beliefs and doctrines. Certainly it would be easy to find specific chapters and verses in the Bible that would show my friends where they were wrong and what they needed to know to become

Christians. Once they had accepted that Jesus as God had died to pay the penalty for their sins, they'd be saved! I was convinced that that was why Jesus was the Messiah, and I knew that he'd been proclaimed Messiah and Christ in the book of Islam, the Holy Quran. I thought I could easily prove Christianity to Muslims by using the Holy Quran and the Bible.

- **Growing up, I believed that Christianity was the right religion.**
- **I thought it taught that the path to heaven was believing the right things about God.**
- **I struggled with that because of how often the Bible recommended good behavior, too.**

CHAPTER 6

....

THE BASIS OF BELIEF

What is it that makes "believers" so certain what we believe is true? Even if you acknowledge that faith is a gift from God and accept that belief is an important part of it, everything that we believe about our religions still had to come from somewhere. One of the basic precepts of religious belief is that it can't be tested. While it's true that few if any of the beliefs can be objectively confirmed, every one of them still had to begin with something someone important either said or wrote down. From there, the path that each point of doctrine takes to each of us has to be traceable and verifiable. If that weren't true, it would mean that the people who teach us everything would have to admit they'd made it up! Our beliefs' beginnings are important because their beginnings give them their power.

Some religions have it easier than others. Many have to rely on uncertain things like ancestral memory or word of mouth to carry information from God to us. That makes their beliefs seem a little unreliable, even to those of us who believe in God in the first place. Others are lucky enough to have a recorded text to follow, and that gives them a real advantage. Christianity, Islam, and Judaism are all religions of the second sort. All of them claim that they can say with certainty that things are the way they say they are because they have God's Word on it, in black and white, or even engraved in stone. That makes it easier to justify what they teach. The idea that any religion truly has The Word Of God is itself a religious belief that's completely untestable; but the fact that religions are based on what that Word says is open to independent verification, and the textual support grants them an apparent objectivity. In the end, though, to claim any sort of objective validity—even amongst those of us who believe in divine revelation—Christianity, Islam, and Judaism can't be different from any other religion. Their beliefs and practices have to be based on the revelations given to them by their prophets and, through the prophets, by their God. The only reason that any of us believes what we do is because we believe that all our religious doctrines are what Jesus, Muhammad, Moses, and the other prophets said while they were still around.

When I set out to prove Christian doctrine by finding the Bible verses that began it all, I didn't think my search would turn out to be very difficult. I'd grown up convinced that the words of the Bible *proved* Christianity and that anyone who disagreed did so because he or she didn't accept what the Book actually said. I hadn't yet realized how easy it is for two people to read the same book and find very different things inside it. The only people who think that the Bible is the Word of God and a good reference for trying to prove anything at all are likely already Christians, and they, whatever their denomination, read it already believing in the doctrines of Christianity. At one time that truth was very much in question, but few today remember the schism between the northern and southern branches of the early Christian church or the way the northern Bishops took control, instituting a list of dogmas called the Nicene Creed to assist them in rooting out the Arian heretics. Those were dark days. Split over the Trinity, the ascendant Greco-Roman branch chose to exclude anyone who wouldn't swear by the Creed, often violently. They've continued to do so on and off for the last two millennia, and the practice of killing dissent (sometimes literally!) may even have affected the evolution of the modern-day Christian, if you believe in that sort of thing. If you punish everyone who disagrees with you, people will be less likely to ask difficult questions, and so will their children.

In Christianity today, the (ostensibly God-given) capacity to believe all the specific things the church claims are true has become proof you're saved from hell and going to heaven. That means if you're a Christian, it's unlikely that you will ever need to find proof for your religious doctrines, because you think that sticking to them is a gift from God and that that's what faith is. The Roman Catholic Church actually calls this the Doctrine of Faith, which makes trying to prove what you believe almost a sin. On the other hand, people who don't think the Bible is the Word of God are unlikely to think that you can prove anything with it except that believers can be a little gullible. No one who reads the Bible is likely to try to use it to confirm the doctrines of Christianity from a perspective of nonbelief. Non-Christians aren't interested, nonbelievers don't think it can be done, and few Christians check very closely, because to most of them, believing in their doctrine *is* faith, and questioning that is a swift ticket to damnation.

In spite of that, I was once a committed, Bible-believing Christian who set out to prove that the Bible certified the beliefs of Christianity. I didn't do it for my own sake, because I already proudly believed everything and believed that I had to continue believing in it all for the sake of my eternal soul. I set out to prove Christianity, using the Bible as my reference, for the sake of my Muslim friends.

My first step was to read an English translation of the Holy Quran. I figured it was a good idea to find out what I was up against. I still remember the fear I felt every day when I sat down to read, prepared for spiritual combat. With every turn of a page, I expected to find some horrible blasphemy that would test my faith. Instead, to my profound surprise, and at least initially to my relief, I found only honor and respect for God and the teachings of all of the prophets. I had always been taught that Allah was the name of a false God, but one of the first things I learned was that to Muslims, Allah simply meant "the Lord." Muslims gave it no more reverence than they did any of God's other titles, like the Most Gracious or the Most Merciful. In fact, I learned that some Muslim scholars had even recommended that "Allah" not be used to refer to God in any language but Arabic, to avoid giving non-Muslims the impression that Muslims thought Allah was the only name of God. I remember thinking that the more I learned, the easier converting them to Christianity seemed to become.

The first Surah that I read, Al-Fatiha 1:1–7, instead of being the satanic invocation I expected, simply said:

> In the name of Allah, Most Gracious and Most Merciful
>> Praise be to Allah, The Cherisher and Sustainer of the Worlds:
>> Most Gracious and Most Merciful: Master of the Day of Judgment.
>> Thee do we worship, and Thine Aid we seek.
>> Show us the straight way, The way of those on whom
> Thou has bestowed Thy Grace. Those whose (portion) is not wrath, and who go not astray.

I was surprised. If I substituted "the Lord" for "Allah," this prayer became the most Christian of supplications. It even talked about grace, a concept I was familiar with from my Christian education. Since I was sure I already knew everything possible about God's grace, I concluded that Muslims simply didn't understand their own book and needed to have it explained to them by someone familiar with the Bible—someone like me.

Every day's study was similar. Instead of finding the blasphemy I had expected, I found love and devotion, prayer, supplication, and respect. I'd believed that Islam was a cruel, fatalistic, and judgmental religion, utterly opposed to Christianity and promising Muslims little hope of forgiveness. Expecting to find proof, I instead found verses like Al-Baqara 2:2–5:

> This is the Book; in it is guidance sure, without doubt, to those who fear Allah; who believe in the Unseen, are steadfast in prayer, and spend out of what We have provided for them; and who believe in the Revelation sent to thee, and sent before thy time, and who (in their hearts) have assurance of the Hereafter. They are on (true Guidance), from their Lord, and it is these who will prosper.

The passage even talked about "assurance of the Hereafter," which confused me because I thought the afterlife came only to those with the correct doctrine. Then I read Az-Zumar 39:53 and An-Nisa 4:110:

> Say: "Oh my Servants who have transgressed against their souls! Despair not of the Mercy of Allah: for Allah forgives all sins, for he is Oft-Forgiving, Most Merciful."

> If anyone does evil or wrongs his own soul but afterwards seeks Allah's forgiveness, he will find Allah Oft Forgiving, Most Merciful.

I had to admit that rather than describing a cruel and rigid judgment, the verses both seemed to promise the same sort of forgiveness that Christians spoke of.

Instead of fatalism, I found Al-Baqara 2:21 and Al-Mujadila 58:22:

> O ye people! Adore your Guardian Lord, who created you and those who came before you that ye may become righteous.

Thou wilt not find any people who believe in Allah and the Last day, loving those who resist Allah and His Messenger, even though they were their fathers or their sons, or their brothers, or their kindred. For such He has written faith in their hearts and strengthened them with a spirit from Himself. And He will admit them to Gardens beneath which rivers flow, to dwell therein (forever). Allah will be well pleased with them, and they with Him. They are the Party of Allah. Truly it is the Party of Allah that will achieve Felicity.

Both verses seemed to say that perfection was not required and that Muslims "became righteous" through faith in God's grace, just as I believed that Christians did. Muslims were even promised God's spirit, just like I knew Christians were! I remember feeling astonished at how all this faith was being squandered at the feet of a false God. I became convinced that Muslims had somehow been arrested in the process of becoming Christian. I decided that their religion would need to be corrected only in a few small points. Then I started to relax; the more I learned, the easier it seemed to get.

After finishing the Quran, I embarked upon a careful review of everything that Jesus had taught. I was sure that was all I would need to convince my Muslim friends to change their minds, as it was the basis of my own faith, too—despite already having received a few clues to the contrary, which I see in retrospect. I'd occasionally experienced pangs of worry whenever I encountered verses like Mark 6:10 or Matthew 5:17:

"Why do you call me good?" Jesus answered. "No one is good but God alone!"

"Do not think that I have come to abolish the Law or the Prophets; I have not come to abolish them but to fulfill them. I tell you the truth, until heaven and earth disappear, not the smallest letter, not the least stroke of a pen, will by any means disappear from the Law until everything is accomplished. Anyone who breaks one of the least of these commandments and teaches others to do the same will be called least in the kingdom of heaven."

Thankfully, I had always been able to disregard the verses and the way they threatened to contradict what I believed. In my Christian education, I had come to understand that the first verse was an example of Jesus' teasing, which could be comprehended only by someone who already knew that Jesus was God. It was a pleasure to laugh with other Christians at God's sense of humor! In the second verse, I had learned to focus on the word "fulfill"; since Jesus had "fulfilled" the Law, none of the rest of us had to. The fact that that interpretation completely contradicted the rest of the verse didn't matter. I just ignored the second half of Matthew 5:17 or assumed that it applied to people with a different doctrine than my own.

Another verse that sometimes caused me anxiety was Matthew 7:21:

> "Not everyone who says to me, 'Lord, Lord' will enter the kingdom of heaven, but only he who does the will of my Father who is in heaven. Many will say to me on that day, 'Lord, Lord, did we not prophesy in your name, and in your name drive out demons and perform many miracles?' Then I will tell them plainly, I never knew you. Away from me, you evildoers!"

When I asked the pastors at my church in Saskatoon about the verse, they assured me that it likely referred to Mormons and could be ignored by the rest of us. I knew a lot of Mormons, and even though it seemed unfair to condemn such good people, I was truly grateful when people assured me that the verse was about them and not me! I blamed their religion and, for the sake of my faith, I figuratively flung them off the lifeboat and moved on. I had always believed that taken as a whole, the Bible supported Christian doctrine fully. I believed that following pure, unadulterated Christian doctrine was the path to pleasing God. Therefore, when I needed to prove Christianity to Muslims, I went to the Bible for support.

You've probably already figured out that my search didn't accomplish what I had expected it to. I had never studied the Bible in its entirety, seeking to support Christianity as the true faith. I had always assumed that people who were smarter than me and had a lot more time on their hands had already done that job. I trusted them. When I finally did my own review of the Bible, I found some things I didn't know, which caused me to reevaluate other things I had misunderstood. I still recall how often my Bible study leaders said, "What Jesus really meant when he said this was …" I still regret how often I said exactly the same thing myself. Instead of learning how to use the Bible to teach Muslims how to become better servants for God, I learned how the Word of God in the Bible had been made to serve Christian doctrine rather than the church serving Jesus' message as it should have.

- **Every religion says it's leading its followers along the true path.**

- **Every religion claims to be following its own books and revelations.**

- **When you look at what the books actually say, they're really not that different.**

CHAPTER 7

....

STEP BY STEP

When I began, I had no doubt that I'd save my Muslim friends from hell by turning them into Christians. My approach to the differences between our religions was quite straightforward. As far as I was concerned, they were wrong, I was right, and Christianity was the victorious doctrine of God, sent to free God's people on earth from sin and damnation! Supremely self-confident (and still blissfully unaware of my arrogance), I decided to be systematic and prove things one at a time, starting with the heavy lifting. I was going to demonstrate exactly where the Bible said Jesus was God. I expected that the direct approach would give me more credibility—and bring me early success as well. I had no doubt whatsoever that Jesus was God, and I was certain that my belief was completely supported by scripture. Since the Bible was full of verses that called Jesus the "Son of God," I had always concluded that obviously meant he had to be God, too.

In fact, the phrase "Son of God" occurred thirty-eight times in the New Testament of my computerized New American Standard Revised Version of the Bible. Right off the bat I noticed that seven of the references had been said by either Satan or other "unclean spirits"—none of whom would be likely to convince a Muslim. I knew that even though a lot of Christians thought Muslims listened to Satan, *Muslims* certainly didn't think they did. That still left me with thirty-one references to work with, but then one of the first "clean" verses came with a bit of a surprise.

According to the footnotes in my New International Version (NIV) Bible, Mark 1:1 didn't really call Jesus the Son of God, at least not in the earliest manuscripts. The reference had apparently been added to the Gospel a few hundred years after it was written. If I used it, I knew I'd probably come to regret it. Although it was tempting to just gloss over what I thought was a minor point, I'd already learned that many of my Muslim friends knew a surprising amount about the Bible. My credibility would suffer if they caught me in even the least appearance of a lie. I remember that I was also a little surprised to read that Gabriel in Mark 1:35 had said only that Jesus would be "called the Son of God" and that instead of the Throne of Heaven, he was to get the "Throne of David" and "rule the House of Jacob forever." That declaration was somehow less emphatic than I remembered.

When I came to the Gospel of Luke, I found that Luke 3:38 actually said that Adam was the "Son of God"! I was sure that I hadn't run into the verse before; either it hadn't been covered in my own catechism or I had missed that class. I wasn't sure what to make of it, but since it obviously didn't strengthen my position, I left it for future personal consideration and kept looking. Yet later in that same book, the priests questioned Jesus: "Are you the Messiah, the Son of God?" Luke said that Jesus replied, "You say that I am." Even though I knew that Jesus had to be teasing, I found it all a little frustrating. His response lacked the sort of conviction I needed; a joke wouldn't be enough to prove my point to someone who didn't already agree with me.

I finally came to the end of my review with the Gospel of John. Even though it contained more references to Jesus as the Son of God than any of the others, none of them were quite emphatic enough either. Jesus talked about the "Son of God" in John 3:17, 5:24, and 11:4, and others called him "the Messiah, the Son of God" in John 11:27 and John 20:31, but none of the verses took the step I was looking for. I hadn't found a verse in any of the Gospels that said being the Son of God was the same thing as being God Himself.

For my plan to work, I had to find an unequivocal verse that said Jesus was God. I was trying to refute the Quran's An-Nisa 4:171:

> O People of the Book! Commit no excesses in your religion: nor say of Allah aught but the truth. Christ Jesus, the son of Mary was (no more than) a Messenger of Allah, and His Word, which He bestowed on Mary, and a Spirit proceeding from Him: so believe in Allah and His Messengers. Say not "Trinity": desist: It will be better for you: For Allah is One

God: Glory be to Him: (Far exalted is He) above having a
son. To Him belong all things in the heavens and on earth.
And enough is Allah as a Disposer of affairs.

I couldn't think of a way that this quote could be made a more emphatic
contradiction of Christian doctrine. By separating Jesus' role as Word and
Spirit from "Jesus as God Himself," it made it sound like Jesus/God was
only the product of Christian hyperbole! To rebut the Quran, I needed
to find a Bible verse with real conviction. I intended to show my Muslim
friends the contradiction between their reverence for Jesus and the Bible
and their refusal to accept what I knew Jesus and the Bible said. Once I
found the proof of Jesus' divinity that I knew was there, I'd be well on my
way to showing my friends they were wrong.

So far, I had been struck by two different things in the Bible's references
to Jesus as the Son of God. The first was the way the phrase was linked to
"the Messiah." Obviously, the two titles had been joined back in the day.
The second was the uncomfortable realization that if the phrase "Son of
God" implied divinity, I'd have to acknowledge many other "sons" as gods
as well. It wasn't just that Luke had called Adam the "Son of God." Isaiah
62:8 actually referred to the entire house of Israel that way, and Paul even
implied that the rest of us were, too! By now, having reread every Gospel
verse that contained the words "Son of God," I realized the phrase would
not be sufficient by itself to establish Jesus' Godhood to Muslims. To do
that, I would have to learn more about the Messiah.

At this point, when I began to intensify my search, I was still a Christian.
I attended church regularly and participated in a weekly Bible study. I
thought that the Bible was right; even more fundamentally, that meant that
the Quran absolutely had to be wrong. Since I had found no reason to
question my religious beliefs, my faith in them was unchanged. Although
I was frustrated by my lack of progress, I felt my failure to find sufficient
evidence for Jesus' divinity in the title "Son of God" was my own fault.
I'd likely been trying to go too far in one step. I decided to start with the
verses that showed that Jesus was the Messiah and then find the ones that
proved that the Messiah was God. This two-step approach made a lot of
sense. Even though it meant that I would have to expand my study into
the Old Testament, it seemed the appropriate thing to do. I knew that I
would benefit from a more complete review of the Bible, and I thought

my arguments would have even more weight with Muslims if they came from the combined teachings of Judaism and Christianity. Certain that I already knew what I was going to find, I never considered the possibility of anything less than success.

I jumped into my study of the Messiah with enthusiasm. The first thing that I learned was that the word *Messiah* only meant "anointed." Priests, prophets, and kings were all anointed with oil to show that they'd been set apart from the rest. Isaiah 45:1 even used the term to describe Cyrus, the King of the Medes and Persians! Although the honor belonged to a relatively small number of people to begin with, my Old Testament said that the Messiah was something even better than the rest of them. It looked like I was finally on the right track.

My *Oxford Companion to the Bible* told me that Jews believed they had been promised a ruler whose reign would bring them everlasting justice, peace, and security. The prophecies they thought referred to him included the following:

Isaiah 11:1–2:
> A shoot will come up from the stump of Jesse; from his roots a Branch will bear fruit. The Spirit of the Lord will be on him—the Spirit of wisdom and of understanding, the Spirit of counsel and of power, the Spirit of knowledge and of the fear of the Lord—and he will delight in the fear of the Lord.

Jeremiah 33:14–20:
> "The days are coming," declares the Lord, "when I will fulfill the gracious promise I made to the house of Israel and to the house of Judah. In those days and at that time I will make a righteous Branch sprout from David's line; he will do what is just and right in the land. In those days Judah will be saved and Jerusalem will live in safety." This is the name by which it will be called: "The Lord Our Righteousness." For this is what the Lord says: "David will never fail to have a man to sit on the throne of the house of Israel, nor will the priests, who are Levites, ever fail to have a man to stand before me continually to offer burnt offerings, to burn grain offering and to present sacrifices."

Ezekiel 37:24–28:

"My servant David will be king over them, and they will all
have one shepherd. They will follow my laws and be careful
to keep my decrees. They will live in the land I gave to my
servant Jacob, the land where your fathers lived. They and
their children and their children's children will live there
forever, and David my servant will be their prince forever. I will
make a covenant of peace with them, it will be an everlasting
Covenant. I will establish them and increase their numbers,
and I will put my sanctuary among them forever. My dwelling
place will be with them; I will be their God, and they will be
my people. Then the nations will know that I the Lord make
Israel holy, when my sanctuary is among them forever."

Genesis 49:10:

"The scepter will not depart from Judah, nor the ruler's staff
from between his feet, until he comes to whom it belongs and
the obedience of the nations is his."

And Numbers 24:17:

"I see him, but not now; I behold him, but not near. A star
will come out of Jacob; a scepter will rise out of Israel. He
will crush the foreheads of Moab, the skulls of all the sons
of Sheth. Edom will be conquered; Seir, his enemy, will be
conquered, but Israel will grow strong. A ruler will come out
of Jacob and destroy the survivors of the city."

They all made for some interesting reading, but none of them predicted
that the Messiah would be God incarnate. In fact, when I read one of the
most important prophecies in the Old Testament for the first time, it became
immediately apparent that, even though the first half of it was quoted in the
New Testament as if it confirmed Jesus' divinity, the rest was completely
incompatible with the idea of a divine Messiah. In 2 Samuel 7:12–15, the
prophet Nathan tells King David:

"The Lord declares to you that the Lord Himself will establish
a house for you: When your days are over and you rest with

your fathers, I will raise up your offspring to succeed you, who will come from your own body, and I will establish his kingdom. He is the one who will build a house for my Name, and I will establish the throne of his kingdom forever. I will be his father and he will be my son."

In the New Testament book of Hebrews, the quote stops there; but in the book of Samuel the original continues:

"When he does wrong, I will punish him with the rod of men, with floggings inflicted by men. But my love will never be taken away from him, as I took it away from Saul, whom I removed from before you."

Only the first half of Nathan's prophecy had found its way into the New Testament. Although that fragment sounded like it predicted a divine Messiah, the rest, if the prophecy referred to Jesus, said that he would sin and that God would even have him flogged for it. That meant that the title "Son of God," if it was based on the prophecy, couldn't have been a declaration of divine origins. God couldn't sin; God had made the rules! I felt crushed. It seemed inconceivable, something worse than dishonest—a heinous sort of betrayal that the second part of the prophecy had been omitted from the New Testament and had never been taught to me.

When I asked my pastor, he blithely told me that the first half referred to Jesus and the second to King Solomon. That would have been wonderful, but it seemed like an obvious contrivance. I knew that there was no record of Solomon ever being flogged, but anyone familiar with the crucifixion story knew that Jesus had been. If Christians were going to split the prophecy, we should have done it the other way around. I examined both passages, researched the history of the verse, and had to conclude that there was no reason to separate the sentences. By separating them, the author of Hebrews and the early leaders of the church had completely changed what they said.

I read, reread, and thought about all the verses about the Messiah. However I looked at them, it seemed clear that the person they predicted could not have been God on earth. To the contrary, to fulfill the prophecies, he had to be both human and humanly fallible. Taken as a whole, the Old Testament said that he would be given the Spirit of wisdom, understanding, counsel, power, knowledge and the fear of the Lord; despite it all, he'd still end up being punished for something. I tried hard to convince myself that human fallibility was a characteristic that God had to take on before He could understand us. I actually had a few people I trusted assure me that God *had* to fail before He could understand how we could. Even then, the idea that the God who created man and woman at the beginning of our time on earth hadn't understood everything about us seemed ludicrous. That said, I probably would have gone that route eventually and found some way to rationalize how a perfect God would have graciously developed the ability to sin (perhaps because He needed to earn the right to deserve His own punishment), except for one thing: I realized that all the Bible said was that the Messiah was a descendant of David established by God to reign on earth over God's people. Try as I might, I couldn't find the verse that explained why I had to believe that the Messiah would be God.

I was becoming more and more confused. The Bible had completely contradicted everything that I had been taught to believe about Jesus. Convinced that I had to be on the wrong track, I searched even harder for verses that would support the idea that Jesus was God incarnate. I thought I'd found one when my New American Standard Revised Version quoted a verse from the Psalms in Hebrews 1:5: "You are my Son; today I have begotten you." In the book of Hebrews, it seemed to be clear that Jesus, as God's son, had to be God, too. However, I couldn't find where the Bible said that Godhood was hereditary.

I don't remember when I first began to ask myself why I'd always accepted that calling Jesus the "Son of God" meant that he was God as well. I'd never really considered the question that way because I'd always been sure that everything else in the Bible had come to the same conclusion from a number of different directions. Since "everything else" had ended up being quite different from what I'd been expecting, I was faced with relying on that one pathway to Godhood all by itself. Suddenly it seemed a lot less reliable. Although the Greek and Roman religions agreed that the sons of gods were at least partially divine, when I actually considered it, the whole concept seemed incompatible with monotheism. I knew that many of the early fathers of the church had been raised and educated in a Greco-Roman culture. Out of respect for them, I could almost bring myself to believe that incorporating that background into my own faith was okay. Maybe those ancient Greek storytellers had known something all along. Yet I knew in my heart that using another religion's beliefs about its many gods to justify my own beliefs about Christianity's one God had to be fundamentally wrong.

It only got worse when I found out that the verse that was quoted in Hebrews 1:5—Psalm 2:7—actually said:

> "I will proclaim the decree of the Lord: he said to me, 'You are my Son; today I have become your Father.'"

The footnotes in my New International Version said that the verse could be translated into English (and, I supposed, Greek) either as "become your Father" or as "begotten you." Apparently, there was conceptually no difference in the original Hebrew. In my NIV, they were both translated in the same fashion as in the Psalm. But if the verse actually meant "become your Father," it seemed to speak more to adoption and exaltation than to conception. God choosing to treat a servant as if that servant were a son said a lot about God, but not so much about the servant.

I really wanted to believe that the Psalm was supposed to be translated "begotten you," but it seemed unlikely that that was what the author had intended. The voice speaking in Psalm 2:7 had already been born. As I understood it, the act of begetting was something inextricably linked to the moment that a life began; it couldn't be just an acknowledgment. Thus, I couldn't even rely on that line of argument to provide the proof I was looking for. The translation I needed to arrive at the meaning I wanted was hard to justify. The theology was even more questionable. It was only when the words were translated as "begotten you" that the verse became capable of supporting the idea that the Messiah was the begotten Son of God. Furthermore, that only made him God if I used the rules of Greco-Roman theo-wrestling.

I had started my quest to correct Islam convinced that the Bible would confirm that Muslims were wrong and I was right. Knowing I was right was the best part of being a Christian! Now, instead of the certain conviction that I was on the path to heaven, I only had questions. I no longer knew where I was going. Only an uncomfortable feeling remained that nothing would ever be the same. I didn't think I was going to be able to get back to where I wanted to be from where I had unexpectedly found myself.

- I tried to make my Muslim friends into Christians by showing them what the Bible said.

- I read the Quran and the Bible carefully, but instead of helping prove I was right, they took the other side!

- I didn't know how I could keep my faith in God if I couldn't have faith in my religion, too.

CHAPTER 8

....

FALTERING FAITH

By now, I was in a bit of a panic. Try as I might to convince myself otherwise, I was being forced to accept that neither the New Testament verses about Jesus being the Son of God nor the Old Testament prophecies about the Messiah supported my own cherished belief that Jesus was God. There had turned out to be a world of difference between Gabriel's proclamation "he will be called the Son of God" in Mark 1:35 and the sort of Son of God that I needed Jesus to be. If Jesus was, as he claimed, the "one anointed to preach Good News to the poor" as prophesied by Isaiah, and if he was the Messiah proclaimed by Gabriel, the apostles, himself, and the rest of the New Testament, then according to the prophecies I had found in the Old Testament, he could not be God too.

I'd begun my journey wanting to prove to my friends that the Bible said Jesus was God, but now I had to do it for my own soul's sake. My family could tell I was upset, and I finally discussed what I was up to with my mother. She reminded me that the verse she used to affirm Jesus' divinity was John 8:58:

> "I tell you the truth," Jesus answered, "before Abraham was born, I am!"

When I heard it had worked for my mom, I wanted to feel relieved. It could have finally been the strong claim to divinity by Jesus I had been looking for: he had used "I Am," the name that God had given to identify Himself to Moses. Whenever I'd considered it before, I'd always assumed that only a Jew who truly believed he was God would do such a thing. I wanted it to be enough; I really wanted to leave my traumatic search behind me, successfully completed, and move on.

Unfortunately, I already knew it wasn't going to be that easy. I'd learned (sometimes the hard way) that I had to look at things more objectively than I was used to before I shared them with my Muslim friends. They tended to ask hard questions! I knew they'd wonder why I thought Jesus had meant that he was God. From their perspective, that was the worst possible sin, and when the question was put that way it did seem like we were reaching. Then I looked into the history of the verse. According to *The Complete Gospels: Annotated Scholar's Version,* a more accurate translation didn't necessarily even end in "I Am"! Robert Miller, editor and member of the famed Jesus Seminar, had written that the following translation was much closer: "As God is my witness, I existed before there was an Abraham." Though this changed my understanding of the verse, it steadied me, too. At least I was going in the right direction. To have existed before Abraham, Jesus had to possess something exceptional. I needed only to find out what that was.

Another verse that my family tried to reassure me with was John 3:16, a favorite among Christians:

> For God so loved the world that he gave his only begotten
> son, that whoever believes in him should not perish but have
> eternal life.

It was good to hear the verse from my relatives and to know that they were still in my corner plugging away. Unfortunately, I had to tell them that I'd already looked at the verse and realized that it wouldn't work on a Muslim. It didn't specify whether it was talking about our belief in Jesus as God, Jesus as Messiah, or Jesus as a prophet. Since Muslims all believed the last two and took issue only with the first, I knew that the verse alone would not be sufficient for them. To make matters worse, I'd looked into the verse's history and found out that an early pope named Jerome had even changed what it said! That was when I learned of the Arian heresy and its pivotal role in the structures and beliefs of the early Christian church. As it turned out, I wasn't the first Christian to have struggled with the Trinity: early in the history of Christianity, a popular leader named Arius from Alexandria in Egypt had argued quite skillfully to support his own interpretation of events. He was convinced that the Holy Scriptures said that God had created Jesus just like everything else. Skillful or not, Arius never managed to convince enough people to change the religion, and his ideas ended up being condemned. They proved surprisingly resilient regardless, and when his followers couldn't be silenced, they had to be brutally suppressed. Afterward, to consolidate belief and prevent further confusion and bloodshed, Pope Jerome changed the original version of John 3:16 (which used *monogenes,* a word that meant "unique" or "special" and could be interpreted either way) to say "unigenitus," which clearly meant "begotten." Thus, the verse originally said exactly the opposite of what I wanted. I couldn't use a verse that meant that Jesus was unique or special; I needed one that said that he was the same as God.

Still not prepared to throw in the towel, I remembered another argument that I had heard used to prove the Bible said Jesus was God. The Book of John included a number of places where Jesus said that he and God were inside each other, such as John 10:38 and John 14:10:

> "But if I do it, even though you do not believe me, believe the miracles, that you may learn and understand that the Father is in me, and I in the Father."

> "Don't you know that I am in the Father and that the Father is in me? The words that I say to you are not my own. Rather, it is the Father, living in me, who is doing his work."

I hoped that I could use those verses to prove divinity by implication; it seemed that for God to be in Jesus and Jesus to be in God, they both had to be one and the same. Unfortunately, that line of reasoning failed pretty quickly. Only ten verses later Jesus said:

> "On that day you will realize that I am in my Father, and you are in me, and I am in you."

That meant that if I wanted to say that Jesus was God because he'd said he and God were inside each other, I'd have to admit that his disciples were God, too! I decided that I would have to read everything else that John had written in the New Testament before I could really attempt to understand what he had meant by *in*. I soon found out that he had been quite explicit in 1 John 2:5–6:

> "But if anyone obeys his word, God's love is truly made complete in him. This is how we know we are in Him: Whoever claims to live in Him must walk as Jesus did."

I quickly gave up on *in*. If John had intended it only to mean following God's commands and trying to emulate Jesus, it wouldn't work for me. So I tried yet another approach. I knew that John 17:22–23 recorded that Jesus had said:

> "I have given them the glory that you gave me, that they may be one as we are one; I in them and you in me. May they be brought to complete unity to let the world know that you sent me and have loved them even as you have loved me."

That passage sounded perfect. I thought I'd finally found the place where Jesus had stated explicitly and unequivocally that he and God were "one." I was filled with hope. He even seemed to be making a distinction between two different sorts of "oneness": that of his followers among themselves and that between him and God. I did a little linguistic research and found out that there were two words for the concept "one" in Greek: *heis* described the numerical concept of "one," and *hen* meant "a unity of essence." With growing excitement, I realized that if Jesus had made a distinction between his oneness with God and his followers' oneness among themselves, then this verse would be an even stronger support for Christian doctrine than I was looking for. To my bitter disappointment, I found that chapters 10 and 17 of John's Gospel had used the same word throughout—it had been *heis*, not *hen*. That meant that Jesus had not differentiated between the two sorts of oneness. For my purposes, *one* was no better than *in*. John 17:22–23 was nothing more than a prayer Jesus had made to God that all his followers would have the same relationship to God as he had.

I eventually had to accept that even with all those mystical, difficult verses taken together, I couldn't prove that Jesus had said that he was God. If the verses meant that, they would have had to apply to the rest of us, too. There are many ways that people can become "one." Couples joined in marriage are described as being one in flesh, possibly referring to sex, but also one in their purpose and goals. Individuals in agreement over some undertaking or disputed point are often described as being one as well. None of those uses connote or denote identity. Likewise, in the Gospel of John, oneness did not mean sameness.

I looked at other stories, too, in hope and desperation. In one of them, Jesus told his disciples that if they saw him, then they saw the Father as well. Near to it was another story where Jesus told his disciples that if they accepted a little child, then they also accepted him. Since Jesus obviously didn't mean that the child was God or that he was that child, I had to concede that this wasn't a personal declaration of divinity either. Although I had always been taught that doing good things for others allowed them to see Jesus in me, I knew that I wasn't God. As I searched in verse after verse after verse, the pattern was always the same. What I wanted to believe had always clouded my interpretation of what Jesus had actually said. I had known all along that the only way I could prove that I was right to my Muslim friends (and by now to myself) was by finding an incontrovertible verse in which either Jesus, an angel, or a prophet declared Jesus to be God. I became despondent.

Cynically, I started to ask myself why I was clinging so hard to Christianity's doctrines in the face of so much evidence that those doctrines weren't supported by the text. If all I really wanted was to believe what the Bible taught me, then I should have been happy. When I had started, I was convinced that my beliefs were exactly what the Bible taught, confirming that my faith would deliver on its promise of an eternally joy-filled existence with God in heaven. Some of my pastors and teachers liked to say that if Jesus wasn't God, then he had to be a liar or a lunatic. I knew that he was neither. Everyone I had ever listened to had always said that the claims that Jesus had made and the things that he had said could not be true unless he was God. Reading the Bible now, I found that what it really said was that Jesus had been a man, strengthened by a spirit from God, but still human and fallible. If that was true, then how could I have any faith in anything else I had been taught?

My beliefs had given my faith a form that I could understand, and I had always believed that form was founded in the Bible. Now, I still wanted to have faith in God, but without the right things to believe and the right reasons to believe them, I didn't know how I could. It had been supremely comforting to believe that that my faith and my religious beliefs were the same and that they were both a gift from God. I remained convinced that if I wanted to go to heaven, I had to believe everything in exactly the same way that I always had. I didn't think that I could get away with changing anything, even though that was what it seemed the Bible said I should do. In a final act of desperation, I pulled out the big guns.

- **I became desperate to prove that Christianity was right because I thought I had to.**

- **I was convinced that if I wasn't following the right religion, I was going to hell!**

- **Instead of reassuring me, the real meaning of the Bible forced me to face how wrong I'd been all along.**

CHAPTER 9

....

FIRMER FOUNDATIONS

Most Christians know that John 1:1 says, "In the beginning was the Word, and the Word was with God, and the Word was God. He was with God at the beginning." As a Christian, I had been certain that John meant that Jesus was God because one of Jesus' official titles was "the Word." I had been excited to discover that Jesus' being the Word was even echoed in the Quran! When I'd begun, I had hoped that this verse was going to be my pièce de résistance with my Muslim friends, but now it was my last-ditch fallback position.

In the Quran, Surah 4:171 proclaims:

> O People of the Book! Commit no excesses in your religion: nor say of Allah aught but the truth. Christ Jesus the son of Mary was (no more than) A Messenger of Allah, *and His Word*, which He bestowed on Mary, and a Spirit proceeding from Him: so believe in Allah and His Messengers. Say not "Trinity": desist.

Even though it contradicted most of the rest of Christian doctrine, particularly the entire concept of the Trinity, this Surah confirmed that one essential point. According to both it and the Bible, Jesus was the Word of God. John 1:1 said that the Word *was* God! Now I was faced with a blatant contradiction between the Old and the New Testaments that was even supported by the Quran. I was terrified that the contradiction would inevitably destroy my ability to believe in anything. Since I was sure that faith was about believing in the correct doctrines of the right religion based on the words of the Bible, I was convinced that the contradiction I'd found would have to destroy my faith in God. That meant I was going to hell. It was hard to have trusted in the church to save me from that fate for so long, only to realize that I had been lied to and lose everything I'd thought I had. Everyone had seemed so earnest and sincere, but at some point, someone must have known what was going on.

Before I gave up, though, I knew that I had to find out what *Word* meant. I looked it up in my *Oxford Companion to the Bible* and discovered that *Word* and *Wisdom* had been synonymous around the time of Jesus. I was amazed to learn that *Word* and *Wisdom* had also been more than just words; they were apparently names for a being that was actually alive. I was even more astonished when I found out that those same Jews had believed that Wisdom had been there and had helped out when God made everything else. Proverbs 3:19 explained:

> By wisdom the Lord laid the earth's foundations, by understanding he set the heavens in place; by his knowledge the deeps were divided, and the clouds let drop the dew.

Even in my state of despair, I found it all fascinating. I followed the *Oxford Companion*'s direction to Proverbs 8:22–30, where Wisdom herself confirmed it all:

> The Lord brought me forth at the beginning of his work before his deeds of old; I was appointed from eternity, from the beginning before the world began. When there were no oceans, I was given birth, when there were no springs abounding with water; before the mountains were settled in place, before the hills, I was given birth, before he made the earth or its fields or any of the dust of the world. I was there when he set the heavens in place, when he marked out the horizon on the face of the deep, when he established the clouds above and fixed securely the fountains of the deep, when he gave the sea its boundary so the waters would not overstep his command, and when he marked out the foundations of the earth. Then I was the craftsman at his side.

My introduction to the Spirit of Wisdom as the firstborn of God's creations came as quite a shock. The answer was so simple. As a Christian, I had always thought that the Holy Spirit was part of the Trinity and therefore a part of God, just like Jesus. Instead, these verses described the Spirit as something that had been created just like the rest of us, but still made it sound as if that created being could fulfill all the criteria set by the opening to the Gospel of John! I started to breathe a little more easily again. If that was really what the Bible said, then I only had to accept that we'd all made a mistake. I found this notion vastly preferable to rejecting the message of every prophet in the Bible, my hope of heaven, and my own faith in God. I quickly dug up everything that I could find about wisdom in my various translations and my *Oxford Companion*. The *Oxford Companion* sent me to two books of Apocrypha called "Wisdom literature."

Two centuries before Jesus the Christ was born, another devout and blessed Jew named Jesus ben Sira studied, lived, and prophesied in and around Jerusalem. He gained great renown as a scholar, and the book he wrote—Sirach, or Ecclesiasticus—was included in the Bible up until the Reformation. Then, according to my *Oxford Companion*, Protestant theologians found only Greek translations of the book, so they decided its origins were questionable and had it and others like it removed. Since then, older Hebrew versions of the text had been discovered at both Qumran and Masada. It seemed to me that the instant the text was found confirmed in its original Hebrew, the reasons for excluding it ceased to exist; in fact, it showed that it shouldn't have been excluded in the first place. In Sirach 24:1–12, Jesus ben Sira proclaims:

> Wisdom praises herself, and tells of her glory in the midst of her people. In the assembly of the Most High she opens her mouth, and in the presence of his hosts she tells of her glory: I came forth from the mouth of the Most High and covered the earth like a mist. I dwelt in the highest heavens, and my throne was in a pillar of cloud. Alone I compassed the vault of heaven and traversed the depths of the abyss. Over waves of the sea, over all the earth, and over every people and nation I have held sway. Among all these I sought a resting place; in whose territory should I abide? Then the Creator

of all things gave me a command, and my Creator chose the place for my tent. He said, "Make your dwelling in Jacob, and in Israel receive your inheritance." Before the ages, in the beginning He created me, and for all the ages I shall not cease to be. In the holy tent, I ministered before Him, and so I was established in Zion. Thus in the beloved city He gave me a resting place, and in Jerusalem was my domain. I took root in an honored people, in the portion of the Lord his heritage.

There was even another book, Wisdom of Solomon, that had gone through the same process of exclusion as Sirach and said virtually the same things. In Wisdom of Solomon 7:25–27, an anonymous Jewish scholar had written:

For she is a breath of the power of God, and a pure emanation of the glory of the Almighty; therefore nothing evil gains entrance into her. For she is a reflection of eternal light, a spotless mirror of the working of God, and an image of His goodness. Although she is but one, she can do all things, and while remaining in herself, she renews all things; in every generation she passes into holy souls and makes them friends of God, and Prophets.

I remember feeling quite angry at the Reformation scholars. In the interests of scriptural purity, they'd decided to leave out so much important information that they'd changed the meaning of the entire Bible! In all my years as a Christian, no one had ever mentioned the creation story in Proverbs or anything else about the Spirit of Wisdom. Yet it was obvious that "she" was able to fulfill everything about the "Word" of the Gospel of John without being God. In retrospect, it seemed unlikely that John had intended anything else. The phrase "and the Word was God. He was with God at the beginning" had always confused me. I had never understood how the Word could "be God" and be "with God" at the same time. With the Spirit of Wisdom, it all made sense.

I had always figured that John 1:1 had been the real beginning of the idea that God could be divided into three in the first place, but Wisdom made the mistake obvious. It was easy to see how the Spirit of Wisdom, as a reflection and image of God, understood by the Jewish scholars of that time to be made solely out of a pure emanation from Him, could be said to "be" God. They had all believed that God, out of His goodness and power, had created Wisdom at the beginning of everything. Saying that Wisdom was God in that context would have made her a kind of subset—just as saying salt is a spice doesn't mean that there are no other spices, or saying that two is a number doesn't mean that all numbers are two. There's no way that John would have been talking about the Trinity: any Jew who had tried to convince the High Priest that God was divisible would have been killed on the spot. Based on what Jesus ben Sira had written in Ecclesiasticus, I could even imagine everyone's excitement, watching and waiting for a sign that Wisdom had finally become manifest among them as prophesied.

I didn't know what to do, where to go, what to think, or who to talk to. However, the panic and despair I had felt earlier had disappeared. I felt that I was close to a real breakthrough. If Jesus, indwelt and supported by the Spirit of Wisdom, could fulfill the prophecies of the Bible and yet not be God, then everything still made sense.

I reread the Book of Proverbs with the Wisdom of Solomon and Sirach. Then I reread all of John's writings and the rest of the Gospels. Then I reread everything else. I realized that there had never been any contradiction between what the Old and New Testaments said about Jesus' relationship to God. Despite what my pastors had said, Jesus was neither God nor a liar nor a lunatic! If John believed that the Spirit sent by God to Jesus had been the same Spirit of Wisdom and Prophecy that was sent to all prophets, then the conflict between Old and New Testaments that I had feared would destroy my faith and send me to hell had never existed.

The doctrine of the Trinity, as it had been taught to me, was that the Holy Spirit, Jesus, and the Father were all aspects of the same divine, eternal, uncreated, one God. Although I had tried my best, I couldn't find any verse in the Bible that actually said that was true. In the Wisdom literature, I had found that doctrine refuted in a way that actually made everything else the Bible said make sense. I finally understood something that my Jewish friends, it turned out, had known all along. The Spirit of Wisdom had been God's first creation, uttered as "God's First Word" or "Breath." After God made her, she was what He then used to complete the rest of creation. Then she had become the Spirit of Inspiration. Wisdom of Solomon 7:22 even said, "For wisdom, the Fashioner of all things, taught me." If the Spirit of Wisdom was what Christians had made into the Holy Spirit, then everything else recorded in the Gospels fit perfectly. I realized that I finally understood what John had meant when he wrote John 1:32:

> Then John [the Baptist] gave this testimony: "I saw the Spirit come down from heaven as a dove and remain on him. I would not have known him, except that the one who sent me to baptize with water told me, 'The man on whom you see the Spirit come down and remain is he who will baptize with the Holy Spirit.'"

When I reread An-Nisa 4:171, I knew that I had finally come to a place where I could rest.

I realized something basic about religion and what had really been at the heart of my problems with it. None of us likes to be wrong about anything. That's just a fact of human nature, but to a religious person it's even more important. If you belong to a religion, being wrong has significant consequences. I'd been fighting, really for my entire life, to prove to myself (and to everybody else unfortunate enough to have to listen to me) that Christianity was "right," and that I was "right," because I thought that I had to be. Even when faced with obvious proof that my religion was self-contradictory, I hadn't wanted to accept what the Bible told me: my beliefs had defined me as a Christian, but as a Christian, they were also the sole basis for any reward I expected to receive. I'd always known that if I ever gave up working so hard to hold on to them, I wouldn't be able to remain the same and neither would my hopes of heaven.

I didn't want to be wrong, and I thought that meant that someone else had to be wrong instead. That's one of the problems with the issue of right and wrong in religion: it predisposes us to look for differences because those differences make us feel safer—at least as long as we can convince ourselves that we're on the correct side of the question. If you look for conflicts, wanting them to be there, then it's inevitable that you're going to find them. To be right, you sometimes have to create the whole idea of wrong in the first place. Then, if you want somebody else to fill that slot for you, you're going to have to create a religion that helps you believe it's true. Those hopes and expectations inevitably end up being imposed on your perceptions of everything. Soon, instead of religions being about what the revelation and the message really were when they began, they start to become more about us and what we want to hear.

I had started out wanting to change what Islam said to my friends, but I had ended up trying to change what the Bible said to me. For me to be right, they had to be wrong, and that meant that we all had to be different. The impact something like that can have on the way we look at other people is bad enough, but the bigger tragedy is the way it can make us see ourselves. One common way to make contrasts between groups more apparent is to focus on the most extreme, radical practices and ideas on the other side. This strategy is popular; it makes distinctions more obvious, and it makes it easier to reassure yourself that the other people are the weird ones. Another method is to choose the most polarizing and confrontational positions yourself. When it first started to look like the messages of the holy books had significant similarities, I had started working harder and harder to prove that they didn't really say the same things at all. Instead of fighting Islam, I ended up fighting with my own faith and with what I believed was the basis of it.

Being right and feeling like you're right are two very different things. If learning that you agree with somebody about God and religion makes you feel less secure in your own faith, then you're going to avoid that knowledge. The quest for truth and the quest for positive affirmation really aren't compatible; if affirmation comes as a consequence of belonging to a group that defines itself by exclusion, then the members of that group will always have to tend toward choices that promote their own distinctiveness, whether they're good choices or not.

I'd been working all my life to keep my doctrines distinct from everybody else's because I thought I had to. When I finally stopped trying to use the Bible to prove that Muslims, Christians, and Jews were different, I found that all our holy books were saying the same things anyway. Trying to keep my beliefs distinct from everyone else hadn't kept me on the right path; in fact, it had almost forced me off it. When I finally accepted that the Bible hadn't said what I thought it had (and stopped trying to force it to say what I wanted it to), the two religions that I thought were supposed to be wrong ended up agreeing with everything that the Bible actually did say! Accepting that even made reading the Bible easier. The Old Testament had said that Jesus would be fallible, punished, and forgiven. I no longer had to tell myself that Jesus was only joking in Mark 10:18 when he said: "Why do you call me good? No one is good—except God alone." It turned out that Jesus had been telling the truth all along.

- My mistake was simple: instead of listening to the Bible and the Quran, I'd been trying to prove that they said what I wanted them to.

- The Bible and the Quran got along better than I thought they would.

- I realized that being right wasn't as important as I'd thought it was.

CHAPTER 10

....

BUILDING BETTER BELIEFS

The "I'm right, you're wrong, and I'll prove it to you!" approach had been full of surprises. I'd been forced to accept that all of the things that I'd been sure made Christianity better than Islam and Judaism weren't even supposed to be part of it. You'd think I would have felt pretty awful, but to my surprise, I actually felt great. I'd been given a crash course on the consequences of playing "doctrinal chicken," and the message had finally been received loud and clear.

When I started, I'd taken the head-on approach for exactly the same reason people play the real game of chicken with their cars. Driving at top speed in opposite directions toward each other is a lot of fun ... for a while. The excitement occurs solely in the approach phase. I'd honestly thought that my search would be an enjoyable experience, and even though it started out well, in the end it wasn't worth it. The real message that was waiting for me pertained to the other similarity between my game and the real chicken. When you play chicken and crash, the severity of the damage is a direct consequence of both the speed and the direction of approach: you get hurt only if you come in hard and fast and manage to be in the same place at the same time as your erstwhile opponent. My experience had been traumatic only because I'd made it that way. We'd all been in the same place all along. If I hadn't backed up and taken a run at everyone, I wouldn't have suffered at all!

Instead of refuting my faith, learning Islam and studying Judaism strengthened my belief in the Bible. The change from constantly struggling to prove that the beliefs of Christianity were distinct from and superior to those of Judaism and Islam, and perpetually having to try and make Jesus and the rest of the prophets support those ideas, was profound. It turned out that I didn't really have to prove anything. I could relax and just accept the holy books and their messages for what they were, which was a lot easier. I'd learned that all three religions were quite compatible, as long as I stuck to what they actually said rather than what other people said about them.

The final message I took home was that I still wanted to trust God. I'd been through the religious equivalent of a train wreck, yet when I did my spiritual pat-down to check that all limbs were still present and accounted for, everything felt the same. When I sat down later and thought about the implications, I was amazed not that I still had any faith, but rather that I'd ever had it in the first place. Despite the fact that I'd been wrong about so much of what I believed, and despite the fact that those beliefs had made my religious practice unnecessarily arrogant, elitist, confrontational, and divisive, it seemed as if God had forgiven me for all of it—even though I hadn't known I'd been wrong and hadn't been able to ask for forgiveness. That was my first inkling that my faith was completely independent from what I happened to be believing at any given time. The way I experienced faith had nothing to do with what I thought I knew about God.

I still wanted to believe something. I also had to test my hypothesis that consensus led to the true path, so I decided to explore what all three religions would tell me about the real implications of Jesus' ministry. Even if he wasn't God, he was still a major figure to at least two of the three. It seemed unlikely that he could ever be removed from his role as the founder and guiding light of Christianity, and in Islam he has always been considered one of the three greatest prophets. His followers are promised a lot in Aal-E- Imran 3:55:

> Behold! Allah said: "O Jesus! I will take thee and raise thee to Myself and clear thee (of the falsehoods) of those who blaspheme; I will make those Who follow thee superior to those who reject faith, to the Day of Resurrection: Then shall ye all return unto me, and I will judge between you of the matters wherein ye dispute."

Both religions agreed that Jesus was the Jewish Messiah, and even though few of the Jews I knew concurred, most of them were more than willing to accord him the respect that they'd give to a rabbi. All three of our religions seemed willing to look for something that Jesus could do for them, even if we couldn't agree on exactly what or how. Nobody seriously doubted that Jesus had been inspired, either. Everybody's holy books said that Wisdom came to God's servants, and everybody agreed that Jesus had been one of the important ones. Frankly, the Holy Quran even seemed to say that we all should pay more attention to what Jesus had said.

I knew that I couldn't blame the Bible for the way Christian scholars had spun it. The only question was whether things had become so obscured over the centuries that it would be impossible to decipher the original message, but that really hadn't been a problem for me so far. Although I'd been frustrated when I first ran into the Muslim contention that the early Christians had played fast and loose with Jesus' actual message, I had found obvious examples in the footnotes and margins of my very own NIV. They'd been there, out in the open, all along. That made it easy for me not to abandon the Christian texts. Finding out what Jesus' real message was hadn't been all that difficult. The Gospels had been surprisingly accurate and informative; only the commentary had been contradictory. With the Spirit of Wisdom as firstborn, strengthening, empowering, and enlightening Jesus, the Bible had become more consistent rather than less so. If I really wanted to believe what it said, the most exciting discovery I'd made was that taken together, the prophecies of the Torah and the Jewish prophets, the Holy Bible, and the Holy Quran had actually supported each other (so far at least). I looked forward to finding out where they were going.

After Godhood, Jesus' crucifixion was the next significant point of conflict between the three, and I had known from the beginning that that would be my next stop. I knew it would be interesting. Many Jews still consider it a tender subject. They've suffered centuries of abuse from irate Christians, angry with them because they killed the Christians' God. Conversely, my Muslim friends seemed to almost cherish their own quibbles with the crucifixion day's events. Their main doctrinal problem was that the idea of one person's punishment being substituted for another's is completely incompatible with the Islamic concept of the intimate relationship we share with God. Most Muslims don't believe that Jesus was crucified; some even call it the cruci-fiction! The Bible and most Christians, on the other hand, are quite firm on the subject.

What the Quran says about the crucifixion can be found in An-Nisa 4:157–158 and Aal-E-Imran 3:54–55:

That they said (in boast), "We killed Christ Jesus the son of Mary, The Messenger of Allah." But they killed him not, nor crucified him, but so it was made to appear to them. And those who differ therein are full of doubts, with no (certain) knowledge, but only conjecture to follow. For of a surety, They killed him not. Nay, Allah raised him up Unto Himself; and Allah is Exalted in Power, Wise—and there is none of the People of the Book but must believe in him before his death. And on the Day of Judgment he will be a witness against them.

And (the unbelievers) plotted and planned, and Allah too planned, and the best of planners is Allah. Behold Allah said: "O Jesus! I will take thee and raise thee to Myself and clear thee (of the falsehoods) of those who blaspheme; I will make those who follow thee superior to those who reject faith, to the Day of Resurrection: Then shall ye all return unto me, and I will judge between you of the matters wherein ye dispute."

When I approached the verses looking for agreement rather than argument, I realized that believers choosing confrontational positions had inflamed the entire controversy. Both sides seemed equally guilty. The most important message that the Quran seemed to be trying to convey was that whatever had happened wasn't the Jews' fault because God had been in control all along. Muslims fixating on disputing the Christian interpretation had been unfortunate; if they'd just gotten the word out that God had arranged it all, they could have saved a lot of Jewish lives and prevented a lot of pogroms. The Quran also seemed clear that *everyone* who argued about exactly what had happened would be running on conjecture—Muslims included. I had to wonder whether those particular verses weren't just a warning to avoid arguing with each other, no matter what the perspective happened to be.

Whatever else, all three holy books agreed that God was in control. In the Old Testament, Isaiah 53:10 said:

Yet it was the Lord's will to crush him and cause him to suffer, and though the Lord makes his life a guilt offering, he will see his offspring and prolong his days, and the will of the Lord will prosper in his hand.

In the New Testament, Jesus confirmed Isaiah's message in Matthew 26:52–53 and John 19:11:

> "Put your sword back in its place," Jesus said to him, "for all who draw the sword will die by the sword. Do you think I cannot call on my Father, and he will at once put at my disposal more than twelve legions of angels? But how then would the Scriptures be fulfilled that say it must happen in this way?"

> Jesus answered, "You would have no power over me if it were not given to you from above."

All three religions seemed happy to accept that Jesus surrendered himself to God, and Muslims and Christians both agreed that God had taken Jesus to heaven. Our arguments were about what had happened in between. Looking at it all myself, I saw a strong parallel with the story of Abraham's obedience to God; there, Abraham's willingness to perform the sacrifice of his firstborn was more important than the actual sacrifice itself. God's reward was based on the intention of His servant and the servant's willingness to give up everything to obey God's commands. It seemed obvious to me that anyone who wanted to argue about the precise mechanism of Jesus' exaltation had missed the point.

Another problem with having to be right all the time in religious arguments is that it's difficult to avoid the temptation to fill in the gaps. Although there are many things our holy books say that are quite explicit, some things aren't. Inevitably, there are a lot of questions the texts don't answer, and our attempts to come up with solutions can lead us into disputes that might remain irresolvable until the end of time if we're not careful. An excellent piece of advice appears in the Holy Quran's Aal-E-Imran 3:7 for anyone trying to understand what is really the Word of God:

> He it is Who has sent down to thee the Book; In it are verses basic or fundamental (of established meaning); They are the foundation of the Book: Others are not of well-established meaning. But those in whose hearts is perversity follow the part thereof that is not of well-established meaning. Seeking discord, and searching for its hidden meanings, but no one

knows its true meanings except Allah. And those who are firmly grounded in knowledge say: "We believe in the Book; the whole of it is from our Lord": and none will grasp the Message except men of understanding.

A respected Muslim scholar named Yusuf Ali once wrote in the commentary to his translation of the verse:

> This passage gives us an important clue to the interpretation of the Holy Quran. Broadly speaking it may be divided into two portions, not given separately, but intermingled.
>
> 1. The nucleus or foundation of the Book, literally "the mother of the Book."
>
> 2. The portion which is not of well-established meaning. It is very fascinating to take up the latter, and exercise our ingenuity about its inner meaning, but since it refers to such profound spiritual matters that human language is inadequate to it, and though people of wisdom may get some light from it, no one should be dogmatic, as the final meaning is known to Allah alone.

I hope nobody who's reading this thinks that he or she is perfect. No matter how hard we try, our ability to understand will never reach that ultimate level. Even if you have the original, untranslated, first-transcribed Word of God in front of you, a normal person can't honestly expect to be right about everything. Unfortunately, some of us are always going to be more wrong than we realize. Human nature being what it is, it's also unlikely that we'll guess correctly when we try to discern how wrong we are. Aal-E-Imran 3:7 is a promise that if you trust God and the revelation you're working from, what's important will be made clear. As a corollary, that also means that if there's room for argument about the interpretation of a particular verse, the absolute meaning can't be as important as we think it is. The verse says that the important stuff is going to be unequivocal.

If you choose to believe that God has gone to all the trouble to provide us with divine guidance, then you should be prepared to believe that He's made it possible to get the gist of the important parts right. More important, we should all realize that it's always going to be a perversion of both faith and revelation to go looking for things to fight about. If God really wants to communicate with us, then it's a bad idea to try to use His Words for anything other than what they're meant for, especially if we're using the Words to confuse others. Whenever I was studying the Quran and the Bible and thought I had found a contradiction, the problem always turned out to be something that I'd thought they said or somebody else had told me they said. If I read the words myself and checked the meaning carefully, there were never any conflicts—even about something as controversial as the crucifixion. The Quran said that everyone who argued would inevitably misinterpret the import of the events of the day. Isaiah 53:10 said that the suffering servant would "see his offspring and prolong his days, and the will of the Lord would prosper in his hand." Neither the Quran nor Isaiah 53 said exactly where Jesus was going to be when those prophecies were being fulfilled.

- **I'd grown up convinced that for me to be right, someone else had to be wrong.**

- **I knew that even though I'd been the one who was wrong, God had always been there for me.**

- **That meant being wrong couldn't have been as important as I'd thought it was, either.**

CHAPTER 11

....

CREATING CONSENSUS

onsensus had passed its first test, and so I continued my search for answers in the rest of the Gospels, cross-checking what was written there with the Old Testament and then seeing whether any of it disagreed with the Quran. My first surprise came in the book of Matthew. I had always thought that the Old Testament prophecy in Isaiah 53:4—"He took up our infirmities and carried our diseases"—was about how Jesus had been an atoning sacrifice for everyone, and that the infirmities and diseases Isaiah was talking about were our sins. But when Matthew referred to the sacrifice in his Gospel, he did so in the context of a series of miraculous healings that Jesus had performed. That meant Matthew had thought Isaiah was talking only about Jesus' healing ministry. Even though both Isaiah 53:4 and Matthew 12:18–21 confirmed that Matthew had identified Jesus as Isaiah's "suffering servant," it was obvious Isaiah hadn't considered "suffering servant" to be another name for God. Isaiah had actually written something very compatible with Islam's view, with God and Jesus distinct each from the other:

> "Here is my servant whom I have chosen, the one I love, in whom I delight; I will put my Spirit on him, and he will proclaim justice to the nations. He will not quarrel or cry out; no one will hear his voice in the streets. A bruised reed he will not break, and a smoldering wick he will not snuff out, till he leads justice to victory. In his name the nations will put their hope."

Later in Matthew (at the Last Supper), I read that Jesus had said the following:

> "This is my blood of the covenant, which is poured out for
> many for the forgiveness of sins."

I realized something else: I had always believed that Jesus was referring to his blood pouring out to wash away sins. That was the whole basis of the New Covenant of Christianity! Terminating the Old Covenant was what made it so different from Judaism. In retrospect, since "poured out" actually modified the noun phrase "blood of the covenant," it looked more like Jesus was linking himself to the old one rather than proclaiming something new. If that was true, then when Jesus alluded to the wine they were drinking, he was confirming that the Old Covenant was still in force. Christians read it the way they do because that makes it seem as if it foreshadows a later event on the hill of Golgotha. There, according to John 19:34:

> One of the soldiers pierced Jesus' side with a spear, bringing
> a sudden flow of blood and water.

By linking the wine to Jesus' blood, Christian scholars have made the verses sound as if they prove that Jesus ended one Covenant and began another, activated by his own sacrifice. If Jesus was linking the wine to the Old Covenant instead, that would mean he wasn't replacing it at all.

I had finally come to the crux of the difference between Christianity, Judaism, and Islam. All of them traced their beginnings back to the deal between God and Abraham. Terminating that Covenant would have terminated the Jewish religion and potentially the very existence of Jews as a separate people. That meant that the Jews required the Covenant to continue, but so did Islam. The Quran, dictated six hundred years after Jesus walked the earth, repeatedly pronounces that the Covenant was still in force then and that it should still be today. If the Bible really had said it wasn't, then the issue would be irreconcilable. The real question I had to answer was twofold: Had Jesus actually thought that he was closing off the Old Testament Covenant between God and Abraham? And had he really believed that he could replace it with his own?

I was right back where I had first started with Christianity when I was ten years old; this time, however, I already knew the answer. Posing the question that way made the answer obvious, even though I hadn't known it at the time. Jesus' own words said that he never even intended to end Judaism. In fact, Matthew 5:17 promised the following:

> "Do not think that I have come to abolish the Law or the
> Prophets; I have not come to abolish them but to fulfill them.
> I tell you the truth, until heaven and earth disappear, not the
> smallest letter, not the least stroke of a pen, will by any means
> disappear from the Law until everything is accomplished.
> Anyone who breaks one of the least of these commandments
> and teaches others to do the same will be called least in the
> kingdom of heaven."

Those words were unequivocal: Jesus had come to confirm that all the
Law and God's promises were still in force and to prove by his own life that
it was possible for a man to satisfy their terms.

The Great Commission recorded in Matthew didn't tell Jesus' disciples
to proclaim forgiveness in the name of Jesus or by the blood of Jesus.
Throughout his entire ministry, he was insistent that he wanted to make
people believers in God, not in him! Jesus told them to proclaim baptism as
an act of repentance, not absolution, and he recommended full compliance
with all God's commands. In my New International Version Study Bible's
translation of the Gospel of Mark, the only reference I found to simple belief
leading to forgiveness was in 16:9–20, but according to the footnotes, those
verses weren't even included for the first hundred or so years. The NIV
also told me that when Jesus promised reconciliation with God in Luke
24:46–49, biblical scholars could only be sure that he had said either:

> The Christ will suffer and rise from the dead on the third day,
> and repentance and the forgiveness of sins will be preached
> in his name to all nations, beginning at Jerusalem.

or

> The Christ will suffer and rise from the dead on the third day,
> and the change of heart that brings about the forgiveness of
> sins will be preached in his name to all nations, beginning at
> Jerusalem.

No matter which of them best represented the actual words of Jesus,
neither version supported contemporary Christianity's idea of forgiveness.
Instead of proclaiming absolution by way of belief, both said that repentance

had to come before forgiveness for Christians, just as it did for Muslims and Jews.

What did happen that day? Most of Jesus' promises were recorded in the Gospel of John. Reading through what he'd said, the first verse I found was John 12:24:

> "I tell you the truth, unless a kernel of wheat falls to the ground and dies, it remains only a single seed. But if it dies, it produces many seeds ..."

It wasn't very helpful. Although Jesus talked about the necessity of death or transformation in a general way, and even foreshadowed an important purpose for his own, he said nothing about the specific outcome. Neither was the next verse I came to, John 12:32:

> "But I, when I am lifted up from the earth, will draw all men to myself."

Even though the verse clearly showed that Jesus knew he'd have a worldwide impact, he didn't say what that impact would be.

I finally found a verse in John 14:3 where Jesus specifically said what he expected to do after being taken away by God. Neither that verse nor a later one—John 16:5–7—said anything about him being a sacrifice of universal absolution.

> "And if I go and prepare a place for you, I will come back and take you to be with me that you may also be where I am."

> "Now I am going to him who sent me, yet none of you asks me, 'Where are you going?' Because I have said these things, you are filled with grief. But I tell you the truth: It is for your good that I am going away. Unless I go away, The Counselor will not come to you; but if I go, I will send him to you."

None of the Gospels had any verses that claimed Jesus was a sacrifice for anyone's sins. In all of them, Jesus taught that God demanded repentance and obedience first. John 15:9–10 was quite explicit:

"As the Father has loved me, so have I loved you. Now remain in my love. If you obey my commands, you will remain in my love, just as I have obeyed my Father's commands and remain in his love."

And so was John 8:29:

"The one who sent me is with me; he has not left me alone, for I always do what pleases him."

In fact, both verses imply that even Jesus had to play by the same rules as the rest of us if he wanted to remain in God's good books!

Rather than predicting the direction that Christianity would eventually go, the Old Testament prophecies confirmed Jesus' self-stated role. Isaiah 49:6 promised:

"It is too small a thing for you to be my servant to restore the tribes of Jacob and bring back those of Israel I have kept. I will also make you a light for the Gentiles, that you may bring my salvation to the ends of the earth."

It was obvious that, instead of bringing a New Covenant, Isaiah had predicted that the servant would restore Israel to the tribes of Jacob and be a beacon for the rest of the world. Clearly it was his message, not his mode of departure, that mattered the most. Given all of the confusion for the last two millennia, it was surprising to see just how clear and concise the verses really were. Then I read what I had always thought of as the longest and most confusing prophecy: the one about the servant in Isaiah 53. It turned out that the passage told me pretty much everything else I needed to know.

Isaiah 53 has always been a favorite for most Christians; it's spawned a bevy of songs and sermons and even some books. Despite that, I had always thought that it was a little self-contradictory. In it, Isaiah prophesied the following:

Who has believed our message and to whom has the arm of the Lord been revealed? He grew up before him like a tender shoot, and like a root out of dry ground. He had no beauty or majesty to attract us to him, nothing in his appearance that we should desire him. He was despised and rejected by men, a man of sorrows, and familiar with suffering. Like one from whom men hide their faces he was despised, and we esteemed him not. Surely he took up our infirmities and carried our sorrows, yet we considered him stricken by God, smitten by him and afflicted. But he was pierced for our transgressions, he was crushed for our iniquities; the punishment that brought us peace was upon him, and by his wounds we are healed. We all, like sheep, have gone astray, each of us has turned to his own way; and the Lord has laid on him the iniquity of us all. He was oppressed and afflicted, yet he did not open his mouth; he was led like a lamb to the slaughter, and as a sheep before her shearers is silent, so he did not open his mouth. By oppression and judgment he was taken away. And who can speak of his descendants? For he was cut off from the land of the living; for the transgression of my people he was stricken. He was assigned a grave with the wicked and with the rich in his death, though he had done no violence, nor was any deceit in his mouth. Yet it was the Lord's will to crush him and cause him to suffer, and though the Lord makes his life a guilt offering, he will see his offspring and prolong his days, and the will of the Lord will prosper in his hand. After the suffering of his soul, he will see the light of life and be satisfied; by his knowledge my righteous servant will justify many and he will bear their iniquities. Therefore I will give him a portion among the great, and he will divide the spoils with the strong, because he poured out his life unto death, and was numbered with the transgressors. For he bore the sin of many, and made intercession for the transgressors.

Reading it again, I realized the passage wasn't at all confusing if I was willing to accept that Isaiah didn't think that the servant was God. Instead, it answered most of my remaining questions. Isaiah had promised that we'd all be blessed by knowledge and by the servant's intercession, not his sacrifice. Isaiah's perspective on the real reason for Jesus' suffering was the most illuminating part of the passage. He had written that it was a "guilt offering." As a Christian, I had always assumed that a guilt offering had to be a general sacrifice of atonement, like the scapegoat sacrifice on Yom Kippur—something done for everyone. I'd also believed that making it and being it had been the primary purposes of Jesus' coming. But looking back in the Old Testament to find out what a guilt offering actually was, I found that what Moses had written in Leviticus 5:14–19 meant that the sacrifice couldn't possibly be universal:

> The Lord said to Moses: "When a person commits a violation and sins unintentionally in regard to any of the Lord's Holy things, he is to bring to the Lord as a penalty a ram from the flock, one without defect and of the proper value in silver, according to the sanctuary shekel. It is a guilt offering. He must make restitution for what he has failed to do in regard to the holy things, add a fifth of the value to that and give it all to the priest, who will make atonement for him with the ram as a guilt offering, and he will be forgiven. If a person sins and does what is forbidden in any of the Lord's commands, even though he does not know it, he is guilty and will be held responsible. He is to bring to the priest as a guilt offering a ram from the flock, one without defect and of the proper value. In this way the priest will make atonement for him for the wrong he has committed unintentionally, and he will be forgiven."

According to the Book of Leviticus, guilt offerings helped only with unintentional sins, particularly concerning one of "the Lord's Holy things." They were literally an offering for guilt, not for actual transgression— meaning that Jesus' suffering was a rite of personal purification. Instead of being a sacrifice of global atonement, the act seemed more likely to arise from the fact that even though he had been good his whole life, Jesus accepted that he had to be flogged, humiliated, and sent to his death by Pontius Pilate as part of his own submission to the sovereignty of God.

Now all I had left to do was find out what Jesus himself had said his intercession was supposed to be for. It was surprisingly easy. Jesus had specifically stated that the result of his followers' faith would be obedience to God and the help of the Spirit. John 14:15–17 recorded that Jesus said the following:

"If you love me you will obey what I command. And I will ask the Father and he will give you another Counselor to be with you forever—the Spirit of Truth. The world cannot accept him, because it neither sees him nor knows him. But you know him for he lives with you and will be in you."

Then, John 16:5–11 expanded and clarified Jesus' words:

"Now I am going to him who sent me, yet none of you asks me, 'Where are you going?' Because I have said these things, you are filled with grief. But I tell you the truth: It is for your good that I am going away. Unless I go away, the Counselor will not come to you; but if I go, I will send him to you. When he comes he will convict the world of guilt in regard to sin and righteousness and judgment: In regard to sin, because men do not believe in me; in regard to righteousness, because I am going to the Father, where you can see me no longer; and in regard to judgment, because the prince of this world now stands condemned."

If Jesus had been planning to pay the blood price for all his followers, I think he would have said so. If it were supposed to be some sort of a test of faith, he probably would have said nothing at all; lying isn't a behavior characteristic of either a prophet or a kind and loving God. Instead, Jesus said plainly how his followers would benefit. He promised that if they loved him, they would obey him, and that if they did, they would receive God's grace. In John 5:28–29, he told them the following:

"Do not be amazed by this, for a time is coming when all who are in their graves will hear his voice and come out—those who have done good will rise to live, those who have done evil will rise to be condemned."

He was very clear that compliance would be required. Then in John 8:31, he said:

"If you hold to my teaching, you are really my disciples. Then you will know the truth and the truth will set you free."

He established that his followers would have to do as they were told. Finally, in John 14:23 he proclaimed:

> "If anyone loves me, he will obey my teaching. My Father will love him, and we will come to him and make our home with him."

Jesus confirmed that the holy books were all in agreement, and the consensus was complete: Christians had been promised the same path to divine reconciliation as the followers of Moses and Muhammad were. Like them, Jesus had taught that we'd all be rewarded for the good that we'd done, not for the precision we brought to our believing. In all the holy books, everyone had been promising the same things, all along.

- **I realized that neither the Bible nor the Quran said that God only wanted us to believe things.**
- **Both books said that the things they taught were intended to help us become better people and better servants of God.**
- **Jesus and Muhammad said the same things in different ways, and both of them promised that God would help, too.**

CHAPTER 12

....

APOSTOLIC ASSENT

N ow that it was clear Jesus had never intended to terminate the Old
Covenant of Abraham, I was left wondering where Christianity
had started its long, slow slide away. One of the biggest surprises
I'd had was how easy it had been to get back to where I was from where
I'd been! It wasn't just idle curiosity; there was one last place I could check
my conclusions to make sure I wasn't headed down some new doctrinal
dead end. The process would have had to begin in the early years of the
church, when the Bible was first being written. That meant I'd likely find
the answer in the Epistles, a series of letters written by Jesus' apostles. I
already knew that I needed to read the Epistles again. Jesus had promised
his first followers the Spirit's help in continuing his legacy. If I was going
to continue taking everything the holy books had said at face value, then I
knew I'd have to find a way to reconcile everything they'd written, too.

I started with the apostle John because I'd always thought of him as a
bit of an enigma. The Gospels implied that Jesus had loved him the most
of his followers, but then said little else about their relationship. I'd always
wondered, since Jesus had put Peter, not John, in charge before he left.

John had left us with 1 John 5:20:

> We know also that the Son of God has come and has given us
> understanding, so that we may know him who is true. And
> we are in him who is true even in his Son Jesus Christ. He is
> the true God and eternal life.

So I had always been sure that John believed Jesus was God. Reading it now, I realized that I'd have to be a little more careful. Since "his" and "him" actually referred to God and not to Jesus, the final "He" could have referred to either. I had also been convinced that John believed God's forgiveness sprung from the substitutive nature of Jesus' sacrifice, because of 1 John 1:7, John 5:12, and 1 John 5:13:

> And the blood of Jesus, his Son, purifies us from every sin.

> He who has the Son has life; he who does not have the Son of God does not have life.

> I write these things to you who believe in the name of the Son of God so that you may know that you have eternal life.

However, the exact way in which John thought each person's salvation would come about—whether through belief alone or through belief-based repentance—had always eluded me. In 1 John 1:9 and 1 John 1:3–5 he presents two different possibilities:

> If we confess our sins, he is faithful and just and will forgive us our sins and purify us from all unrighteousness.

> We know that we have come to know him if we obey his commands. The man who says, "I know him," but does not do what he commands is a liar, and the truth is not in him. But if anyone obeys his word, God's love is truly made complete in him. This is how we know we are in him: Whoever claims to live in him must walk as Jesus did.

On the questions of Jesus' divinity and the path to salvation, according to these passages, it honestly looked like John could have gone either way.

What John had really intended became clearer as I slowly worked my way through everything else he'd written, looking for verses about Jesus, sacrifice, forgiveness, and salvation. In 1 John 3:7–10, he proclaimed the following:

> Dear children, do not let anyone lead you astray. He who does what is right is righteous, just as he is righteous. He

who does what is sinful is of the devil, because the devil has been sinning from the beginning. The reason the Son of God appeared was to destroy the devil's work. No one who is born of God will continue to sin, because God's seed remains in him; he cannot go on sinning, because he has been born of God. This is how we know who the children of God are and who the children of the devil are: Anyone who does not do what is right is not a child of God; neither is anyone who does not love his brother.

Here, I realized that John had actually melded the ideas of repentance and obedience with adoption and family. According to him, it was by following God's rules that we all became God's children. Then, when I came to 1 John 3:4–6, I saw something else. It said:

Everyone who sins breaks the law: in fact, sin is lawlessness. But you know that he appeared so that he might take away our sins. And in him is no sin. No one who lives in him keeps on sinning. No one who continues to sin has either seen him or known him.

My teachers had actually used those verses to prove that Jesus was a sacrifice to take away the *penalty* for our sins. However, I knew that interpretation would work only if I pretended I didn't already know that 1 John 2:5–6 had clarified that "in Jesus" or "in God" referred to fidelity, not possession. In truth, John had only intended to say that if you really wanted to follow Jesus, you would have to stop doing things that you knew were wrong.

Although I could find plenty of verses where John had written that belief in Jesus brought on forgiveness in a general sense, he explained in more specific terms that belief led to confession and repentance and that those were the bases of any real reconciliation. As for thinking Jesus was the Son of God, it turned out that he considered me (and everyone else) to be the sons (and daughters) of God, too! For example, 1 John 3:1–3 said:

How great is the love the Father has lavished on us, that we should be called children of God! And this is what we are! The reason the world does not know us is that it did not know him. Dear friends: Now we are children of God, and what we will be has not yet been made known. But we know that when he appears, we shall be like him, for we shall see him as he is. Everyone who has this hope in him purifies himself, just as he is pure.

It had been an interesting year. When I had gone looking for a way to show that the Messiah was God, I'd had to accept that Jesus was only supposed to be a very special man. When I went to the Gospels to prove that Jesus had said that he was God and that his death would redeem humankind, I'd found out that he'd actually said he had come to bring us all the help of the Spirit. Now in John's letters, expecting to find the roots of modern Christianity, I saw that the difference between what I'd expected and what he'd written was pretty much the same as it had been everywhere else. Even John wasn't responsible for modern Christianity.

Next came the apostle Paul. When I was growing up, I had been taught various things about him and his work. The Lutherans had told me that he was an authoritarian; the Baptists had acclaimed him as the one who'd liberated Christians from the Law! It had always been fun to chuckle about what that said about Lutherans and Baptists. But I wasn't sure what I'd find on my own. Given the strength of feeling Paul generated, I'd always just gone with the spin of whomever I was listening to. Whatever else, I had been convinced that Paul had thought that Jesus was God because of Philippians 2:6 and Colossians 1:15–16:

> Who, being in the form of God, did not consider equality with God something to be grasped.

> He is the image of the invisible God, the firstborn over all creation. By him all things were created: things in heaven and on earth.

The truth was, Paul had always confused me a little, too, since he had also written 1 Corinthians 11:7:

> A man ought not to cover his head since he is the image and glory of God.

It had always seemed just possible that Paul thought the rest of us were God, too.

When I actually sat down and read everything he'd written, I realized that one of the reasons Paul was so difficult to understand was something I'd run into before: the Spirit of Wisdom changed everything. Paul had trained under some of the greatest teachers of his time. Like most academics, he seemed to enjoy complicated language and phrasing, but the real problem seemed to be one of context. Since the Wisdom books had been written around the time Paul had lived and hadn't yet been excluded from study, he would undoubtedly have been familiar with their content. Back then Jewish scholars said that the Spirit of Wisdom was the firstborn of God's creations, an image of God, and an active participant in the process of creation. When Paul said that Jesus was the firstborn through whom all else was created, he was only describing Jesus in the same way as the Spirit of Wisdom. Achieving Godhood from there would have been quite a stretch. Likewise, since he'd also said that man was the image and glory of God, saying that Jesus was the image of God couldn't have meant he thought Jesus was all that different from the rest of us. As a Christian, I had always been sure that I understood Paul. Now, after everything I had gone through the last year, I realized that I had never understood him at all.

The Spirit of Wisdom helped explain many difficult passages. I'd always accepted that Philippians 2:6 proved that Paul believed Jesus had been God in heaven and then become a man on earth—then I'd tried my best not to think about it too much. It had always made me uncomfortable; no one had ever been able to explain to me how God could choose not to grasp at equality with Himself! It made much more sense to deal with it in the context of the Spirit's prophesied incarnation, juxtaposed with the Creation story.

A recurring theme throughout Paul's letters was that Spirit was good and flesh was bad. He also seemed convinced that the two had become separated because of the fall of man. In the garden, Adam and Eve had grasped at equality with God, and as punishment they'd been expelled from heaven, bringing dishonor to all humankind. Paul believed that Jesus had redeemed us by fulfilling the Law, and in doing so had redeemed flesh as well, returning it to its appropriate relationship with Spirit. Viewed through that lens, Philippians 2 actually shed some light on how Jesus did this. Instead of proclaiming the unity of the Father and the Son, Paul was only saying that instead of being expelled from paradise and forced into the flesh on earth like Adam and Eve, the Spirit of Wisdom had come among us willingly.

Had Paul really tried to make any significant changes to the religion Jesus had left behind? His perspective was certainly different, and he did talk a lot about Jesus in the context of his being a sacrifice, but he didn't seem to think his sacrifice had much to do with absolution. For him it functioned more as an attention-getter! Although he had written, "Through Jesus forgiveness is proclaimed" in Acts 13:38, it seemed wrong to say that the verse meant anything more than it actually said. Romans 2:6–8 seemed to indicate Paul hadn't intended to disagree with Jesus at all. There he'd written:

> God will give to each person according to what he has done. To those who by persistence in doing good seek glory, honor and immortality, he will give eternal life. But for those who are self-seeking and who reject the truth and follow evil, there will be wrath and anger.

Despite how often he wrote that Jesus had died for all of humanity and that we were all "justified" by his blood, Paul never actually described the process in a way that contradicted how Jesus himself had said salvation would come. Like Jesus, he proclaimed that everyone would be judged on the basis of his or her own behavior and faith: that made his comments quite confusing. Parts of the Book of Romans even seemed to imply that Paul somehow figured that sin was actually created by the Law in the first place! I was relieved when I read Ephesians 1:13 and Romans 8:9–17; they finally gave me strong additional confirmations that Paul had intended only to teach what Jesus had taught. The verses both promised redemption by way of obedience, with the help of the Spirit.

> And you also were included in Christ when you heard the word of truth, the gospel of your salvation. Having believed, you were marked in him with a seal, the promised Holy Spirit, who is a deposit guaranteeing our inheritance until the redemption of those who are God's possession—to the praise of his glory.

You, however, are controlled not by the sinful nature, but by the Spirit, if the Spirit of God lives in you. And if anyone does not have the Spirit of Christ, he does not belong to Christ. But if Christ is in you, your body is dead because of sin, yet your spirit is alive because of righteousness. And if the Spirit of him who raised Jesus from the dead is living in you, he who raised Christ from the dead will also give life to your mortal bodies through his Spirit, who lives in you. Therefore, brothers, we have an obligation—but it is not to the sinful nature, to live according to it. For if you live according to the sinful nature, you will die, but if by the Spirit you put to death the misdeeds of the body, you will live, because those who are led by the Spirit of God are the sons of God: For you did not receive a spirit that makes you a slave again to fear, but you received the Spirit of sonship. And by him we cry "Abba, Father." The Spirit himself testifies with our spirit that we are God's children. Now if we are children, then we are heirs—heirs of God and co-heirs with Christ, if indeed we share in his suffering in order that we may also share in his glory.

As I neared the end of his story, I discovered that Paul hadn't even thought that he had diverged significantly from Judaism. When King Herod Agrippa (the Herod appointed by Caligula) questioned him before he went to Rome, Acts 26:15–23 records that Paul told him the following:

"Then I asked, 'Who are you, Lord?' 'I am Jesus, whom you are persecuting,' the Lord replied. 'Now get up and stand on your feet. I have appeared to you to appoint you as a servant and as a witness of what you have seen of me and what I will show you. I will rescue you from your own people and from the Gentiles. I am sending you to open their eyes and turn them from darkness to light, and from the power of Satan to God, so that they may receive forgiveness of sins and a place among those who are sanctified by faith in me.' So then, King Agrippa, I was not disobedient to the vision from heaven. First to those in Damascus, then to those in Jerusalem and in all Judea, and to the Gentiles also, I preached that they should repent and turn to God and prove their repentance by their deeds. That is why the Jews seized me in the temple courts and tried to kill me. But I have had God's help to this very day, and so I stand here and testify to small and great alike. I am saying nothing beyond what the prophets and Moses said would happen—that the Christ would suffer and, as the first to rise from the dead, would proclaim light to his own people and to the Gentiles."

Despite all the apparent contradictions, Christians eventually came to base so much of their religion on Paul that he's often even called the second founder of Christianity. One of the biggest surprises I found was that the man Jesus had intended to found his church had warned them not to pay Paul too much attention. In 2 Peter 3:16, Peter cautioned his followers:

He writes the same way in all his letters, speaking in them of these matters. His letters contain some things that are hard to understand, which ignorant and unstable people distort, as they do the other scriptures, to their own destruction.

I could only wish that someone had mentioned that passage to me before.

In the end, the only verses that my Bible claimed John and Paul had written that actually disagreed with what Jesus had said turned out to be nothing more than the most popular alternatives among the many that were available when the Bible was being compiled. The main text of my NIV claimed that 1 John 2:2 and 1 John 4:10 said:

He is the atoning sacrifice for our sins, and not only for ours but also for the sins of the whole world.

This is love: not that we loved God, but that he loved us and sent his Son as an atoning sacrifice for our sins.

Without a doubt, both verses were strong supports for contemporary Christian doctrine. Likewise, according to my Bible, Romans 9:5 recorded that Paul had written:

Theirs are the patriarchs, and from them is traced the human ancestry of Christ, who is God over all, forever praised!

It also claimed that in Romans 3:25, he had declared:

God presented him as a sacrifice of atonement, through faith in his blood.

Clearly, these four verses made it look like it had been John and Paul who had first begun to slip away.

According to my NIV, though, the four verses had something else in common: each had footnotes admitting that there were multiple interpretations available. The footnotes clarified (in small print) that instead of proclaiming Jesus to be our atoning sacrifice, John might actually have said this:

He is the one who turns aside God's wrath, taking away our sins, and not only ours but also the sins of the whole world

Or he might have said this:

This is love: not that we loved God, but that he loved us and sent his Son as the one who would turn aside his wrath, taking away our sins.

There was a big difference between the two versions. Only one of them claimed that Jesus had taken away anyone's punishment. I already knew that when John wrote "taking away sins" he only meant telling people to stop doing things they knew were wrong.

My NIV study Bible also admitted that Paul might really have intended to say one of the following:

Theirs are the patriarchs, and from them is traced the human ancestry of Christ, who is over all, God be forever praised!

Theirs are the patriarchs, and from them is traced the human ancestry of Christ, God who is over all be forever praised!

> God presented him as the one who would turn aside his
> wrath, taking away sin, through faith in his blood.

Any one of those alternatives—with God and Jesus playing distinctly different roles and receiving distinctly different levels of adulation—was also completely compatible with what had been taught by Jesus and was still being taught by Judaism and Islam.

Throughout my review of the Bible, I'd been surprised by the amount of tampering I'd found, but I'd always been able to give the people who'd done it the benefit of the doubt. A lot of the changes could have been well-meaning attempts at clarification, and the modifications that Pope Jerome made to John 3:16 had at least prevented some bloodshed. These modifications were different: in each case, one of the versions had to have started with a lie. In researching how the versions that had been promoted were chosen, I learned that it had been by a sort of vote, where the frequency of the versions available was simply counted. Experts conferred, but it was usually the most common version that was finally perpetuated. That meant that no one had tried to find out which version was actually correct. The process they'd followed would work only if you wanted to choose the most popular versions instead.

If people had really had the desire, figuring out which version was right would have been easy. John and Paul had left behind pages of text, not just about what they were trying to say but also about why they were trying to say it. The valid versions of the verses would only have had to agree with everything else the men had written. Truth be told, Paul and John would have had to mention something as important as an atoning sacrifice more than once in their writings. Paul had been quite clear when he summarized his ministry to Herod, and he'd somehow left that part out. John's letters actually carried one of the strongest warnings about the dangers of messing with Jesus' message in the entire Bible! 2 John 7–11 said:

> Many deceivers, who do not acknowledge Jesus Christ
> as coming in the flesh, have gone out into the world. Any
> such person is the deceiver and the antichrist. Watch out
> that you do not lose what you have worked for, but that you
> may be rewarded fully. Anyone who runs ahead and does
> not continue in the teaching of Christ does not have God:
> Whoever continues in the teaching has both the Father and

the Son. If anyone comes to you and does not bring this teaching, do not take him into your house or welcome him. Anyone who welcomes him shares in his wicked work.

Given that, it seemed unlikely that John would have done what he'd forbidden everyone else to do.

At long last, I came to the apostle Peter, a moment I had been looking forward to all along, since Jesus had said that Peter would be the foundation of his church in Matthew 16:18:

"And I tell you that you are Peter, and on this rock I will build my church, and the gates of hell will not overcome it."

I thought that Peter was a good place to finish. He had always been my favorite apostle. Although in church everyone focused on his flaws, I'd found they made him the most human of the lot. Despite those flaws, he showed a powerful yearning to become better than he was, making him easy to relate to.

Since one of his alleged failings had been an unfortunate tendency to correct mistakes that he thought Jesus was making, I wasn't surprised when he didn't proclaim Jesus to be God any more than John and Paul had. If he'd honestly thought Jesus was God, I doubt he would have thought Jesus could make mistakes. Instead, in Acts 2:22, Luke recorded that Peter had told a crowd this:

"Men of Israel, listen to this: Jesus of Nazareth was a man accredited by God to you by miracles, wonders and signs, which God did among you through him."

In Acts 22:36, he announced to another group:

"Therefore, let all Israel be assured of this: God has made this Jesus, whom you crucified, both Lord and Christ."

In Acts 3:13 Peter was quoted as saying:

"The God of Abraham, Isaac and Jacob, the God of our fathers, has glorified his servant Jesus."

Finally, in 1 Peter 1:21, he wrote this:

> Through him you believe in God, who raised him from the
> dead and glorified him, and so your faith and hope are in
> God.

All those verses together confirmed for me that Peter was convinced Jesus was nothing more than a very blessed man.

Nothing in the New Testament indicated that Peter thought Jesus had been a sacrifice of absolution either. He was actually quoted in Acts 2:38 as saying:

> "Repent and be baptized in the name of the Lord Jesus Christ
> so that your sins may be forgiven and you will receive the gift
> of the Holy Spirit."

Then in Acts 3:19, he commanded Jesus' followers in this way:

> "Repent then, and turn to God, so that your sins may be
> wiped out, that times of refreshment may come from the
> Lord."

His intended message was confirmed for me when I found that Luke had written in Acts 3:26 that Peter said:

> "When God raised up his servant, he sent him first to bless
> you by turning you from your wicked ways."

And in support, I found that in 1 Peter 1:13–17, he had written the following:

> Therefore, prepare your minds for action; be self-controlled;
> set your hope fully on the grace to be given you when Jesus
> Christ is revealed. As obedient children, do not conform to
> the evil desire you had when you lived in ignorance. But just
> as he who called you is holy, so be holy in all you do; for
> it is written: "Be holy, because I am holy." Since you call on

a Father who judges each man's work impartially, live your
lives as strangers here in reverent fear.

I honestly didn't think I could have said it any better myself.

I was tired after my long quest for the real meaning of the Gospels,
but I knew I was finally done. I'd looked everywhere and checked every
word, and I'd found the same message repeated again and again. The only
conclusions I was left to draw were that neither the man whom Jesus
had made the heir to his legacy and founder of his church, nor his best
friend, nor even the man whom many of today's Christians consider the
cofounder of Christianity, ended up saying anything different from what
Jesus, Moses, or Muhammad had. If any people could have noticed that
they'd been following the Creator of the universe around, surely it would
have been these three.

- **John, Peter, and Paul didn't say anything substantially different
  from what Jesus had said.**

- **None of them expected Christianity to become distinct
  from Judaism.**

- **The apostles understood that instead of replacing Judaism, Jesus was
  calling the Jewish people back to the path he thought they should be
  on and then reaching out to others from there.**

CHAPTER 13

....

JESUS' CHRISTIANITY

I think it's obvious that Christianity—at least as it was originally envisioned by Jesus—wasn't supposed to end up so incompatible with Judaism and Islam. The path I took to reach that realization began with an exploration of the real roots of the Trinity, just as Muhammad and the Quran said it would, and those roots are planted firmly in Judaism and the Old Testament. The Trinity makes some aspects of the Christian experience easier to describe and explain, but 1600 years of Christian insistence that there be no other way to understand God's nature than as the Trinity has had consequences that are hard to justify. That insistence has required the exclusion of scriptural passages of pivotal importance (not to mention the exclusion of millions of earnest believers) and stifled centuries of dialogue. Belief is a profoundly personal aspect of an individual's expression of faith, and Christians have as much right to believe what they choose as anyone, but modern Christianity's claim that Jesus is the sole path to paradise (revoking earlier Covenants and rendering any future prophecy redundant) doesn't sit very well with Jesus' own honest acceptance of his role in the relationship between God and man. In the transfiguration, he seemed quite comfortably equal to the earlier prophets of Judaism. None of them worshiped him, and that was obviously okay with him at the time. It's true that he declared:

> "I am the Way, and the Truth and the Life; none shall come to the Father but by me."

But given everything else he said, the words seem more likely to have been an endorsement for the "Way of God" Jesus taught, the "Truth of the

Word" he preached, and the shining example of righteous living he left behind rather than a personal declaration of divinity. While most of us will agree that Way, Truth, and Life are all powerful religious tropes, they're all still a far cry from "I Am God Incarnate: Maker of Heaven and Earth."

Growing up, I had always believed that Christianity was better than any alternatives because of its differences. Thus, when I first decided to explore Islam, I set out to prove that my way was *the* way. I read the Bible and the Quran expecting to find that they taught two, or perhaps even three, completely incompatible religions. What I found instead were two books that, when studied together, said virtually the same things. They presented me with a vision of different people with different needs given different religions to help them work together, all of them serving God in their own way.

It turned out that what had set Christianity apart—things like the New Covenant and "Jesus-as-God"—were based on some pretty questionable and inventive interpretations. I had to accept that there really wasn't sufficient support for them in either the Old or the New Testament to justify the sort of profoundly divisive distinctiveness that's become so important to Christianity over the years. Without those extras, the Christianity of Jesus and the apostles became a much kinder, gentler, and less confrontational religion. Instead of making it harder for me to believe, knowing both holy books actually made it easier. Rather than relying on something as ephemeral as belief and as mechanistic as sacrifice by proxy, I finally understood what Hosea 6:6 and Psalm 40:6–7 said:

> For I desire mercy, not sacrifice, and acknowledgment of God rather than burnt offerings.

> Sacrifice and burnt offering you did not desire, but my ears you have pierced (or opened), burnt offering and sin offerings you did not require. Then I said, "Here I am, I have come—it is written about me in the scroll."

Whether you believe in God or not, the message of the holy books is the same. The only thing that belief changes is what you're going to do about it. I think all three texts are clear that Jesus was sent by God and born to a virgin to be the "once and future" Messiah that the Jewish scriptures describe. Personally, I even think it's safe to say that the Spirit who lit on Jesus at his baptism was the same Spirit of Wisdom that has always been with the prophets of God. There's also no disagreement over Jesus having had a special relationship with the Spirit, although I don't think anyone can pretend to understand exactly what that relationship was. The Apocryphal books of the Bible seem to predict some sort of incarnation, and the Quran implies something similar. Jesus taught faith, repentance, and obedience, just like Moses, Muhammad, and the rest of the Semitic prophets. All of them have promised help from the Holy Spirit, too. However, it's important to remember that even according to the Gospels, God is the One who decides who gets that gift, not Jesus. None of the holy books deny that Jesus was condemned to death by crucifixion by Pontius Pilate or that he went willingly to his fate, submitting himself to God. Finally, both Islam and Christianity agree that in return for his own faith and fidelity, God lifted Jesus up to heaven to be with Him instead.

Islam reinforces Jesus' real message. There's no question that the Bible's record of that message is strong, coherent, and consistent. When I went to find proof and support for my Christian faith within its pages, it made me Muslim! The fact that both books confirm each other was an unexpected miracle. I'm where I am today not only because without the support of the words of the Bible I simply couldn't justify believing in Christianity anymore, but also because Islam is what Jesus taught, too. Although I miss the "deal" that Christianity offered, it's not the deal God offered anyway.

Even when I still believed that the Bible taught that Jesus was God incarnate, Jesus' prayer in the garden of Gethsemane had always troubled me. There, Jesus asked God to spare him the next day's arrest, trial, torture, and condemnation:

> "Abba, Father, everything is possible for you. Take this cup
> from me. Yet not what I will, but what You will."

If Jesus had really been God, I sometimes wondered why he'd made such a distinction between what he and God wanted. My confusion regarding his mingled divinity and humanity had even turned out to be a weak spot in my attempts to share his story. Although most Christians didn't seem troubled by it, my non-Christian friends often questioned whether Jesus' indecision might have been feigned! They asked whether his suffering could have been all that bad, since as God he would have known the severity, duration, and outcome, and likely would have been able to call upon greater-than-human resources of strength and perseverance.

When I finally accepted Jesus' humanity, his story stopped being a source of confusion and became a profoundly eloquent illustration of the goodness of God: that Jesus, though only a man, was able with the help of the Spirit to fulfill Jewish Law sufficiently to be exalted and raised by God to heaven just as He'd promised he would be. To me, Jesus' submission and his trust in the mercy and power of God Most High is a perfect example of what the Spirit makes us all capable of, free from the mockery of those who can only question whether Jesus suffered at all. When I was young and feared God's judgment, I took comfort in my parents and their assurance that God's son had taken my punishment onto himself. Now, as a Muslim, I find reassurance in the words of Jesus himself. One of his greatest gifts was his insight that among the infinite perspectives from which God Most High considers each of us is the regard of a father and the love that a father has for his child.

Far from coming to terminate the Covenant, the Jesus of the Gospels was always bent on directing Judaism back toward it and a real relationship with God, away from the perception that Abraham's legacy had been replaced by rigid adherence to ritual. Instead of condemning Jewish intellectuals like the Pharisees outright, he actually quoted them quite often (particularly in his own explication of Rabbi Hillel's "golden rule"). Perhaps he did this to remind them of their own wisdom and precedents, but certainly he did it to create a place for both himself and his lessons within their teaching. Instead of replacing the original Covenant, his words in the Gospels confirmed the importance of the Covenant and its commands.

Instead of revoking Jewish Law, both Jesus' words and his life serve as an irrefutable reminder to believers that no matter how perfect our compliance with those Laws might be, all of us in the end will have to put our trust in God alone. Even nonbelievers still see Jesus as one of the greatest inspirations in human history because of what he said and what he did. The message of Jesus and his apostles was a message of hope and literal inspiration, its popularity enhanced by its unspoken confirmation of the absolute equality each of us, no matter who we are, enjoys under God. Even more important to its success was that in exalting Jesus for his humble submission, God proved once and for all that He was good for His side of the deal!

That message was preserved for centuries, but gradually success rather than submission became the main message of Christianity. The doctrine of salvation by faith, shared by all of Christendom, promises its followers paradise even if they do nothing but believe it's already theirs. It teaches that since forgiveness and exaltation both come from acceptance and gratitude for Jesus' sacrifice, those who follow him need make no great effort to live as he lived. While that's understandably appealing, it's also profoundly at odds with Jesus' austerity and the path that he recommended others follow.

Christianity's popularity and burgeoning influence in the world today is often used to promote Christianity as "God's choice." The argument some make is that by trusting wealthy Western Christians with "the kingdoms of the world, and all their splendor" (Matthew 4:8), God has shown the religion that will carry His blessing into the next millennium. The problem with that argument: the one who promised that sort of temporal supremacy in the Bible was Satan, when he was trying to tempt Jesus to worship him instead of God! Based on that precedent, popularity and success should have been the last things Christians wanted. Their quest to achieve those two qualities to help the message spread has to have contributed to the gradual shift of Christianity's course from the path that Jesus laid. He certainly wasn't concerned about those sorts of things, and the people who knew him weren't either.

Beginning with the Greek Apollos and the book of Hebrews, and continuing through every new culture that Christianity has been taken to, Christianity has consistently sought to be easy to understand and accessible; to Christianity, understanding and accessibility have been of the utmost importance. Taking Jesus' own condemnation of the reliance on Law to heart, and at least initially understanding that that meant only God's mercy mattered, early Christians knew they had to try to explain it in ways everyone could relate to. Gradually, the explanations and the act of understanding the message became more important than the message itself. The message changed to suit that interpretation, and faith slowly, gradually, and inexorably became dogma.

It's hard to know whom to blame. The vast majority of the players seem to have had the best of intentions. Even Emperor Constantine, who sometimes comes across as a bit of a villain, may have only been doing his best in what were very difficult times. Whatever his motivations, it was only after he chose Christianity as a tool for uniting his empire that things really began to change. Constantine needed the religion to be attractive to all of his subjects, and although Jesus' ideas about generosity and servanthood had gone over relatively well among slaves and the middle classes, something more would have been needed to sell it to the wealthy and powerful elite. Paradise in return for belief in a man-God who sacrificed himself for humanity would have fit into the Promethean mold of Greco-Roman ideology a lot more easily; that may be why that's what they finally got.

It's well accepted that Constantine was responsible for the decision to recast the winter solstice as "Christmas" to help make the loss of the popular festival of Saturnalia easier to accept. He replaced the fish, a symbol of God's kindness and care for everyone, with the cross, a symbol of bloody sacrifice strikingly similar to the handle of a sword; his agents oversaw the refurbishing of statues of Zeus in Ephesus to give us a blue-eyed, blond-haired, markedly less Jewish Christ; and he ruthlessly put down dissent. Most say that Constantine was behind the suppression of the Arians that began on his watch, and it was certainly his support for the Greek bishops in Nicaea that gave us all the Catholic Creed we use today. Most of the verse substitution in Scripture seems to have gone on around his time, too. Jesus had predicted that Mammon, the God of the marketplace, would lead people away from his path. Instead of driving the market from the temple like Jesus did, Constantine's Christianity allowed popularity to dictate the church's doctrine. In turn, this allowed Mammon and the market to define the religion Christianity became, and the marketplace to define its God.

Gradually, "I believe" became more important than "I'll do what he said" because Jesus himself said (and directly experienced) that no matter what you do, in the end you still have to rely on God to accept it. Since that sort of reliance is a product of faith, and since that makes the eternal outcome of any action relatively independent of what was actually done, a more nuanced application of what Jesus said seems inevitable. Believing is so much easier than doing that it's worked out to be a pretty good growth strategy; marketability has ruled Christianity ever since.

Doctrine was supposed to be what Christians were good at! Believing the right things in the right way has become their own particular path to peace with God. Figuring out the correct thing to believe has been so important to them that people have fought and killed and died over questions of interpretation. In retrospect, though, you have to wonder: since they were following the man who had taught them the Beatitudes, "Blessed are the meek," "Blessed are the humble," and "Blessed are the merciful," shouldn't they have realized there might be a better way of peacemaking? Whenever the church was split, Christians always tended to fight and then go with the winning side. Instead, perhaps they should have considered that the best people to listen to might not be the ones most violent, aggressive, or skilled in the arts of war.

- **Christianity, Judaism, and Islam say the same things about God and us.**

- **Creating a more popular religion wasn't ever what Jesus had in mind.**

- **Wanting to be popular was what made Christianity start to change, centuries after Jesus was gone.**

Christianity taught me:

Different religions can serve God in different ways.

Being different doesn't make them wrong.

PART III

INTO ISLAM

CHAPTER 14

....

ONE ISLAM?

After all that reading and thinking, it was nice to rest quietly in Islam for a few years. My faith in God felt strong, and I was completely comfortable in my new spiritual home. In the 1990s, we Muslims looked pretty good. Most people remembered that Osama bin Laden and al Qaeda had been the good guys in Afghanistan, and it was easy to discount the low murmur of violence, political unrest, racism, and quiet misogyny everywhere else. I figured that I'd trust God, keep to myself, and leave well enough alone. I thought that all of those problems existed in just a few countries on the other side of the planet anyway, and I figured they'd stay there. Then September 11, 2001, came along, and it became impossible to ignore the fact that even apparently committed Muslims could be made to serve evil. Christianity had shown me how the drive to be different can make you lose touch with who you really are. Islam was going to demonstrate just how disruptive a great idea like unity can be.

When I first realized that I'd always been Muslim, I was reading the Quran alone. Initially, I began with no leaders or community and no idea where to find them. I honestly expected to discover one giant group of believers, all united by our quest to serve God. Unity is important in Islam. According to the Quran, it's one of the most important signs that you're on God's path, and in my first Little Mosque on the Prairie in Saskatoon, united was pretty much how we felt. We were a small group, everyone knew who everyone else was, and we got along pretty well despite the occasional disagreement (we actually represented quite a few different schools of thought and interpretation). In retrospect, it was a good place for me to begin and has colored my experiences ever since. We proved unity is possible.

Since then, like every Muslim, I've had my face rubbed in the fact that most of the time, we really don't get along very well at all. Today's Islam illustrates how the quest for unity can tear people apart and how Muslims can become quite nasty when we're fighting to make each other recognize that we're the ones who should be in control. There's a sad, ironic joke that circulated after the destruction of the World Trade Center, when people were still arguing about how it had happened, who was responsible, and why. A lot of people pointed out that if it had really been organized solely by Muslim men, they'd still be sitting in their first meeting, paralyzed, unable to agree which one of them should be in charge!

Unity actually describes many different things. The word itself means "the state of oneness." Christianity and the Gospel of John are good examples of how confused you can become trying to understand that particular concept! Unity connotes harmony and the joining of separate entities in the pursuit of some shared goal, and it's an aesthetic concept of both beauty and completion. In Islam, instead of beauty, harmony, shared purpose, love, or respect, unity has come to mean following the person in charge; moreover, "striving for unity" has become nothing more than trying to figure out who that's supposed to be.

Proud as I am of my religion, I'll admit that compared to us, the Christians seem like an awfully cohesive bunch lately. One obvious contrast is that the passion with which they approach their internal arguments has flagged over the centuries. The distinctions between the various Christian sects are still as real as they've ever been, but today they actually seem to serve as a buffer between the various factions and groups. They allow groups to agree to disagree without having to discuss exactly what it is they disagree about, and they're rarely, if ever, used to justify mayhem or murder. The same can't be said for modern Islam. I was shocked when I first began to explore the depths of feeling that our own divisions engender. The Islam that I fell in love with is the Islam of the Holy Quran, the Hadiths (Muhammad's collected sayings), and the Sunnah (a record of the things he did); I was swept into Islam by the Word of God with its interpretation and practice brought to life in the words and the life of the last Prophet, recorded and preserved by those who knew him best. To me, that sort of Islam is exemplified in one of the most precious stories recorded in Islam, the "Gabriel Hadith." Its Islam is big enough for everyone. (The additions of translations for Islam, Iman, and Ihsan are my own.)

One day, while we were sitting with the messenger of Allah, there appeared before us a man whose clothes were exceedingly white and whose hair was exceeding black; no signs of journeying were to be seen upon him, and none of us knew him. He walked up and sat down by the Prophet. Resting his knees against his and placing the palms of his hands on his thighs, he said "O Muhammad, tell me about Islam (Submission)." The messenger of Allah said: "Islam is to testify that there is no God but Allah and Muhammad is the messenger of Allah, to perform the prayers, to pay the Zakat, to fast in Ramadan, and to make the pilgrimage to the House if you are able to do so." He said: "You have spoken rightly" and we were amazed at him asking and saying that he had spoken rightly. He said: "Then tell me about Iman (Faith)." He said: "It is to believe in Allah, His angels, His books, His Messengers, and the Last Day, and to believe in divine destiny, both the good and the evil thereof." He said: "You have spoken rightly." He said: "Then tell me about Ihsan (Virtue)." He said: "It is to worship Allah as though you are seeing Him, for while you see Him not, yet truly He sees you." He said: "Then tell me about the Hour." He said: "The one questioned about it knows no better than the questioner!" He said: "Then tell me about its signs." He said: "That the slave-girl will give birth to her mistress, and that you will see the barefooted, naked, destitute herdsmen competing in constructing lofty buildings." Then he took himself off and I stayed for a time. Then the Prophet said: "O Umar, do you know who the questioner was?" I said: "Allah and His Messenger know best." He said: "He was the Angel Gibreel, who came to you to teach you your religion."

There are three sources of prophetic guidance in the religion of Islam. The first and most obvious is the Holy Quran, which Muslims believe is a true record of the "Mother of the Book," the source of inspiration that sits with God in heaven. Alongside that, and assisting Muslims in its interpretation, are the Sunnah and the Hadiths. The high status of the Gabriel Hadith in the Sunnah of the Prophet is similar to that of the first

Surah, Al-Fatiha, Arabic for "the Opener" or "the Opening," with regard to the rest of the Quran. The Gabriel Hadith might well have been the Prophet Muhammad's final exam! It's probably the most inclusive expression of the religion of Islam that there is, and it's noteworthy that it was given specifically to Umar, a man considered by many Muslims today to have been the original Salafi (a currently popular conservative Muslim school of thought), renowned for both his conviction to Islam and his assertive inflexibility in the way he practiced it.

Contrasting with the Gabriel Hadith is another Hadith warning Muslims about the consequences of controversy, disagreements, and divisions. Although it's not recorded in either of the two most authoritative collections of Hadiths, its authenticity is generally considered to be above question because it comes to us through so many different chains of transmission. It says:

> My community will experience everything that the Children of Israel had experienced, following in their footsteps exactly, so much so that if one of their number had approached his mother publicly for sex, one of my community will do the same. The Children of Israel divided into 72 sects. My community will divide into 73 sects, and all of them will be in the Hellfire save one." The people then asked him: "And which one will that be?" He replied: "The one that follows what I and my Companions are upon right now."

Despite the fact that the bulk of this Hadith seems to rebuke the holier-than-they attitude most Muslims today seem to have toward most Jews, the majority of Muslim interest and attention has been concentrated on which of our sects is the "right" one. Most think that the rest are condemned because Aal-E-Imran 3:104–105 commands the following:

> Let there arise out of you a band of people inviting to all that is good, enjoining what is right and forbidding what is wrong: They are the ones to attain felicity. Be not like those who are divided amongst themselves and fall into disputations after receiving clear Signs: For them is a dreadful penalty.

Al-Anaam 6:159 further confirms:

As for those who divide their religion and break up into sects, thou hast no part in them in the least: Their affair is with Allah: He will in the end tell them the truth of all that they did.

Despite a thousand years of trying to find unity, and affecting the history of the entire world in the process, it's obvious that nothing we've tried has worked very well. In retrospect, that shouldn't really come as a surprise. If you believe that Muhammad could see the future, then you should realize it was inevitable. According to the Hadith of the seventy-three sects, Islam was doomed to fragmentation. One of the problems with prophecy is that knowing what's going to happen never lets you actually prevent it from happening; if that were possible, it wouldn't be prophecy! A prophet's predictions are primarily meant to help you learn from your mistakes sooner and faster. To Muslims who believe in the religion of Islam, it was preordained that we would break apart; otherwise, the Prophet Muhammad wouldn't have said we would.

Virtually the first question any Muslim is ever asked is "What sort of Muslim are you?" I honestly hate the question, because to answer it you have to personally choose one particular designation and at least indirectly endorse one group over every other one. If the questioners agree with me, they're comforted (perhaps inappropriately), and if they don't, I'm condemned—at least in their hearts. The trouble is, no matter the answer, we're all trying to do the right thing! Every Muslim I know, regardless of which sect he or she belongs to, hopes and prays that it is the right one. Every one of us is in the group we are because we are convinced that it is on the straight path. Every sect today thinks that they're correct and the rest are wrong. If they (as a group) didn't think so, they'd change. If we (as individuals) didn't agree, we'd join a different group. To me, the tragedy of modern Islam is really threefold: that the question can be asked at all, that there are so many different answers, and that they matter as much as they do.

The emphasis Allah placed on unity now might not seem to have been such a good idea. It hasn't done us a lot of good so far, and it has likely even contributed to some of our problems. The arguments that we've had among ourselves have been complex, complicated, and hard to understand, but their outcome has become unquestionable. We are a broken Ummah (an Arabic word that means "community" or "nation" and signifies the entirety of the People following Islam), just as Muhammad said we would become, and every one of us is convinced that we're right and everyone who disagrees with us is wrong. None of us have been able to convince the rest to agree with us, and instead of helping us find any sort of resolution, the arguments, disagreements, and distinctions have grown and multiplied. In the last couple of centuries, they've become so heated and profound that many Muslims have started to believe that anyone who disagrees with them has to be a heretic. Tragically, some of us have even begun using that to justify violence, war, and atrocity. Our zeal to stay on the right path and to stick to the correct beliefs and practices—a zeal that we might have hoped would help us avoid sectarianism—has actually caused the very thing that we have been striving to prevent. In addition, it now serves as a prime justification for murder among Muslims. Ironically, most of the time both the murderer and the murdered are dedicated, committed, and convinced that they're following Islam!

- **Muslims know that we're supposed to stick together.**
- **Most of us assume that means we have to agree with each other.**
- **The struggle for unity has caused most of our battles with each other for the last thousand years.**

CHAPTER 15

....

FAILED TESTS

When Muhammad first revealed Islam to the Arab tribes of Medina and Mecca, unity wasn't such a problem. The first Muslims had a living Prophet with them to answer their questions, and they had his example to guide what they did. They were unified by their obedience to Muhammad and the words of the Holy Quran. It would have been easier back then to know what to do when An-Nisa 4:59 commanded:

> You who believe, obey Allah and obey the Prophet and those of authority among you. If ye differ in anything, amongst yourselves, refer it to Allah and His Messenger, if ye do believe in Allah and the Last Day: That is best, and most suitable for final determination.

Both secular and religious leadership were joined in the person of the Prophet. The earliest Ummah had a hierarchy and structure that was self-evident to everyone; it shared one culture and had one relatively small community in which to practice its faith. The Islam of the Ummah of Muhammad was at its most perfect when it first began.

Muhammad died when he was sixty-two, and Islam continued to grow. There was still only one Ummah united by one caliph for many years afterward, even though not everyone was happy about it. That unhappiness festered and was perhaps the main reason why only the first four caliphs carry the title "Rightly Guided." Abu Bakr was the first, recognized as God's vice-regent on earth whether everyone liked it or not. For the earliest Muslims, a caliph derived his authority from Allah through Muhammad's revelation and passed it inevitably on to his designated successor upon his death. Since Muhammad had made Abu Bakr his deputy while he was still alive, Abu Bakr was the obvious first choice, but there was already some muttering.

In fact, today's Sunnis and Shiites remember those days very differently. Shiites have always questioned the validity of Abu Bakr's caliphate. Their name is actually a contraction of the Arabic phrase that means "the Party of Ali," and they've always thought Abu Bakr's election was a little too hasty because it was instigated by Umar (the second caliph) while Muhammad's son-in-law, Ali, was still in mourning. From their perspective, that decision was questionable. Umar had apparently once told Ali that the Qurayshi tribe didn't want the caliphate to pass directly into the rest of Muhammad's family because it would have given them too much control. Since Muhammad had described Ali as his "successor, brother, and heir," Shiites have always felt that Ali should have been the first caliph, regardless.

Despite the politics and intrigue, Abu Bakr led the Ummah, and most people feel that he led it well. Islam grew on his watch. Likewise, after he designated Umar as his successor, the vast majority of Muslims recognized Umar's authority, and Islam continued to grow. Unfortunately, things then got more complicated. Umar chose not to designate a successor, but left it up to a council of Qurayshi tribal leaders. Although it was a common way of choosing leaders prior to Muhammad, Umar's decision allowed politics to return with a vengeance, literally. The council elected Uthman, a member of the Umayyads, one of the largest clans in the Quraysh. The Umayyads were used to power, and Uthman's rule was marred by allegations of nepotism. While it's true that Uthman was a wealthy caliph and that his tribe benefited from his position, most scholars have absolved him of any blame, either because they didn't think the nepotism even happened or because they thought his actions were appropriate; he was caliph, after all. Unfortunately, the situation looked bad at the time, and Islam faced its first significant trial when Abu Bakr's son led a revolt in which Uthman was killed.

Ali was finally elected caliph, but he immediately faced a rebellion ignited by Umayyad vengeance and led by the Companions Talhah, az-Zubayr, and even Aisha, widow of the messenger of Allah himself. Ali defeated the rebels in the Battle of the Camel, but the rebellion itself continued until he finally agreed to an arbitrated settlement, in which his own negotiator, in a ruse, publicly deposed him. The other negotiator immediately declared his own Umayyad candidate, Mu'awiyah, caliph! Although Ali refused to surrender under those circumstances, his authority was undermined nonetheless and his followers melted away. He ended up being assassinated. The failure of the Ummah to support and defend both Uthman and Ali marked the first significant check to the growth of Islam and the birth of the first real divisions within it.

Our earliest schisms were over politics, but since the leadership of Islam was also a religious issue, the schisms were religious as well. We haven't been able to separate religion from politics since. The beginnings of Shia are an excellent example. The Umayyads were unpopular among many non-Arab Muslims. They believed in something called client dependency—the unfortunate idea that (despite the divinely declared equality of all Muslims) an individual didn't have any real status unless he or she could attract an Arab mentor. The idea of client dependency went over well among the Arab elite, but it didn't work out for anyone else. In fact, it pretty much created the political divisions between the nascent Sunnis, the supporters of Ali, and the Kharijites (another early group of Muslims who thought they were different from the rest). The party of Ali didn't support the practice because Ali was against it, and the Kharijites gave their support (initially at least) to Ali because they shared some of his more egalitarian beliefs. Condemning client dependency became a politically popular rallying point to attract non-Umayyad subjects who felt they were being mistreated. It made both the Shiites and the Kharijites powerful, separate political entities, as well as separate religious ones.

After Ali, it was left to Mu'awiyah (the man whose maneuvering had weakened Ali, of all people) to try and keep the Ummah alive. Mu'awiyah isn't remembered as having been particularly noteworthy for his righteousness, but his self-restraint was remarkable. It was that self-restraint that brought us together again, if only for a while. There's likely a lesson for all of us in his caliphate, as many Muslims then and now would probably have thought themselves justified in rejecting his leadership based on their own estimations of his piety. But whatever you might think of Mu'awiyah, under his command, Islam regained its drive and began to spread again. He brought Hasan, the son of Ali, back into the fold, and he skillfully negotiated with anyone who would listen, using force only as a last resort. He instituted the Umayyad dynasty by obtaining the support of his followers in advance for the succession of his own son, Yazid. The caliphate remained primarily hereditary, at least in practice, until it ended in 1924.

After Umar, the caliphate didn't bring us all together ever again. Many have blamed the caliphs themselves, but the fault likely lies with the rest of us.

Even during the time of the rightly guided caliphs, the precedent had been set in the minds and the hearts of the Ummah to deny the authority of those we didn't choose to recognize either religiously or politically. It is interesting to chart the course of Muslim history and the spread and success of Islam against the extent to which the caliphate held the support of the people in the ensuing centuries. Unfailingly, whether the caliph is remembered as righteous or not, it is the level of support that the Ummah gave him and the extent of rebellion our caliph had to deal with that predicted our corporate wealth, health, and influence. That difference just makes sense; whenever we have succumbed to the voices of rebellion, our Ummah has been inevitably diminished. Since the end of the caliphate, Islam hasn't done well without a recognized leader. In his absence, we have become even more preoccupied with the struggle for that leadership among ourselves to the point that we've become pretty much useless for anything else—despite the fact that we're supposed to be the servants of God. Throughout the world, Muslims languish and suffer and starve at least partly because we can't get along.

Striving for doctrinal purity hasn't brought anyone a lot of success either. As it was with our political leadership, the Ummah was the most religiously united when it was only beginning. If anyone had questions about what was right or wrong when the Prophet was alive, he or she had direct access to Muhammad, and his authority to answer and interpret was undisputed. Even Jews and Christians came to him to settle their arguments! He died, and Islam spread. As it grew, the lines of communication grew longer and new cultures were assimilated. The Quran and the Sunnah had already been collated, but many Muslims, seeing how rapidly the Ummah was growing, became concerned about the potential impact of that growth without a centrally accepted school of thought. It seemed inevitable that variations and misunderstandings would creep in or that a question would come up in two different places at once that would require a judgment call. If two parts of the Ummah arrived at two wildly divergent answers to the same question, chaos could ensue.

A little chaos, or at least variations of some sort, shouldn't have been a surprise; even the Prophet himself hadn't expected the Quran and his Sunnah to be comprehensive. In a farewell audience before sending Mu'az bin Jabal away to be governor of Yemen, Muhammad is recorded to have asked him how he would make his decisions. In a famous Hadith that served as the basis for a significant amount of early Islamic jurisprudence, their dialogue is recorded to have gone something like this:

Mu'az answered: "I shall decide according to the Book of God." "And then what?" the Prophet asked. "Then according to the practice of the Apostle of God," Mu'az replied. The Prophet again asked: "and if there is nothing in the practice of the Apostle of God?" Mu'az answered: "Then I will make a personal effort ('Ijtihad'), use my own judgment, and act according to that." And this the Prophet approved, saying: "Praise be to God who enabled the envoy of the Apostle of God to say what has satisfied him!"

Ijtihad (a Muslim striving to make responsible choices based upon his or her own understanding of Islam, in the absence of clear guidance from either the Quran or Muhammad's example) sounds like a good idea in theory, but the practice was another matter. Obviously, some people's capacity to study, understand, and form judgments would be better than others. Az-Zumar 39:18 promised:

Those who listen to the Word and follow the best meaning in it: Those are the ones whom Allah has guided, and those are the ones imbued with understanding.

However, it also confirmed that there was such a thing as a "best" interpretation. That meant the leaders of Islam had a problem. Many new Muslims (then and now) wouldn't even have Arabic as their first language and couldn't be expected to understand it with the same ease as one who had grown up Arab. Cultural references would be confusing, historical allusions could be missed, and in the end, the all-important "best" meaning and interpretation could be lost to the expanding Ummah.

For Sunni Muslims, the gates of Ijtihad have officially been closed for centuries, but they never really opened very wide at all for anyone. Sunni and Shia explanations vary, but their practice was quite similar: both groups acted quickly to officially limit the capacity to interpret and judge the meaning of the Quran and the Sunnah to a very few practitioners. Sunni Muslims developed the idea of following one particular scholar's interpretations in the emulation of the earliest Muslims—called *taqleed*—because Muhammad had said that the Muslims who were most like him and his Companions would be the best. This required a lot of scholarly interpretation, as the Companions themselves didn't always agree. To simplify things, most

Sunni scholars have limited the accepted list of Ijtihadists to Umar, Ali, Ibn Mas'ud, Ibn Umar, Ibn 'Abbas, Zayd ibn Thabit, and Aisha, but even this group wasn't very unified. After the death of the Prophet, some of them actually went to war against each other. Moreover, Mu'az bin Jabal, whose Ijtihad was commended by the Prophet, isn't even on the list! By contrast, the Shia practice of Ijtihad was based on the idea of the "Infallible Imams" descended from Ali: instead of limiting the right to interpret the meaning of the Quran and the Sunnah to some of the Companions, they chose to limit it to the family of Ali and their successors instead.

Many Muslims, both Shiite and Sunni, blame a Muslim named al-Ghazali and his book *The Incoherence of the Philosophers* (about the incoherence of the *other* Muslim philosophers) for finally ending Ijtihad. Shiites often describe the process in terms of a Sunni conspiracy, but the truth is that Ijtihad was never really officially sanctioned at all. The idea of empowering Muslims to read and understand the Quran and the Sunnah and to be responsible for their own actions went over about as well as Luther's Protestant Reformation went over in the Vatican. Centralized interpretation of God's will has always been safer, at least for the centrists. It's been the official practice in one form or another for our entire history.

In retrospect, the idea that Islam could be unified by scholarship was risky at best. In every field of human endeavor, some of us have always been able to make names for ourselves by disagreeing with everyone else, and it's quite possible to make the same facts support different conclusions if you look at them the right way. In defense of the scholars, most obviously believed that centralized interpretation was a good way to prevent arguments and wars, but it obviously hasn't worked as well as we would have liked. There's really no excuse for the way most Muslim groups and nations have responded to the command not to break up our religion into sects: by oppressing and suppressing different points of view and outlawing groups they didn't agree with, forcing them out, legislating the interpretation of God's Holy Word, and in effect attempting to control the meaning itself.

Legislating religion has never worked well for anyone for long. Laws about belief—or oppression and ostracism—inevitably create an atmosphere of dissent and rebellion. Given both human nature and divine revelation, Muslims should have known better. Most scholars agree that that's why Allah revealed Al-Baqara 2:256:

> Let there be no compulsion in religion: Truth stands out clear
> from error: whoever rejects evil and believes in Allah hath
> grasped the most trustworthy handhold that never breaks.

According to this passage, legislating religion is actually forbidden—not that that's made any difference to our practice. As a whole, we've had little difficulty finding ways to get around that particular prohibition and even less difficulty finding reasons to do so. Our leaders may have had the best of intentions, hoping to prevent the Balkanization of Islam into the succession of armed camps we now find ourselves in, but instead of preventing the catastrophe, they unfortunately may have contributed to it.

All our political maneuverings and doctrinal efforts have gradually come to naught. Instead of fostering unity, Muslims have progressively fractured Islam into a series of increasingly divided camps. The passage of time has fossilized those divisions and made reconciliation more and more unlikely. At some point, some Muslims began branding Muslims with whom they disagreed with "heretics" and "apostates." An awfully destructive minority among us has taken that as permission to use physical force and even murder to correct everyone else's "innovations."

It's been a rough few centuries, and we've finally come to a point where most Muslims accept that some of us think it's okay to judge, condemn, and kill each other. At their mildest, disagreements over doctrine and interpretation can justify insult and backbiting, even though we're told, in Al-Hujraat 49:12:

> O ye who believe! Avoid suspicion as much as possible: for
> suspicion in some cases is a sin: And spy not on each other,
> nor speak ill of each other behind their backs. Would any of
> you like to eat the flesh of his dead brother? Nay, ye would
> abhor it... but fear Allah: For Allah is Oft returning, and
> Most Merciful.

At their worst, our arguments have become an excuse for murder, even though the Holy Quran tells us that murder, whether it's of another Muslim or of any other human being, is one of the worst sins there is.

- The earliest Muslims were unified whether they agreed with each other or not.

- After Muhammad died, Muslims first started fighting over politics, even though our leaders were supposed to be ordained.

- We've been fighting over religion ever since, even though that's always been forbidden, too.

CHAPTER 16

....

TRIALS

There's a series of Hadiths among those collected by the scholars Muslim, Dawud, and Abu 'Awana describing the evils that would fall upon Islam after the Prophet was taken away. They all agree with the core message of the Hadith of the seventy-three sects—that we'll end up fragmented—but they're more specific about the steps we'll follow to get there. The word that's generally translated as "evil" in this context is the Arabic word *fitnah,* and while it does mean evil, it means a lot more as well: "test," "temptation," "trial," and "division." I think these fitnah the Hadiths actually describe are a series of preordained events sent to separate the good among us from the bad or to help us recognize the good and the bad within ourselves. The Hadiths go into some amazingly precise detail about how it will all happen and why, and what some of the consequences will be.

The *Sahaba* (an honorific reserved for one of Muhammad's respected Companions) Hudhayfah, a famous source of many Hadith and Sunnah, reported:

> The people used to ask the messenger of Allah about the good things; but I used to ask about the evil things, fearing that they may overtake me. So I said, "O Messenger of Allah! We had lived in the times of ignorance and evil; then Allah granted us the excellence which we are now enjoying, and He has sent you. Will there be, after this excellence, any evil like that which preceded?" He replied: "Yes, O Hudhayfah! Learn the Book of Allah and follow what is in it! Learn the Book of

Allah and follow what is in it! Learn the Book of Allah and follow what is in it!"

I asked him, "What is the way for protection from it?" He replied: "The Sword!"

I asked, "Will there be any good remaining after that evil and fighting?" He replied: "Yes, there will be a leadership and a Jamaa'ah (group or assembly) accompanied with dirt and corruption. And there will be hatred."

I asked, "What is that dirt?" He replied: "Leaders following ways other than my Sunnah, and guided by other than my guidance. You will approve of some actions, and disapprove of others. There will arise from amongst them men whose hearts are the hearts of devils in human bodies."

I asked, "What is the tainted treaty?" He replied: "The hearts of many people will not go back to that love whereupon they had previously been."

I asked, "Will there be any evil after that good?" He replied: "Yes, there will be a blind and deaf turbulence; callers to the gates of Hell. Whoever responds to their call, they cast him into it."

I said, "O Messenger of Allah, describe them to us." He replied: "They are from our own skin, and they speak our tongue."

I asked, "O Messenger of Allah, what do you command me with if that should happen in my lifetime?" He replied: "If you find at that time a Caliph for Allah upon the earth, then adhere to the Jamaa'ah of the Muslims and their commands. Listen to the leader and obey him, even if he whipped your back and took away your wealth—listen and obey."

I asked, "What if they the Muslims did not have a Jamaa'ah or an Imam?" He replied: "Desert all of those parties and run away over the earth. It would be better for you, O Hudhayfah, to die whilst you cling to the branch of a tree, than to follow any of them."

Al-Hafidh Ibn Hajar (a well-known early transmitter of Hadith and Sunnah) reported at-Tabaree (another well-known scholar and transmitter) as saying: "This Hadith indicated that when the people divide into parties in the absence of a Caliph, no particular group should be followed. If one can, he should desert all the parties for fear of falling into evil."

What was the nature of the fitnah that cost us our unity? That question has received a lot of speculation over the years. The Prophet described it as a return to the ignorance that preceded his revelation, a time of paganism, animism, polytheism, and tribalism leading to strife, conflict, and war. All of those things ended through Muhammad; after his time, all of them returned, at different times and to varying extents. The most common interpretation of this Hadith has been that it warns about idolatry and polytheism. The only trouble with that is that polytheism, idolatry, and even the inappropriate veneration of Muslim saints were never widespread enough to split the Ummah. The Ummah always knew that those practices were wrong. None of those practices caused any wars either, although I suspect allegations of polytheism, idolatry, or inappropriate saintly veneration were used to justify a lot of wars that were going to occur anyway.

Before anyone can say that a problem has returned to afflict a community as big as the entirety of Islam, the problem has got to be close to ubiquitous. The only characteristic of the *jaahilayyah* (an Arabic word that means "ignorance of divine guidance") that returned in sufficient force to plague the entire Ummah was politics. Tribal politics had started most of the wars before Muhammad, and politics have been behind most of our wars ever since. Of all of the candidates for the fitnah in question, politics and its consequences are the only things that fit the description we were given: something that would return to infect and divide the entire Ummah. Political dissension returned very quickly; it cost us the caliphate, and it's been behind everything that's divided us since.

Hudhayfah was offered four recommendations to help him pass the test. First, the Prophet told him to learn the Quran and the Sunnah and follow what was in them three times to identify the two sources' singular importance. Then he told him to obey the caliph whether he thought that the caliph was good or bad, even to the point of using his sword to defend him. Finally, Muhammad warned Hudhayfah that if he couldn't find a caliph, he should follow no one, in order to avoid being led astray. In retrospect, if we'd all taken Muhammad's advice, that would probably have worked out pretty well! If we had read and studied the Quran and the Sunnah, we'd have known better what to do. If we'd all supported the caliph no matter what we thought of him, we'd likely still have one. If we'd all been more ready to use our swords in his defense, we'd have been less likely to use them on each other. Finally, if we'd all run away from anyone who told us to do any different, we'd have had to remain one unified Ummah, despite our disagreements, even today. It's obvious that the first fitnah began almost immediately after Muhammad died. Factionalism, divisions, politics, and dissension returned quickly when Muslims began to question whether the caliph they had was the right one.

Our ongoing battles over leadership have arguably been the most destructive force in all of Islam. Everyone has selected Hadith, Sunnah, and valid arguments to convince themselves they're right, but none have done much good convincing anyone else. The Shiites are likely correct about what our Prophet's own preferences would have been; his love and reverence for his daughter, son-in-law, and grandchildren are obvious and unquestionable. To counter, Sunnis can point to occasions when Muhammad allowed his personal preferences to be overruled for the sake of the greater good. One of the most memorable examples was when he wanted to perform the funeral prayer for the non-Muslim son of a dear friend. Umar (the man most often vilified for preventing Ali from becoming the first caliph) actually stood up in front of the Prophet with his arms outstretched over his head to physically prevent him! And Muhammad allowed him to. He never made the mistake of thinking his way was better than the way of Islam, and he never confused the two.

Our caliphs were never expected to be perfect. The word *caliph* in Islam is often thought to mean our righteous "ruler," "sovereign," or "king." As God's vice-regents on earth, there's no question that the caliphs were the most directly responsible to God for leading the rest of us in obedience to God's Will. However, "righteous" is something that *caliph* was never meant to mean! While the root word of *caliph—khalafa—*does mean "agent, substitute, or successor," implying a series of representatives, derivations of the word are used in many places in the Quran with different connotations— not all of them good. *Khalafa* also implies diversity, contradiction, and variation. As a ruler, a caliph could be either good or bad. A Hadith of the Prophet narrated by Abu Hurayrah confirms this:

> Leaders shall rule you after me, the God-fearing of them ruling you with God-fearingness and the profligate ruling you with wickedness. So listen to them and obey them in everything that is right; for if they do well, it will count for you and for them, and if they do badly, it will count for you and against them.

Hudhayfah was commanded to obey the caliph and to defend him with his sword, whatever he thought of him personally, for a reason. The caliphate was meant to unify Islam, whether the caliph himself was good or bad.

If any of us actually believe the Hadiths and Sunnah we've used to justify what we've done to our religion, we should realize that there's ample evidence that Muhammad had at least some idea of what was going to happen after his death between Umar, Abu Bakr, Uthman, Mu'awiyah, Ali, his beloved daughter, and his cherished grandchildren. He even told Mu'awiyah that he smelled his own blood on him! Despite all our hindsight, something obvious seems to have escaped most of us: even with his God-given foresight, Muhammad never took any of the steps that he could have to prevent any of the events from happening. He could have killed Mu'awiyah. He could have driven Umar away. He could have done any number of things, but instead, he kept everyone close to him and made sure each person had an honored place. He loved everyone despite his or her faults, and he never split the Ummah. Muhammad trusted God enough to know that what was going to happen would only happen because it had to. He had the big picture.

That big picture underlies one of the most easily misunderstood concepts in Islam: the relationship between the mosque and the state. In the West, we assume there have to be walls between the two of them to protect citizens and believers from the abuse of the two sources of power used together. It was supposed to be quite different for Muslims. In Islam, religious and secular leadership were supposed to be joined in the person of the caliph for a reason. Despite the potential that arrangement has for expediting mass manipulation, it was kept free of abuse by the nature of the caliphate itself. In Islam, religious leadership is about responsibility, not power. In Islam, power, dominion, and ultimate authority belong only to God. The secular power of Islamic leadership was minimized and controlled by the caliph's own fear of Allah. Although outsiders may question the wisdom of centering Islamic government around the caliphate, the arrangement was never meant to be one that could be abused by corrupt men—at least not for long.

In Islam, secular and religious authority were supposed to be joined together only when that leadership comprised the caliph and his appointees, and only to the extent that the instructions were actually Islamic. It's noteworthy that Hudhayfah was told to obey the caliph whether the caliph abused him or not; it wasn't necessary to tell him to ignore the caliph if the caliph told him to abuse anyone else. As a Muslim and a Sahaba, Hudhayfah would have known that already. That way, the power of the caliph was limited by everyone else's fear of Allah, too. Additionally, since Islamic leadership was supposed to be ordained, we weren't supposed to have too much influence over who the caliph was, either. Regrettably, since the rightly guided caliphs, we've all allowed personality, prejudice, and our own preferences to decide our leaders for us. That's the essence of politics, and the caliphate was never supposed to be contaminated by any sort of political process.

So we began the first fitnah. We never should have played politics with religion in the first place. Because we did, politics cost every caliph the unanimous support he was supposed to have and thus left him weakened. The authority of the caliphate eroded gradually and progressively until finally we didn't have one. Without a caliph, we no longer have anyone meant to lead and unify us, let alone anyone who actually does. Hudhayfah was told that without a caliph, he should follow no one. Instead, even when we had a caliph, we tried to choose our own leaders based on our preferences. That practice has inevitably led each of us further and further away from the rest.

You get quite a few problems when you join politics to religion. First, the mixture affects the sort of leadership you get. Any leader you can choose to follow or not isn't really a leader at all. No matter what they start out as, politicians all end up as servants, supplicants, and sycophants for as long as they need outside support. There's a reason why American presidents look forward to their second terms! As long as leaders' positions are dependent on the opinions of their followers, then they aren't really leading; all their apparent power is only the result of an ongoing popularity contest. The difference between a leader and a representative is simple: you do what a leader says to you, and representatives do what you say to them. Granting religious authority—which presupposes an external and objective standard of what's right and what's wrong—to someone you choose merely because they're going to do what *you* want them to is not the best way to get good guidance through tough choices.

Second, politics always divides people. Obviously, as long as our maneuvering continues, we're never going to be unified. There's no way that everyone's going to choose the same leader. We will always want different things. As predicted, we began the time of the "tainted treaty." This time has been marked by a fractured false sort of leadership that's had some good in it, but that has always been accompanied inextricably by corruption within and hatred without because of our power games. With the quick return of politics, when we started to choose our leaders based on whether they'd do what we wanted, we got, just as Muhammad warned Hudhayfah would happen, "leaders following ways other than my Sunnah, and guided by other than my guidance." Some of us have decided to follow some of them, and many of us have approved a few of them, but none of us have ever been able to approve of everything about any of them. To me, the "tainted treaty" seems to eloquently describe the last thousand or so years of Islamic history. Although we have all tried to find the right person or persons to lead us—someone who could join responsibility and power with personal popularity, based on fulfilling our own preferences—we've instead found nothing but more division, uncertainty, and chaos.

There's also the question of personal responsibility. One of the reasons I declare that Muslims should study the Quran and the Sunnah for themselves is that some of us have been following each other straight into hell! We need good, dedicated, scholarly teachers; we always have, and we always will. Even though few of us (hopefully) need someone to tell us simple and obvious things (like, for example, whether adultery is a bad idea), we do need help with more difficult questions about finer points of law and practice. There's even a good argument for adhering to one particular school of *fikh*, or Islamic legal interpretation. Let's say you get directions from two people for a walk to the opposite corner of a city block. One of them tells you to go right, then left, and the other one tells you to go left, then right. If you follow either set of directions, you'll end up in the same place, but if you mix them up instead, you'll only get hopelessly lost! The trouble with following scholars starts when we choose to believe that because we're using different directions, our destinations aren't the same. None of the real scholars ever claimed to be the only ones who knew how to get anywhere.

The difference between learning from someone who knows more than you do and following such a person is really about the extent of personal responsibility you retain. The bottom line in Islam is that we're all responsible for our actions. We're not allowed to convince ourselves that anyone but Allah is infallible. That should affect our approach to the opinions of scholars. If I learn things from someone who knows more than I do, I am still responsible to God for what I do with that knowledge. I'm also both able and willing to learn from and benefit from the lessons of other

teachers. Few academics will ever agree about everything, and everybody
has his or her own perspective. Alternatively, if I choose to make myself
subject to a teacher, and instead of simply listening I choose to follow
and obey him or her, I make the teacher responsible for my actions. By
elevating the teacher above me, I also prevent myself from benefiting from
the wisdom of others; followers can only go in one direction. That's why
the act of learning keeps me responsible to God and open to others, and
why choosing to follow a scholar can easily become nothing but an attempt
to abrogate that responsibility. My choosing to believe in anyone but God
closes my mind to people with a different point of view from mine, even
though they may be right. It also sets me apart from everyone who hasn't
made the same choices I have.

I have never met a Muslim I couldn't learn from, and I have never met
a man, woman, or child who didn't have something to teach me if I was
willing to give him or her my attention. Some points of view I agree with
and some I don't, but everything and everyone shows me something I need
to know. Personally, I believe that that's why God puts them into my path
in the first place. We've had a lot of different perspectives over the years:
Wahabean, Sufi, Shia, Sunni, Kharijite, Ahmadiiyya, Ismaili, Ilawi, Ali-
Alahi, Zaydi, Zahari, Hanafi, Hanabali, Maliki, Shafi, Ibadites, Fatamids,
Shakii, Babii, Baha'i, Nusari, Sevener, Twelver . . . in Islam—the list goes on
and on. They all have two things in common: all of them think they're
onto something, and none of them think that they're wrong. The truth is
that they all have a point, but the result of our belief that any of them is
"right," in the absolute sense that we're supposed to reserve for God, should
be apparent to everyone. Every division we've undergone has left us with
another sect that has had something they're right about that holds them
together. However, they've also had something everyone else thinks they're
wrong about that sets them apart.

I have read and reread the Holy Quran, the Hadiths, and the Sunnah
year after year. I have listened at the feet of wise men, women, and children
whenever I've found someone who thought he or she had something to
say. In all their halakahs, khutbahs, sermons, and lessons, I have found the
same theme consistently repeated: as a Muslim, I am expected to obey (in
descending order) God, God's Prophets, the meaning of God's Word and
revelation, and then those in authority over me—as long as obeying them
doesn't bring me into conflict with the rest. Nowhere am I given permission
to follow and obey those whom I choose to, whether I think they're right or

not. In fact, doing so is mocked and condemned in the pages of the Holy Quran itself! Choosing only one teacher brings us prejudice, closed minds, and hatred. Learning from many teachers brings us openness, scholarship, wisdom, perspective, and love. Following many leaders brings division, dissension, and conflict. One leader brings us unity, even if we don't agree about everything. According to what our Prophet told Hudhayfah, there's a simple explanation for why we've found ourselves where we are today: we didn't take his advice. We haven't learned the Quran and the Sunnah for ourselves, we lost the caliph because we preferred politics to prophecy, and we have chosen to follow lesser men and women in an attempt to abrogate our own responsibility to God Most High. We've failed to benefit from the wealth of wisdom that surrounds each of us to help us change and grow. Instead we've chosen to remain on the path that makes us most comfortable with who we are; it's human nature.

- **Muhammad predicted everything that has happened to us.**

- **He said that we'd fight over religion and politics until we forgot what was important.**

- **Our leaders weren't ever supposed to be perfect, and neither were we.**

CHAPTER 17

....

TRIBULATIONS

Eventually, the first fitnah of politics made the People of Islam vulnerable to the second fitnah that Muhammad warned Hudhayfah about:

> I asked, "Will there be any evil after that good?" He replied: "Yes, there will be a blind and deaf turbulence; callers to the gates of Hell. Whoever responds to their call, they cast him into it."
>
> I said, "O Messenger of Allah, describe them to us." He replied: "They are from our own skin, and they speak our tongue."

Throughout the world, believing, dedicated Muslims have been killing innocent men, women, and children in what they think is the name of Islam. We should all know better. Based on what they're doing and saying, few if any of the leaders can actually be Muslim, and according to the Hadiths we have on the subject, they might not even be human. Muhammad's prophecy described them to Hudhayfah as "sharing our skin and speaking in our tongue," but he was clear that despite their appearance, these "callers to the gates of hell" would be "men with the hearts of demons," springing out of the spiritual turbulence of our last thousand years as a fitnah for all humankind. Muhammad warned Hudhayfah that they'd be able to lead believing Muslims astray, and so they have. Muslims have become murderers throughout the world. The worst failure of today's teachers of Islam is that so many Muslims honestly believe that killing innocent people guarantees that the killers will go to heaven when they die.

So many misguided Muslims believe it's okay to kill people because they believe in the evil ones guiding them—men that the Prophet Muhammad said would act like demons masquerading in Arab skin and speaking lies in the Arab tongue. You can tell who they are by what they say and what they do. We should all know that murder is wrong, but those leaders tell us it's okay. The fact that they have encouraged the slaughter of women and children, regardless of their faith, in the name of their own version of Islam should be all the evidence we need to understand the true nature of their souls. Muslims should know better. We should be able to simply ignore them or bring them to justice ourselves. Instead, we encourage them or even help them.

The last thousand years of Islam and the first fitnah have made us susceptible to manipulation by the lies of men and women who we think know more about the Holy Quran and the Sunnah than we do. They prey on our ignorance. The extent to which blind obedience to scholars and schools has replaced deeper wisdom, understanding, and learning enough to make good choices has made many think that disagreements should divide us rather than teach us something about the limits to human wisdom. Those conflicts and divisions in turn have promoted the idea that hatred and condemnation can spring from wisdom just as much as love and understanding can. Finally, even hatred, standing alone—whether it's of Jews, Christians, Americans, or even other Muslims—has come to be seen as a sign of wisdom.

I know I'm not going to make a lot of friends with this chapter, particularly among the membership of al Qaeda. Opinions like mine rarely go over well in those particular circles. The truth is, they have a point: trusting the opinion of anyone else about something as important as the Will of God just because he or she can quote the Holy Quran was never really a good idea. I think we can all agree that there needs to be more individual diligence and responsibility. In defense of my right to write what I've written, I can only say that everyone should check everything out for himself or herself. The only right that any of us have to share our thoughts on Islam derives solely from how much and how hard we've studied and from the value of what we have to say.

Even today, some Muslims still claim that you can't really understand Islam if you're not an Arabic-speaking Arab. That idea goes to the heart of why we're divided, because if we choose to discount a person's point of view based upon his or her race, then we automatically create a racist religion. We also repeat the mistake that resulted in the schism between

Sunni and Shia Muslims. Islam is for everyone: Muhammad's last sermon made it clear that there's no place for racism within it. According to the words of the Holy Quran, our Arab brothers and sisters weren't created to perfect the message that Muhammad revealed. According to the Quran, they're perfected by it, just like the rest of us. Only submission, obedience to God's commands through His Word and His Prophets, makes any of us better than we are. Az-Zumar 39:27–28 is quite clear on this subject:

> We have put forth for men, in this Quran, every kind of Parable, in order that they may receive admonition. It is a Quran in Arabic, without any crookedness therein: In order that they may guard against evil.

Allah revealed the Quran so that it would be read, understood, and obeyed. The Quran was revealed to the Prophet Muhammad in Arabic as a blessing, not a reward. Fussilat 41:44 explains:

> Had we sent this a Quran in a language other than Arabic, they would have said: "Why are not its verses explained in detail? What! A book not in Arabic? And a Messenger an Arab?"
> Say: "It is a guide and a healing to those who believe; and for those who believe not, there is a deafness in their ears, and it is a blindness in their eyes: They are (as it were) being called from a place far distant!"

Az-Zukhruf 43:3 corroborates:

> We have made it a Quran in Arabic, that ye may be able to understand and learn wisdom. And verily, it is in the Mother of the Book, in Our Presence, High in dignity, full of wisdom. And verily it is on the Mother of the Book, in Our Presence, High in dignity, full of wisdom.

And finally, Ibrahim 14:4 confirms:

> We sent not a messenger except to teach in the language of his own people, in order to make things clear to them. Now Allah

> leaves straying those whom He pleases and guides whom He
> pleases: And He is exalted in Power, full of Wisdom.

I sometimes wonder whether conversational Arabic might sometimes make it harder to understand the real meaning of the Quran. The Arabic of the Quran is a complex language, with its words joined by shared roots that can affect the nuances of what those words mean. In conversation, we all tend to assign one meaning to each word, sometimes to the exclusion of deeper connotations. The depth of the information that the Quran delivers makes it more like poetry than prose. True understanding requires careful study; the Book deserves it. The idea that simply speaking Arabic makes you more of an authority on Islam only makes people even more vulnerable to manipulation. This is the same way that the control of the translation and interpretation of the Bible in the early days of the Christian church helped the Vatican maintain its control over non-Latin-speaking Christians.

As God's servants, Muslims are only as righteous as our obedience makes us. Ignorance is no excuse. Bad advice isn't either. The race of a man or a woman has little or no bearing on his or her trustworthiness. Al-Hujraat 49:14 commanded the Prophet:

> The desert Arabs say, "We believe." Say, "Ye have no faith; but
> ye only say, 'We have submitted our wills to Allah.' For not
> yet has Faith entered your hearts. But if ye obey Allah and
> His messenger, He will not belittle aught oft of your deeds:
> For Allah is Oft-Forgiving, Most Merciful."

The only completely trustworthy sources of guidance and instruction are the Quran and the Sunnah themselves.

Even in Islam, if scholars tell you that God wants you to kill someone, that's not the same as God saying it to you, no matter how beautiful their recitation, how full their beards, or how archaic their dress code. They might be right. Every Muslim knows we might be expected to do something for God that we'd rather not do. The trouble is, those scholars might be wrong, too, and it's not worth the risk. Muhammad told us that human life is more sacred than the Kabah in Mecca! One of the central principles of Islam is that every Muslim is responsible to God for his or her own behavior. We're expected to obey those in authority—but only to the extent that their commands are just, righteous, and good. Obedience to the caliphate was (perhaps sometimes) an exception, but we haven't had a caliph for years and so all the predictions of the Prophet have come true. We have had a succession of leaders who haven't really had the authority to lead the Ummah; some have even been obviously evil. In the chaos we've found ourselves in, it's been hard for the Muslim on the street to discern the good from the bad. Every leader, group, school, and sect among us have some way to explain why ultimate temporal authority should be theirs. Those rationalizations have been accepted by some of us and rejected by others, but never either rejected or accepted by all of us. It's made us all very confused.

Many of Islam's leaders and scholars have done their honest best. Some people have had something good to contribute to the Ummah as a whole, but because they're only human, they've all been wrong sometimes as well. Because we haven't all been able to support or condone everything that they've done, we've fragmented. Because none of them have ever really had the authority of the caliphate, no matter what we've thought, none of us have ever been absolved of our primary responsibility to God Most High by our obedience to them. Because we never gave appropriate authority to our caliphs when we were supposed to, we haven't had anything to protect us. Since the time of Ali, we've had nothing but disruption and corruption following the leadership of those we've chosen to follow, with our right to make that choice never actually approved by God. Because we've tried to follow our own preferences and prejudices instead of the Will of God, we have been drawn to hate each other. Eventually, as Muhammad predicted, we forgot the love that once set the Ummah apart from the rest of the world.

Because we've confused the proper order of Islam, we've created an Ummah that's replaced obedience to the Words of God and the Prophet with obedience to the words of men who claim to be able to interpret the commands of God for us. We now find ourselves living through a fitnah— an evil, a trial, where, according to the words of our own Prophet, we are plagued by demons masquerading as Arab men. Al Qaeda and their minions are calling us to the gates of hell, and we're flocking to them! They justify our evil acts and their hypocrisy by perverting the words of the Holy Quran and the beautiful Arabic tongue. It's because so few of us know any better that their lies can make us commit crimes against the Word of God and against our fellow man.

There's really no question whether many of the world's Muslims are going through a tough time. Non-Muslims think it's evidence that God's rejected us. Some of us have even come to the point where we question our faith, but that's not what the Quran says we should do. Muslims are supposed to know that God doesn't necessarily reward anyone in this life. The things that happen to us here don't necessarily have to make sense to anyone. Remember the story of Ayoub, or Job? He endured a series of horrid trials simply because God knew he could, and God wanted to use him as an example of a truly good man. In the end, God made everything better than before, as a reward. Any trial we undergo will end up being good for us. Aal-E-Imran 3:178–179 is clear:

> Let not the Unbelievers think Our respite to them is good for themselves: We grant them respite that they may grow in their iniquity; but they will have a shameful punishment. Allah will not leave the Believers in the state in which ye are now, until He separates what is evil from what is good. Nor will Allah disclose to you the secrets of the Unseen, but He chooses of His messengers for the purpose whom He pleases. So believe in Allah and His Messengers; and if ye believe and do right, ye have a reward without measure.

According to the Holy Quran, this life doesn't matter much in the grand scheme of things anyway. Al-Ahzab 33:185–186 tells us:

> Every soul shall have a taste of death: Only on the Day of Judgment shall you be paid your full recompense. Only he who is saved far from the Fire and admitted to the Garden will have attained the object of Life: For the life of this world is but goods and chattels of deception. Ye shall certainly be tried and tested in your possessions and in your personal selves; and ye shall certainly hear much that will grieve you, from those who received the Book before you and from those who worship many gods. But if ye persevere patiently and guard against evil—then that will be a determining factor in all affairs.

In agreement, Al-Baqara 2:155 confirms:

> Be sure we shall test you with something of fear and hunger, some loss in goods or lives or the fruits of your toil, but give

glad tidings to those who patiently persevere and who say,
when afflicted with calamity; "To Allah we belong and to
Him is our return."

The Quran doesn't even promise that the "best" Muslims will enjoy the
best of everything in this life. Actually, it says that God would give the best
of this world to the worst people if God didn't know how hard that would
make it for the rest of us to be good! Az-Zukhruf 43:33–35 assures us:

And were it not that all men might become of one evil way
of life, We would provide for everyone that blasphemes
against Allah most Gracious silver roofs for their houses and
silver stairways on which to go up and silver doors to their
houses and thrones of silver on which they could recline
and also adornments of Gold. But all this were nothing but
conveniences of the present life: The Hereafter, in the sight of
thy Lord, is for the Righteous.

The good news is that I think we can get out of the pit we've dug any
time we want to. First, we have to ask, why do we have fitnah in the first
place? Honestly, what purpose can tests possibly serve if God is really
Omniscient, Omnipotent, and Omnipresent? The God Muslims believe in
and serve certainly doesn't need a test to find out what sort of people we
are. If the process of trial and separation isn't for God's sake, then it has to
be for ours. Next, ask yourself, what are we supposed to get out of trials
and temptations? The fact that our situation and that of the Christians are
so very different is actually a clue, because both Jesus and Muhammad
predicted that their followers would face certain hurdles and that some
of us would fail. Christians were warned about the dangers of wealth and
power; Muslims were told about the dangers of disunity. Just as Jesus
predicted, wealth and the love of money and power are what have driven
Christians away from his path. It should be obvious that the inability of
Muslims to get along with each other is what's driven us away from ours.
At some point—God alone knows when—it'll finally get bad enough to be
obvious to everybody. Someday, the war the wealthy Christian West has
declared on the poor of the world to protect its own prosperity will have
to wake Christians up to the way they now serve Mammon. Perhaps the
way the Muslim marriage of politics and the power of religion has broken

us into our present ridiculous collection of warring clans may finally wake us up as well.

There is no such thing as harmless politicking, and there are few sins worse than that of leading credulous Muslims away from the body of Islam by pretending to know something that you don't. If we've finally come to a point where it's obvious that al Qaeda is only a path to hell masquerading as a faithful believer's supporting foundation (its name is an abuse of the Arabic language), and if their abuse of Arab politics, pride, and people finally makes Muslims everywhere realize that we are swiftly becoming the people described in Al-Baqara 2:8–12, then perhaps something good will finally have come of it after all.

> Of the people there are some who say: "We believe in Allah and the Last day"; but they do not really believe. Fain would they deceive Allah and those who believe, but they deceive only themselves and they realize it not! In their hearts is a disease; and Allah has increased their disease: And grievous is the penalty they incur, because they are false to themselves. When it is said to them: "Make not mischief on the earth," they say: "Why, we only want to make peace!" Of a surety, they are the ones who make mischief, but they realize it not.

- **Muslims have been fighting over the Quran for the last thousand years.**

- **We've been so busy fighting over who's right about what the Quran says that we've forgotten to read it.**

- **Fighting over the path has driven us so far from it that many of us don't even recognize it anymore.**

CHAPTER 18

....

TRUE UNITY

There's got to be a good reason why God commanded Muslims to strive for unity. To a believer, there's no question that God knew what would happen when He made the universe or that He shared some of that information with His Prophet. Both Allah and Muhammad knew that despite the Quran's commands to the contrary, we'd fall apart. Those commands weren't sent to mock us, although it might seem at times that they do. To Muslims, the Quran will always be a blessing, never a condemnation. Like everything else in it, those words were given for guidance. They were meant to lead us back to the Way when we got lost, as we inevitably would and have. According to the Holy Quran, unity is one of the best indications that the Ummah is on the right track. Unity is what will give us back respect, influence, and power. Unity is eventually what's going to lead us from the gates of hell.

Even today, many of us still think that everything would have been better if we had been able to accept the one right caliph in the beginning and if the succession of the caliphate could have continued. Some think we should try to find a caliph now. That presupposes that the events of the last millennia were a mistake, but if they were really predicted, then what happened did because it had to. That doesn't mean that we haven't made mistakes. Our errors were inevitable; we're only human, after all. Prominent among them is likely the way we've assumed that making the message of Muhammad and the Quran subordinate to our own wishes was really what God meant. As an Ummah, we haven't yet realized that prophecy is inevitable, the predictions of prophets always come true, and that trials and tribulations are gifts sent to teach us the errors of our ways.

Understanding the sort of unity we're destined to find in Islam really centers on these questions: Is our religion inclusive, as it seems to be described in the Gabriel Hadith, or is it exclusive, as most interpretations of the Hadith of the seventy-three sects would imply? Is Islam a broad and turbulent river whose current sweeps along everyone who jumps in? What is the nature of the "straight path" that we all beseech Allah to place us on in Surah Al-Fatiha, and how can we be sure we're on it? It should be easy. The Prophet told us that we should emulate him and his Companions. Since the Prophet is the Muslims' best guide, the only questions really are: What did he mean? How do we do what he said? What is the characteristic of the Companions that made them different from what they were before Islam was revealed?

The one thing that we can be certain of about our quest is that we haven't yet found the one true Way of God. We've spent the last fourteen centuries looking for an exclusive, perfect path, politically and doctrinally, and it hasn't done us any good. Even the Companions weren't unified by anything other than the fact that whatever they did, they did because they were striving to serve God. That was why they all obeyed the Prophet, and that was why they listened to, revered, and followed the lessons of the Holy Quran. It wasn't so much what they did that united them as why they did it. It's important to realize that their differences weren't even a bad thing as far as Muhammad was concerned. If Islam were really meant to be exclusive, he wouldn't have said, "Differences and disagreement in my community is a Mercy!"

I think we have to accept that disagreements are unavoidable. If that weren't the case, we wouldn't have been given verses like Aal-E-Imran 3:7:

> He it is Who has sent down to thee the Book: In it are verses basic or fundamental, of established meaning; they are the foundation of the Book: Others are not of well-established meaning. But those in whose hearts is perversity follow the part thereof that is not of well-established meaning. Seeking discord, and searching for its hidden meanings, but no one knows its true meanings except Allah. And those who are firmly grounded in knowledge say: "We believe in the Book; the whole of it is from our Lord": And none will grasp the Message except men of understanding.

According to this verse, it isn't the fact that there may be different interpretations of portions of God's Word that is wrong, only the discord that can result from believing that following one interpretation or the other makes us different from each other. There's no question we're going to make mistakes. Otherwise, why would Al-Baqara 2:286 command us to pray:

"Our Lord, do not impose blame on us if we forget or err."

If you believe these Ayat (*Ayah* is the Arabic word for "miracle" and the way Muslims designate individual verses of the Quran) and Hadiths, you can't make significant, important, or fundamental errors if you're humble enough to admit what you don't know and just stick to the stuff you're sure you understand. According to An-Nisa's commands, if we do find that we disagree, we're supposed to refer to the words of the Quran and the Prophet, not our favorite teachers or our friends. In Islam, even if we make mistakes or find ourselves compelled to make choices we fear might be wrong, we're forgiven as long as we're doing our honest best. In fact, just about the only unforgivable sin when you're interpreting the Word of God seems to be getting it wrong on purpose or wanting to create divisions and distinctions over disagreements about doctrine and dogma.

Creating our own unchangeable rules and laws and claiming that they come from God is one of the worst possible sins. Even the Prophet was commanded to say only what he had been told to. Al-Hijr 15:89–93 commands:

And say: "I am indeed he that warneth openly and without ambiguity"—(of just such wrath) as We sent down on those who divided (scripture into arbitrary parts) (so also on such) as have made the Quran into shreds (as they please). Therefore, by the Lord, We will, of a surety, call them to account for all their deeds. Therefore, expound openly what thou art commanded, and turn away from those who joined false gods with Allah.

Al-Araf 7:28–29 expands on this:

Say: "The things that my Lord hath indeed forbidden are: Shameful deeds, whether open or in secret: Sins and trespasses

against truth or reason: assigning of partners to Allah, for
which He hath given no authority and saying things about
Allah of which ye have no knowledge."

Both Ayat make it clear: although it's possible to lie about what's in the
Quran, it's not a very good idea if you want to follow what it says. That only
makes sense. If you believe in divine revelation, then you have to believe
that there's a purpose to it all. Islam is the religion of frail and fallible
humans submitting to a perfect God. God knows that we're going to get it
wrong sometimes. Whether we're Shia or Sunni, Wahabean or Sufi, Ismaili
or even Ahmadiyyah, we are all striving to obey Allah, God Most High.
Even the Holy Quran says we're going to disagree. Understanding religion
and interpreting the revelations we've been given isn't always easy. When
we're uncertain, God tells us to refer the question to the Quran and the
Sunnah, just as the rightly guided Companions did. Even then, the answer
might be open to interpretation. Sometimes we'll need an expert opinion
from scholars, mullahs, and Imams, but we have to accept that they're all
just as human as we are and won't ever be absolutely right. Anyone who is
striving to obey the Quran and the Sunnah won't ever be absolutely wrong
either. If we accept guidance from each other in that spirit, it won't break
up our religion into sects. We can learn from each other. We should listen
to each other. We really don't have much choice.

The irony of it all, at least to a Quran-believing Muslim, is that the Holy
Quran has told us the one thing that can return us all to the path of unity
once and for all. It's the same thing that worked for the warring, contentious
Arab tribes of Mecca and Medina when the Prophet Muhammad first
came to them. Those fractious, argumentative, and polytheistic tribes of
the Arab peninsula who were sent the Holy Quran through the Prophet
Muhammad were never united by politics or doctrine, and it's really not
a surprise that we won't be either. We've tried! Aal-E-Imran 3:102–103
explains what really happened:

O ye who believe! Fear Allah as he should be feared, and
die not except in a state of Islam. And hold fast all together,
by the Rope Which Allah Stretches Out for you, and be not
divided among yourselves; and remember with gratitude
Allah's favor on you: For ye were enemies and He joined your
hearts in love, so that by His Grace ye became brethren; and

ye were on the brink of the Pit of Fire and He saved you from it. Thus doth Allah make his Signs clear to you: That ye may be guided.

The only thing that joined the first Muslims together and that made them brothers and sisters to each other, as well as Companions to the Prophet of God, was love. They often argued, even when Muhammad was still alive, and they certainly fought after he died. Despite that, it's obvious from reading the histories that the love they felt for each other never changed. Aisha bitterly regretted her rebellion against Ali and his caliphate to the day she died, and she told everyone that Ali had been right all along. One of the most beautiful stories demonstrating the love the Companions had for each other comes to us out of those times in the history of Uthman and Ali. Ali knew Uthman was likely to be assassinated and that Ali would become caliph afterward. If he had really wanted Uthman dead, he could have sat back and done nothing. Instead, he sent his own sons, Hasan and Husayn, to defend Uthman with their lives. When Hasan was wounded, Uthman sent them both away because he couldn't bear to see their blood shed on his behalf, particularly by other Muslims. Then, despite the instructions of their father, the sons of Ali did what Uthman told them to do, proving that he was their caliph, too.

Unity has always been a gift from God Most High, with God's gift of love for each other a grace for every Muslim who receives it. Again and again, the Quran commands Muslims to put their trust in Allah and reminds us that Islam is a journey, not a destination. Paths are defined by where they're going, not where they start. Every Muslim knows that our goal is heaven and that the Quran and the Sunnah are directions there. One of the first Ayat in the Holy Quran, Al-Baqara 2:21, says:

O ye people! Adore your Guardian Lord, who created you and those who came before you that ye may become righteous.

Repeatedly, the Quran tells Muslims the importance of righteousness and what it is. Al-Baqara 2:177 is clear:

It is not righteousness that ye turn your faces towards East or West; but it is righteousness to believe in Allah and the Last Day, and the Angels, and the Book, and the Messengers; to spend of your substance, out of love for Him, for your kin, for orphans, for the needy, for the wayfarer, for those who ask, and for the ransom of slaves; To be steadfast in prayer, and practice regular charity, to fulfill the contracts which ye have made; and to be firm and patient, in pain (or suffering) or adversity, and throughout all periods of panic. Such are the people of truth, the God-fearing.

Righteousness isn't just what we believe. Throughout, the Quran is clear that treating others well is an essential part of it. Al-Anaam 6:151 promises Muslims that choosing to do good is the step of faith that in turn allows us to be taught and led:

Say: "Come, I will rehearse what Allah hath (really) prohibited you from": Join not anything as equal with him; be good to your parents; kill not your children on a plea of want—We provide sustenance for you and for them—come not nigh to shameful deeds, whether open or secret; take not life, which Allah hath made sacred, except by way of justice and law: Thus doth He command you, that ye may learn wisdom.

It's important to note that the Quran never says righteousness has anything to do with forcing others to do or to believe what you think they should. Instead, that practice is summarily condemned in one of the most triumphant passages in the entire Holy Quran, Al-Baqara 2:255–256:

Allah! There is no God but He—the Self-subsisting, Eternal. No slumber can seize Him nor sleep. His are all things in the heavens and on earth. Who is there that can intercede in His presence except as He permitteth? He knoweth what (appeareth to His creatures as) before or after or behind them. Nor shall they compass aught of His knowledge except as He willeth. His Throne doth extend over the heavens and the earth, and He feeleth no fatigue in guarding and preserving them for He is the Most High, the Supreme (in glory).

Let there be no compulsion in religion: Truth stands out clear from Error; whoever rejects Evil and believes in Allah hath grasped the most trustworthy handhold, that never breaks. And Allah heareth and knoweth all things.

In this passage, Allah declares His supreme majesty and confirms He's more than capable of keeping an eye on everything.

The Kabah is a sign to all Muslims of Allah's extravagant way of keeping His promises. All around the world, five prayers a day, Muslims bow towards Mecca, and from around the world Muslims come by the tens of millions to worship and pray there, just because God promised Abraham that his temple would be remembered. We should probably trust that God will be able to keep the rest of his promises too. Al-Baqara 2:148–150 declares that Allah will bring us together:

> To each is a goal to which Allah turns him; then strive together (as in a race) towards all that is good. Where-so-ever ye are, Allah will bring you together. For Allah hath power over all things.
>
> From whence-so-ever thou startest forth turn thy face in the direction of the Sacred Mosque; that is indeed the truth from thy Lord. And Allah is not unmindful of what ye do.
>
> So from whence so ever thou startest forth, turn thy face in the direction of the Sacred Mosque; and where-so-ever ye are, turn your face thither: That there be no ground of dispute against you among the people, except those of them that are bent on wickedness; so fear them not, but fear Me; and that I may complete my favors on you, and ye may (consent to) be guided.

Through these Ayat, God confirms that good works are an essential component of the Muslim path, but He doesn't say anything about our beliefs or practices, save only one: He's quite clear that anyone who questions the Islam of someone who prays towards Mecca is wrong to do so. The Gabriel Hadith, revealed to teach Umar his religion, says that the six things a Muslim must believe in are the authority of Allah, His angels, His books and His messengers, and His control of our destiny, both the good and the bad. That means to arrive at our final destination, Muslims must believe that God has a plan and that He's in control, not that we understand everything that He's doing, or why, or how. As for exactly what constitutes modest dress, whether shrimp are Halal, and who was the best of the Prophet's Companions, we're never all going to believe exactly the same things in exactly the same way, nor are we going to have the same priorities:

God made us all different, and Muhammad said that those differences are a blessing, not a fitnah. The path of Islam is big enough for us all.

According to the Holy Quran, love is what bound the first generations of Muslims to each other and held Islam together when we started. It's still the only thing that can make us one Ummah now. Love is what made the Companions and their children different from what they had been before the revelation of Islam. Losing that love is the thing that Muhammad predicted would bring about the trials that followed after he was gone. Before Islam came, the Companions were all on the brink of the pit, just like we're on the brink of it now. Muhammad told Hudhayfah that one of the consequences of the first fitnah would be Muslims forgetting the love that we once had for each other. More than anything else, that's what's put us where we are today. If we still loved each other the way Muslims used to, we could never have done the things that we have done to each other—no matter how much we disagree. If we still loved each other at all, we couldn't help but be kinder to everyone else, too. The Holy Quran says that Arab tribes of Muhammad's day were saved from hell by God's gift of love to them toward each other. A little of that same love could go a long way toward saving us all now.

The sign of God's love, according to the words of the Holy Quran, is unity. I think that's why unity has always been so important in Islam. Perhaps things are finally bad enough that it's obvious to all of us that we're not going to come together any other way. We're all too far apart. If unity remains the indicator that's been given to Muslims to confirm that we're actually headed in the right direction, then unity's still what we're supposed to be striving for. The good news is that the Quran says doctrine and politics weren't what unified Islam in the first place; love was! God's love created the Ummah of Islam in the time of ignorance among the Arabs of the peninsula. Given how badly our own ideas have worked out, we should maybe try what worked for them.

Unity means many things, but the main thing that it's always meant is oneness, not sameness. The completion and harmony of unity is what you get when you combine different and separate things to create a complete and sometimes completely different whole. Embrace diversity! Love each other! In today's Islam, those are both revolutionary concepts, but you have to admit that we can't do much worse than we're doing now. A rope is long, with many places to hold on. Islam is the same way. We all want to be on the straight path. That doesn't mean that it has to look like the same path to every one of us or that we're all in exactly the same place on it. There are a billion Muslims in the world. Even if we are all trying to approach God, we all started in different places. Even if we all end up in the same place, the paths we take will have to be different because we're all different and we all embark at different times and in different ways. Accepting our own diversity is just a matter of accepting the way things are.

Our disagreements might even tell us more about Islam than the things we agree on. If two people who've studied and truly care about Islam can disagree, then it's possible they're both right. That would explain why the Prophet told us that our differences are a mercy from God, when it's obvious that arguing about them has been anything but. Thinking we're perfectly right about anything is awfully close to elevating ourselves into Allah's place—the only unforgivable sin in Islam! True unity, and the love of diversity it engenders, can repair or prevent our divisions, but it should also keep us from taking our opinions and ourselves too seriously. Unity protects us from replacing submission to God with submission to ourselves or to anyone else. God's authority is supreme. If we allow others to usurp it, we fail the most basic test. If, on the other hand, we accept that we won't ever agree about everything (and sometimes we won't even agree about anything!) and we realize that that doesn't make those who disagree with us wrong, apostate, or non-Muslim, then God willing, we can all be brothers and sisters in Islam again—the way we're supposed to be.

- **The Quran says that the only thing that unified the first Muslims was love.**

- **Learning to get along with people you don't agree with keeps you humble.**

- **It should also protect you from thinking that believing what's right matters more to God than doing what's wrong.**

CHAPTER 19

....

REAL HARMONY

Given what's been happening around the world lately, the image of a unified Islam isn't likely to bring a lot of comfort to anyone. We've all been plagued by men who've wanted nothing more than to make the rest of us submit to them, and been blessed by only a few who've really wanted to submit to God Most High. Violent jihadists in the last few decades have tried to bring Islam together under their banner to make the billion or so believers follow them. Their rhetoric and tactics have given us all a bad name, and we never should have allowed it to go as far as it has. If any one of them really had any sort of authority, then there might be some justifiable cause for concern, but they don't and never have. Without a caliph, there's literally no one on earth with the authority to lead Islam. In the absence of a caliph, the authority of God as expressed through the Quran and the Sunnah is supreme, and these texts should be sufficient to restrain us from the sorts of things that we've been guilty of lately.

When Jesus eventually comes back, if the Sunnis are right, then he will be the next caliph. Few Christians seem aware that according to Hadiths we have on the subject, Jesus will be both judge and war leader over the righteous Ummah: we're all actually looking forward to the Second Coming. Alternatively, if the Shiite scholars are correct, then as I understand it, our next caliph will end up being their Hidden Imam. I have absolutely no idea what the relationship between their Mahdi (the leader they expect God to send back) and Jesus is going to be like, but I do know the Shia will acknowledge Jesus' authority too. Whatever's going to happen then, there's not much use for much speculation now; I suspect we're all going to have to wait and see.

Until then, Muslims have our Islam, the Quran, and the Sunnah to restrain us from either believing whatever we want or doing whatever we want. An-Nisa 4:135–136 commands us:

> O ye who believe! Stand out firmly for justice, as witnesses to Allah, even as against yourselves or your parents or your kin, and whether it be against rich or poor, for Allah can best protect both. Follow not the lusts of your hearts, lest ye swerve, and if ye distort justice or decline to do justice, verily Allah is well acquainted with all that you do.
>
> O ye who believe! Believe in Allah and his messenger and the scripture which he hath sent to His messenger and the scripture which He sent to those before him. Any who denieth Allah, His angels, His Books, His messengers and the Day of Judgment hath gone far, far astray.

Lately, the "lust" that's been getting us into the most trouble is the lust for revenge—for what's been going on in the Holy Land or in Iraq and Afghanistan. Al-Maeda 5:45 commends forgiveness instead:

> We ordained therein for them (the Jews): "Life for life, eye for eye, nose for nose, ear for ear, tooth for tooth, and wounds equal for equal." But if anyone remits the retaliation by way of charity, it is an act of atonement for himself. And if any fail to judge by the light of what Allah hath revealed, they are no better than wrongdoers.

Even if you can't find it in your heart to forgive your enemy, life is sacred. Muslims are allowed to kill only in self-defense or to prevent friends and family from being driven from their homes. Revenge and vigilante-style justice aren't ever approved, whether we want them to be or not. Ayat like Al-Anaam 6:151 are clear:

> Say: "Come, I will rehearse what Allah hath prohibited you from. Join not anything as equal with Him. Be good to your parents. Kill not your children on a plea of want—We provide sustenance for you and for them. Come not nigh to shameful deeds, whether open or secret, and take not life, which Allah

hath made sacred, except by way of justice and law: Thus
doth He command you, that ye may learn wisdom."

If we obey the Quran and the Sunnah, not only will we have to stop
killing each other, we'll probably have to get along better with everyone
else, too.

There are many Ayat that command Muslims to fight, but in the
absence of a caliph, none of them justify anything offensive or expansionist.
Preemptive strikes are only preemptive if you know exactly what's going to
happen. Murder in the name of politics or anything else but immediate self-
defense leaves us personally responsible to God for the sins that we commit
when we injure others. Although we're all supposed to respect authority
only so far as their commands are just, that doesn't justify armed rebellion
if we decide that we disagree with them! Instead, it should make us tend
toward exactly the sort of political stability and gradual democratization so
many of us are so vehemently trying to reject right now. Islamic government
is supposed to be based on a process called *shura*, which means "mutual
consultation." That sounds an awful lot like democracy to me. Whatever
else, Islam has always demanded the rule of law among women and men,
with peace and justice for all. If that's not the picture of Muslims in most
people's minds today, the fault is our own.

The failed tactics that we've used to seek unity in Islam—striving for a
unity of "sameness under ourselves" rather than "oneness under God"—
haven't worked very well among Muslims, but they've had catastrophic
effects on our relationship with non-Muslim faiths. No matter the quality of
their leadership at the time, for the first few centuries of the Islamic empire,
Muslims founded, lived in, and maintained some of the most progressive,
inclusive, and diverse civilizations in the history of humankind. Umar, the
second caliph and arguably the prototypical "rigid" Muslim, went to great
lengths to ensure that Christians and Jews were treated as equals and to
show his respect for their religions. He once ordered that a Christian be
allowed to beat a Muslim who had struck him after losing a footrace, and
he refused to pray in the church in Jerusalem to ensure that later Muslims
wouldn't declare it a mosque and confiscate it. He even ordered that land
stolen from a Jew in order to build a mosque be returned and that the
mosque be torn down! But as our arguments have forced us further apart,
our relations with other peoples, cultures, and religions have degenerated
as well. Finally, we've come to the point where it sometimes seems as if

hating Christians and Jews has become the only thing we can still agree about. Ayat critical of Christians and Jews, the "People of the Book," are freely quoted and even more freely interpreted in virtually every mosque on the planet. Some Imams even use false Hadith to claim that the Prophet flew into a rage whenever he saw a cross!

Muhammad's own words, in his decree to the Christians of Najran, declare his true position:

> To the Christians of Najran and the surrounding territories, the security of God and the pledge of His Prophet are extended for their lives, their religion and their property ... to those present as well as to those absent, and others beside. There shall be no interference with the practice of their faith or their observance, nor any change in their rights or privileges. No bishop shall be removed from his bishopric nor any monk from his monastery, nor any priest from his priesthood. They shall continue to enjoy everything, great and small, as they hitherto did. No image or cross shall be destroyed. They shall not oppress, nor be oppressed. They shall not practice the rights of blood-vengeance as in the Days of Ignorance. No tithes shall be exacted from them, nor shall they be required to furnish provisions for the troops.

A lot of things that Muslims are supposed to say to Christians and Jews are surprisingly conciliatory. "Death to the infidels" just isn't on the list. Aal-E-Imran 3:64–71 defines the minimum basis for peaceful coexistence in terms that none of us could ever disagree with:

> Say: "O People of the Book! Come to common terms as between us and you: That we worship none but The Lord; That we associate no partners with Him; That we erect not from among ourselves lord and patrons other than The Lord." If they turn back say ye: "Bear witness that we at least are Muslims, bowing to the Will of The Lord." Ye People of the Book! Why dispute ye about Abraham when the Law and the Gospel were not revealed 'til after him? Have ye no understanding? Ah! Ye are those who fell to disputing even

in matters of which ye have no knowledge! It is The Lord who knows, and ye who know not! Abraham was not a Jew, nor yet a Christian; But he was true in Faith, and bowed his will to Allah's (the act of Islam) and he joined not Gods with Allah. Without a doubt, among men, the nearest of kin to Abraham are those who follow him, as are also this Prophet (Muhammad) and those who believe: And Allah is the Protector of those who have faith.

Quite opposed to the rage-filled warrior spreading Islam by terror and the sword, the Holy Quran is very specific about the lengths that we should go to get along with non-Muslims when we're discussing religion. An-Nahl 16:125 stresses that we should be polite, and Al-Anaam 6:108 confirms that we should never be insulting:

Invite all to the Way of thy Lord with wisdom and beautiful preaching, and argue with them in ways that are best and most gracious: For thy Lord knoweth best, who have strayed from His path, and who receive guidance. And if ye do catch them out, catch them out no worse than they catch you out: But if ye show patience; that is indeed the best course. Patience is from Allah; nor grieve over them and distress not thyself because of their plots. For Allah is with those who restrain themselves and do good.

Revile not ye those whom they call upon besides Allah, lest they out of spite revile Allah in their ignorance.

Today, those Ayat are often ignored. Instead, Al-Tawbah 9:29 and 9:73 are frequently quoted by Muslims and non-Muslims alike as the two most violent and disturbing Ayat in the entire Quran:

Fight those who believe not in Allah, nor the Last day, nor hold that forbidden which hath been forbidden by Allah and His Messenger, nor acknowledge the Religion of Truth, from among the People of the Book, until they pay the Jizyah with willing submission, and feel themselves subdued.

O Prophet! Strive hard against the Unbelievers and the Hypocrites, and be firm against them. Their abode is Hell— An Evil refuge indeed.

Few take the time to remember that these Ayat were revealed in response to tales of a two-hundred-thousand-strong army of Christians massing in the north and threatening to sweep down and rid the world of Muslims. The Roman army slaughtered Muhammad's envoy and seemed bent on nothing less than complete extermination. That didn't happen: instead, a small Muslim army of three thousand men fought an elite Roman force thirty times its size to a standstill and the rest of the force simply melted away. Then, instead of commanding Muhammad to hunt the Christians down or to carry the war to every other Christian in the world, Al-Tawbah 9:29 actually limited Muhammad's response and brought peace to the entire region.

The other often-quoted verse, Al-Tawbah 9:73, doesn't even apply to Christians or Jews! In Islam, before you can be classed among the "Unbelievers" (*Kuffaara*), you have to knowingly and openly reject something you know is true. To be labeled a hypocrite, you have to perform the rejection in private. In the Quran, both words were used to refer to Muslims who first accepted Islam and then later rejected it when the going got rough.

Because both Ayat were among the last to be revealed, some Muslim scholars use them and the principle of abrogation based on Al-Baqara 2:106 to claim that Al-Tawbah contravenes the roughly one hundred and thirty Ayat commending peaceful coexistence:

None of our revelations do We abrogate or cause to be forgotten, but We substitute something better or similar: Knowest thou not that Allah Hath power over all things?

Were the principle of abrogation to be so universally true, it would mean that the Quran contradicts itself! Such an occurrence would inevitably weaken the validity of the entire book, but examined in the context of the Ayat that precede it, Al-Baqara 2:106 is clearly addressing Jews and Christians, proclaiming God's right to use the Quran to clarify His message to them. It's true that while the Quran was being revealed and the Ummah was taking shape, a few verses were clarified and a few rules changed. Alcohol went from disapproved to condemned, the penalty for adultery changed, and the Qibla moved from Jerusalem to Mecca. Each event had both an Ayah and a Sunnah, an act of the Prophet, to make the change clear. When Al-Tawbah 9:29 and 9:73 were revealed, these verses let Muslims know they'd prevail, reminded them to stick together, and limited their response to non-Muslim aggression.

For centuries after these verses were written, no Muslim behaved as if they said anything else; Al-Baqara 2:106, too, always justified and promoted peaceful dialogue. Muhammad set out from Medina with an army, and they expected a war. When the conditions outlined in Al-Tawbah were met without bloodshed, instead of carrying war to the Christians, Muhammad signed treaties. I agree with Muslim scholars that every Ayah in the Quran is there for a reason best understood by examining the lives of Muhammad and his Companions. I'm concerned that today's innovative interpretations contradicting the Prophet are misleading many Muslims into both unbelief and hypocrisy, and misleading more credulous Muslims is one of the worst sins there is.

Even peaceful conversation can get us into trouble sometimes. When we talk about religion with non-Muslims, and particularly with Christians and Jews, we should probably do everyone (including ourselves) the courtesy of using their books instead of or at least in addition to ours. When we preach from the Quran to people who don't believe in Islam, it often turns into an exchange of insults. We should avoid it. This means we're going to have to study more, but that's a good idea anyway. Muslims are supposed to acknowledge the authority of the prophets who came before, and that practice can help us all avoid the unpleasant spectacle of disrespecting each other's holiest records. Al-Maeda 5:47 tells us:

> Let the people of the Gospel judge by what Allah hath revealed therein. If any do fail to judge by the light of what Allah hath revealed, they are no better than those who rebel.

Some of the most pointless arguments we get into are over which book, prophet, or word for "God" is better. It's obvious that won't be resolved by us. Muslims in particular shouldn't have any issues with the holy books and prophets that Christians and Jews prefer. In fact, one Ayah makes it quite plain that God appreciates the earnest efforts of all three religions! Al-Hajj 22:39–40 proclaims:

> To those against whom War is made, permission is given to
> fight, because they are wronged—and verily Allah is Most
> Powerful for their aid—They are those who have been
> expelled from their homes in defiance of the right for no cause
> except that they say, "Our Lord is Allah." Did not Allah check
> one set of people by means of another there would surely
> have been pulled down monasteries, churches, synagogues
> and mosques, in which the name of Allah is commemorated
> in abundant measure. Allah is Full of Strength, Exalted in
> Might and able to enforce His Will.

Muslims have become quite excited in the last few decades about numerical "codes" embedded in the Quran that seem to confirm its veracity. Investigation has apparently shown that the entire text is written in both Arabic and base-19 numeric simultaneously, with letters, words, and phrases repeated in multiples of nineteen throughout the text. I've never taken the time to confirm it for myself (nor do I know how I would), but if it were true, that sort of thing would obviously require an impressive, God-like sort of intellect. Since nineteen is the smallest prime that's equal to the sum of its digits added to the product of its digits ($[1 + 9] + [1 \times 9]$) it seems an appropriate choice for the signature of the One Complete and Indivisible God. In Islam, Christianity, and Judaism, the number seven seems to signify the completion of God's act of creation. As the eighth prime number, nineteen could also symbolize something even greater than that. That sort of symbolism, and the miracle it would take to implant it into our Holy Book, makes Islam and the Quran more believable, if you like proof. Few Muslims seem to be aware that similar numerical tools are used by the Jews to verify the authenticity of their Torah. Both holy books carry their own confirmation. Even though Christianity has greater difficulty than the other two when it comes to confirming its texts, the church's honest efforts in that direction should be encouraged. While they're at it, the rest of us should probably try to trust that God will make it come out right in the end.

Islam has no more business trying to replace the other two religions than Christianity does. The Quran is very clear that we'll never be one religion. Al-Baqara 2:145 promises:

> Even if thou wert to bring to the people of the Book all the
> Signs together, they would not follow thy direction, nor art

thou going to follow their direction; nor indeed will they follow each other's direction.

Rather than condemning either Judaism or Christianity, the message of the Quran claims to correct and refute falsehoods that can creep into any religion. It's those falsehoods the Quran condemns, whether they're found among Jews, Christians, or other Muslims. Our final destination is the same, and the Quran confirms that the responsibility for our eventual reunion rests with God alone. Surah 2:148 proclaims and commands:

> To each is a goal to which Allah turns him: Then strive together as in a race towards all that is good where-so-ever ye are. Allah will bring you Together. For Allah Hath power over all things.

Many verses in the Quran are critical of Christians and Jews. These have been very popular among Muslims lately, but if you actually look at them, what they condemn are specific scriptural interpretations or particular times that Christians and Jews have failed to live up to their own prophets' commands. One currently popular Ayah seems to imply that Jews are "apes." Recently, an Imam in a mosque in my own country of Canada got quite famous for a while after quoting "Be ye apes, despised and rejected" as if it were meant to be applied to all the Jewish people living today. In fact, Al-Baqara 2:65 condemns a specific group of Jews for the very specific and very Jewish sin of Sabbath-breaking:

> And well ye knew those amongst you who transgressed in the matter of the Sabbath: We said to them: "Be ye apes, despised and rejected."

Another, more extensive retelling of that story in Al-Araf 7:163–170 even contains a confirmation of God's ongoing and eternal commitment to the Jewish people:

> Ask them concerning the town standing close by the sea. Behold! They transgressed in the matter of the Sabbath. For on the day of their Sabbath their fish did come to them, openly holding up their heads, but on that day they had no

Sabbath, they came not: Thus did we make a trial of them, for they were given to transgression. When some of them said: "Why do ye preach to a people whom Allah will destroy or visit with a terrible punishment?"—Said the preachers: "To discharge our duty to your Lord, and perchance they may fear him." When they disregarded the warnings that had been given them, we rescued those who forbade evil, but We visited the wrongdoers with a grievous punishment, because they were given to transgression. When in their insolence they transgressed all prohibitions, we said to them: "Be ye apes, despised and rejected." Behold! Thy Lord did declare that He would send against them, to the Day of Judgment, those who would afflict them with grievous Penalty. Thy Lord is quick in retribution, but He is also Oft Forgiving, Most Merciful. We broke them up into sections on the earth. There are among them some that are righteous, and some that are the opposite. We have tried them with both prosperity and adversity: In order that they might turn to us. After them succeeded an evil generation: They inherited the Book, but they chose for themselves the vanities of this world, saying for excuse: "Everything will be forgiven us!" Even so, if similar vanities came their way, they would again seize them. Was not the Covenant of the Book taken from them, that they would not ascribe to Allah anything but the truth? And they Study what is in the Book. But best for the righteous is the Home in the Hereafter. Will ye not understand? As to those who hold fast by the Book and establish regular Prayer—never shall We suffer the reward of the righteous to perish.

Jews are never summarily condemned in the Holy Quran. It says that they, like everyone else, are both good and bad. The Ayah Al-Araf 7:159 tells us:

Of the people of Moses there is a section who guide and do justice in the light of truth.

Other passages, such as Aal-E-Imran 3:113–116, confirm this:

Not all of them are alike: Of the People of the Book are a portion that stand for the right; they rehearse the Signs of Allah all night long, and they prostrate themselves in adoration. They believe in Allah and the Last Day; they enjoin what is right, and forbid what is wrong; and they hasten in the emulation of all good works: They are in the ranks of the righteous. Of the good that they do, nothing will be rejected of them: For Allah knoweth well those that do right.

To properly balance the Ayat that are critical of Jews, you need only recall some of the many Ayat that are even more critical of hypocritical Muslims.

The religion of Judaism isn't condemned in the Quran either. The Quran is quite clear that the standard that Jews are held to is going to be that of their own religion, not ours. Al-Maeda 5:44 assures us:

It was We who revealed the Law to Moses: Therein was guidance and light. By its standard have been judged the Jews, by the Prophets who bowed as in Islam to Allah's will, by the Rabbis and the Doctors of Law: For to them was entrusted the protection of Allah's Book, and they were witnesses thereto: Then fear not men, but fear Me, and sell not My signs for a miserable price. If any do fail to judge by the light of what Allah hath revealed, they are no better than the Unbelievers.

Many Hadith also confirm that, whenever he was asked to judge or settle disputes between Jews, the Prophet preferred to use Jewish law to do it.

Instead of condemnation, the Quran commends unity among all people of faith, based not on identity of belief but on simple acceptance of the overwhelming sovereignty of God. Instead of the dissolution of two of our three religions, it demands harmony among the People of the Book based on our descent from Abraham. An-Nisa 4:123–126 promises:

Not your desires, nor those of the People of the Book can prevail: Whoever works evil, will be requited accordingly. Nor will he find, besides Allah, any protector or helper. If any do deeds of righteousness—be they male or female—and have

Faith, they will enter Heaven, and not the least injustice will be done to them. Who can be better in religion than one who submits his whole self to Allah, does good and follows the way of Abraham, the true in Faith? For Allah did take Abraham for a friend. But to Allah belong all things in the heavens and on the earth; and He it is that encompasseth all things.

Angry Ayat, like Al-Maeda 5:18, are meant to refute a specific idea, not condemn an entire people:

Both the Jews and the Christians say: "We are sons of Allah, and His beloved." Say: "Why then doth He punish you for your sins? Nay ye are but men—of the men He hath created He forgiveth whom He pleaseth, and He punisheth whom He pleaseth: and to Allah belongeth the dominion of the heavens and the earth and all that is between: and unto Him is the final goal of all."

Confrontational Ayat, like Al-Jumua 62:6, give Muslims a way to respond in arguments to confrontational claims from the other side.

O ye that stand on Judaism! If ye think that ye are friends of Allah to the exclusion of other men, then express your desire for Death, if ye are truthful!

Warning Ayat, like Al-Maeda 5:51, only sound like good advice, given the state of the world today:

O ye who believe! Take not the Jews and the Christians for your friends or protectors; they are but friends and protectors to each other.

Finally, truly condemnatory Ayat—such as Al-Maeda 5:82, "Strongest among men in enmity to the Believers wilt thou find the Jews and the pagans"—must always be considered in the context of Ayat like Surah 7:159, which acknowledges those among the people of Moses "who guide and do justice in the light of truth."

Given that so much of the message of the Holy Quran is sent to Jews as Jews, it's got to be obvious that our collective attempts to enforce our own religion and will upon them is wrong. The tactics we have so often chosen condemn us by our own holy book as hypocrites. They even allow violent retaliation against us, by our own rules! Muslims are certainly allowed to kill violent aggressors in defense of their lives, their religion, or their homes, but everyone else has that right too.

The Quran has a specific message, and it's clear how that message is supposed to be delivered. None of the books were sent to put any one of our groups in charge of everyone else, because they all say that God is in charge. They're there to help us to get along. The message of the Quran to Christians is a simple one, and we should deliver it as it stands. An-Nisa 4:171–172 probably sums it up best:

> O People of the Book! Commit no excesses in your religion, nor say of Allah aught but the truth. Christ Jesus the son of Mary was no more than a Messenger of Allah, and His Word which he bestowed on Mary, and a Spirit proceeding from Him: So believe in Allah and His messengers. Say not "Trinity": Desist! It will be better for you: For Allah is One God; Glory be to Him: (Far exalted is He) above having a son. To Him belong all things in the heavens and on earth. Enough is Allah as a Disposer of Affairs. Christ disdaineth not to serve and worship Allah, nor do the angels, those nearest to Allah; Those who disdain His worship and are arrogant, He will gather them all together unto Himself to answer.

Born miraculously to the Virgin Mary, indwelt and empowered by the Spirit, sent to show how both God's grace and mercy and the Law could come together in a man who submits himself completely to the Will of God—according to the Holy Quran Jesus came to be the Jewish Messiah, as prophesied. He was tortured by Pontius Pilate and condemned to death, knowing that death and torture weren't something he deserved, but knowing that God alone knew what was really going on and that God was in control. Perhaps confused by the turn of events, he chose not to rebel, but instead submitted himself to God in his prayer in Gethsemane. In return, instead of ending up dead in his grave, he was exalted and taken up to heaven by God, leaving behind only his message and his legacy: his own Gospel and Sunnah of submission and faith.

That legacy should have been sufficient to redeem all humankind. Al-Maeda 5:65–66 laments:

> If only the People of the Book had believed and been righteous, We should indeed have blotted out their iniquities and admitted them to Gardens of Bliss. If only they had stood fast by the Law and the Gospel, and all the revelation that was sent to them from their Lord, they would have enjoyed Happiness from every side. This is among them a party on the right course; but many of them follow a course that is evil.

Instead of submission and faith, we have all seen Jesus' main legacy become the celebration of Christmas, a festival of conspicuous consumption at the winter solstice, and Easter, commemorating the belief that, instead of trusting in God's mercy, Christians should trust their own ability to coerce forgiveness from a promise that was never made to substitute for their just punishment the murder of the man-god that Jesus never was. It'll be yet another miracle to add to his list if Jesus isn't more than a little miffed with them when he gets back!

Christianity has become preoccupied with belief. It is that preoccupation, and the extent to which Christians have elevated belief over Jesus' actual message, that has resulted in most, if not all, of the innovations that the Quran disagrees with. Truthfully, though, Muslims have been no better. Our own preoccupation with striving to be sure that everyone believes the same things in the same way has resulted in our own errors and innovations. The two religions are the opposite sides of the same coin. We have both promoted belief about our holy books over actual fidelity to them as a way of promoting ourselves, even though we have had those books available to guide us properly all along. We really stand as warnings to each other, not judges or executioners. Our holy books assure us that our prophets and our God can look after all that without needing our help.

Just like Christians, Muslims look forward to Jesus' Second Coming, when we will all join him in serving God and opposing Satan. A triumphant Hadith (graciously translated for me by the famous Canadian scholar, author, and educator Dr. Arafat El Ashi) predicts a definitive end to all our battles:

Abu Hurayrah reported Allah's Messenger (may peace be upon him) as saying: "The Last Hour would not come until the Romans would land at al-Amaq or in Dabiq. An army consisting of the best of the people of the earth at that time will come from Medina to counteract them. When they will arrange themselves in ranks, the Romans would say: 'Do not stand between us and those Muslims who took prisoners from amongst us. Let us fight with them'; and the Muslims would say: 'Nay, by Allah, we would never get aside from you and from our brethren that you may fight them.' Then will they fight and a third part of the army would run away, whom Allah will never forgive. A third part of the army, which would be constituted of excellent martyrs in Allah's eye, would be killed and the third who would never be put to trial would win and they would be conquerors of Constantinople. And as they would be busy in distributing the spoils of war amongst themselves after hanging their swords in olive trees, Satan would cry; 'The Dajjal has taken your place among your family!' They would then come out, but it would be of no avail. And when they would come to Syria, he would come out while they would be still preparing themselves for battle drawing up the ranks. Certainly the time of prayer shall come and then Jesus (peace be upon him) the son of Mary would descend and would lead them in prayer. When the enemy of Allah would see him, it would disappear just as salt dissolves itself in water and if Jesus were not to confront them at all, even then it would dissolve completely, but Allah would kill them by his hand, and he would show them their blood on his lance (the lance of Jesus Christ)."

Both religions believe that Jesus will return to us some day, and when that day does come, it will be obvious to everyone who's been right and who's been wrong. Muslims should all be prepared that he's not going to be very happy with a lot of the things we've been doing either. If we do as the Quran says, we'll live alongside everyone else who's honestly trying to get along in peace. If we don't, we'll have no one to blame but ourselves for what happens to us in this life and in the next. Abu Hurayrah once narrated:

Allah's apostle said, "By Him whose Hands my soul is in, surely Jesus the son of Mary will soon descend amongst you and will judge mankind justly, as a just ruler. He will break the Cross and kill the pigs and there will be no Jizyah (a tax on non-Muslims). Money will be in abundance so that nobody will accept it, and a single prostration to Allah in prayer will be better than the whole world and whatever is in it."

He added:

"If you wish, you can recite this verse of the Holy Book: There is none of the people of the Scriptures (Jews and Christians) but must believe in him, Jesus the man and apostle of Allah, before his death. On the Day of Judgment he will be a witness against them."

- **If Muslims stop fighting over who's right, we'll get along with everyone else, too.**

- **With the Quran and the Sunnah, the earliest Muslims lived with vibrant diversity.**

- **The Quran and the Sunnah can show today's Muslims how to live with other people, too.**

The lesson of Islam is:

Different people can serve God in different ways, too.

Being different doesn't make them wrong, either.

PART IV

WORKING
WITH JUDAISM

CHAPTER 20

....

THE HOLY LAND

In spite of the way Muslims, Christians, and Jews have been behaving toward each other, in the past we've mostly kept it in the family. Now, finally and lamentably, that relative respite for the rest of the world has come to an end. The trigger for the current escalation has been Israel and the different ways our three religions interpret what's been happening there. Our collective, long-standing, and only occasionally acknowledged war with each other over the destiny of the Holy Land now threatens the rest of the world, too. All three sides claim the moral high ground and profess to be selflessly serving nothing less than the Will of God. The sad truth is that the battle between Christianity, Islam, and Judaism over the Middle East has very little to do with God and everything to do with politics and power, and the influence politics and power have on religion and on us. We should have been able to avoid it. We're fighting over who's right and who's in charge, when we are all supposed to know that God is.

A lot of us, no matter what our religion, believe that one of the main reasons that Jews exist at all is so that they can live in Israel. To many Jews, it's both a contractual obligation and the reward for their compliance with that contract. That's actually not a point of contention for them with either Islam or with Christianity. According to the Holy Quran and the Holy Bible, they're right! The issue is really one of why, when, and how. For all of us, our dispute is over the Covenant and what it actually says. Islam and Christianity both have their own ideas about the deal Abraham made with God, but we all agree that a deal was made. None of us are really supposed to have any issues about the fact that the Holy Land is one of the rewards for Jewish compliance with what God and Abraham agreed.

The differences between us are more complicated. Christianity has decided that when Jesus fulfilled the Covenant, believing in him became the only appropriate way to adhere to its terms. On the other hand, many Muslims believe that because most Jews have failed to live up to the Covenant so far, they've lost the right to claim Israel at all.

Some Muslims even think that Islam has replaced Judaism and that Judaism's promises have become a thing of the past. As popular as that notion is in some circles, simply discarding Judaism isn't a very good idea for any of us. The Quran doesn't claim to replace or revoke God's deal with the Jews any more than Jesus did. In fact, much of the Quran's message to the Jews is a reminder to them to stick to it! Al-Baqara 2:40–46 calls to them:

> O Children of Israel! Call to mind the special favor, which I bestowed upon you, and fulfill your Covenant with Me, as I fulfill My Covenant with you, and fear none but Me! And believe in what I reveal, confirming the revelation which is with you, and be not the first to reject Faith therein, nor to sell My Signs for a small price: Fear Me, and Me alone. And cover not Truth with falsehood, nor conceal the Truth when ye know what it is. And be steadfast in prayer: Practice regular charity; and bow your heads with those who bow down in worship. Do you enjoin right conduct on the people, and forget to practice it yourselves? And yet ye study the Scripture? Will ye not understand? Nay, seek Allah's help with patient perseverance and prayer: It is indeed hard, except to those who bring a lowly spirit—who bear in mind the certainty that they are to meet their Lord, and that they are to return to Him.

The way our different traditions tell the story of Abraham and Lot illustrates how adept we've become at looking at the same things and seeing them in very different ways. I first became fascinated with Judaism when I heard an old rabbi in Saskatoon use the story to delineate the differences between our religions and the way we perceive our relationships with God. The rabbi's wisdom humbled me; he obviously knew what he was talking about, and his familiarity with faiths other than his own was beautiful. I was participating in an interfaith conference, representing the Muslim perspective, and the rabbi's expertise immediately made his perspective the most useful one in the room. Like my awakening to Islam, it made me realize that, even though I'd thought I knew everything I needed to know when I was growing up as a Christian, I still didn't know as much as I thought I did.

As the rabbi described it, the plot elements of the story are the same for all of us. Abraham lived in the country, and Lot lived in the twin cities of Sodom and Gomorrah. The other residents of those cities were a very (very) bad bunch. According to the Quran, Lot was actually there trying to convince them to change their ways, but they wouldn't listen. God decided to destroy Sodom and Gomorrah and dispatched some angels, and Abraham met them on their way there. All of our versions then agree that Abraham pleaded with God on behalf of Lot and Lot's people. The difference between the stories really centers on the different ways that our religions describe the true nature of God and the way that those differences influence the outcome that Abraham achieved.

Muslims are clear about our own version of the story. The angels were sent to warn Lot to get out, and Abraham's pleading didn't change anything. As far as Muslims are concerned, God always knows what He's going to do, and the dialogue that Abraham had with God was for Abraham's benefit — it taught him more about his own place in creation. In Islam, God is perfect and in control and can't make mistakes, despite what we might sometimes think. Most Christians, on the other hand, are clear that Abraham's pleading resulted in Lot's rescue. They'll generally interpret the whole story as an example of the redemptive function that one person can play in the life of another, and gloss over the whole question of whether God was about to make a mistake or not.

Before I start to explore the Jewish interpretation of the story of Lot and Abraham, I want to make it clear that composing this chapter has given me more anxiety than anything else I've done in this book. Using the Bible to refute the Trinity and to show Muslims, Christians, and Jews how much we have in common without it was actually quite easy. I expect that even the most devout Christian will at least appreciate the care I've taken to explore Jesus' real message and commend adherence to it. Likewise, I'm not really afraid of the Muslim response: how can any Muslim hate another Muslim for claiming that Allah wants us to love each other? But I am concerned about how my attempts to direct constructive criticism at Judaism will be perceived.

I've tried to discuss my thoughts with some rabbis, and I've learned that all our differences come down to how we deal with the Covenant, how we interpret God's instructions, and what we do when things go wrong.

There's no question that Jewish scholars have had a lot of time for thinking. Of the three traditions that have come down from Abraham, Judaism is the oldest. Its scholars, doctors, teachers, and lawyers have had thousands of years to pore over its texts and traditions, gleaning all the wisdom from them that they can. It gives a serious student a lot of ground to cover. Most of the Jews with whom I've discussed the path that Judaism has taken seem sure that I'll never be able to figure it all out. Many of them seem quite willing to accept that it's so very complicated that they'll never be able to completely understand it either! That may be the problem.

The hardest thing for me to understand is why they've chosen to make the way they exercise their faith so complicated when the message that's been repeated most often to them by their prophets is the opposite: it's not really supposed to be complicated at all. God takes all of four sentences to set the deal up, and the Babylonian Talmud's Tractate 31a records that Rabbi Hillel, perhaps history's most famous Pharisee, when challenged by a Roman centurion to recite the entire Torah while standing on one foot, summarized it as follows:

> "What is hateful to you, do not do to your neighbor. That is the whole Torah; all the rest of it is commentary. Go and learn."

Jesus changed the wording a little in Matthew 7:12:

> "So in everything do to others what you would have them do to you, for this sums up the Law and the Prophets."

But he still kept it simple. Complex as Judaism has become in the millennia since, one thing stands out clearly: many of those following today's versions of the faith have allowed it to become just as guilty of justifying the slaughter of innocents in the Holy Land as Christianity and Islam have become everywhere else in the world.

I'm sure that the story of Lot, Abraham, and God is used to illustrate many different lessons in the Jewish religion. The one that caught my ear in Saskatoon was that when He set out to destroy Sodom and Gomorrah, God's initial divine plan would have taken out Lot as well. Abraham wheedled, bartered, and argued, and finally changed God's mind. Even though the rabbi described this in terms of God choosing to allow us to participate in perfecting an imperfect world, the underlying message was clear: from Judaism's perspective the story of Lot and Abraham proved that God sometimes chose to make mistakes.

Finding a way to explain how a perfect God could create an imperfect universe is a recurring theme in Judaism. Karen Armstrong's book *The History of God* records that the great sixteenth-century Jewish scholar and mystic Isaac Luria of Safed explained it as a consequence of God's choosing to withdraw himself from Creation in order to give the universe room to exist. He told his followers that God had created a void where He wasn't and that because of His decision to exclude Himself, humankind was the only way God's will could become manifest. Centuries earlier, Rabbi Akiva had told his followers that God made some people poor to make the rest help them, confirming that even according to one of the greatest minds in the history of Judaism, God left creation in a less than perfect state so we could change it. It's a wonderful principle, but it sets a dangerous precedent. Some people are poor, and everyone knows that it's good for those who have more to help out, but the idea that you can use that to explain *why* they're poor is a logical leap of profound consequence. Both Isaac Luria's and Rabbi Akiva's perspectives make the universe and God's management of it susceptible to critical appraisal: if we don't like something, not only can we assume that God gave us the capacity to competently discern what's wrong (and made the repair our responsibility), but we can also conclude that the flaws are God's fault rather than our own!

The story of Lot, as recorded in the Old Testament, discloses two dialogues: one between Abraham and God, and another between God and Himself. In Genesis 18:16–33 it goes like this:

> When the men got up to leave, they looked down toward Sodom, and Abraham walked along with them to see them on their way. Then the Lord said, "Shall I hide from Abraham what I am about to do? Abraham will surely become a great and powerful nation, and all nations on earth will be blessed through him. For I have chosen him, so that he will direct his children and his household after him to keep the way of the Lord by doing what is right and just, so that the Lord will bring about for Abraham what he has promised him."
>
> Then the Lord said, "The outcry against Sodom and Gomorrah is so great and their sin so grievous that I will go down and see if what they have done is as bad as the outcry

that has reached me. If not, I will know." The men turned away and went toward Sodom, but Abraham remained standing before the Lord.

Then Abraham approached him and said: "Will you sweep away the righteous with the wicked? What if there are fifty righteous people in the city? Will you really sweep it away and not spare the place for the sake of the fifty righteous people in it? Far be it from you to do such a thing—to kill the righteous with the wicked, treating the righteous and the wicked alike. Far be it from you! Will not the Judge of all the earth do right?"

The Lord said, "If I find fifty righteous people in the city of Sodom, I will spare the whole place for their sake."

Then Abraham spoke up again: "Now that I have been so bold as to speak to the Lord, though I am nothing but dust and ashes, what if the number of the righteous is five less than fifty? Will you destroy the whole city because of five people?"

"If I find forty-five there," he said, "I will not destroy it."

Once again he spoke to him, "What if only forty are found there?"

He said, "For the sake of forty, I will not do it."

Then he said, "May the Lord not be angry, but let me speak. What if only thirty can be found there?"

He answered, "I will not do it if I find thirty there."

Abraham said, "Now that I have been so bold as to speak to the Lord, what if only twenty can be found there?"

He said, "For the sake of twenty, I will not destroy it."

Then he said, "May the Lord not be angry, but let me speak just once more. What if only ten can be found?"

He answered, "For the sake of ten, I will not destroy it."

When the Lord had finished speaking with Abraham, he left, and Abraham returned home.

When you read the story, there's really no reason to conclude that God was going to kill innocent people or that Abraham changed God's mind. Nowhere does God say anything like, "You're right! I wonder why I didn't think of that!" There's no compelling reason to interpret it any other way, either. Looked at from one perspective, it seems that Abraham just wore God down. It's possible to read the exchange in three very different ways, and that's what Judaism, Christianity, and Islam often do. Our own preferred interpretation depends on what our respective religions are trying to make of it. The Christian version is completely consistent with Christianity. To them, God allowed Abraham to intervene for the sake of Lot, and it changed his life. It's supposed to foreshadow Jesus. On the other hand, I've listened to a variety of rabbis, Orthodox and otherwise, speak on the topic, and they all agree that Abraham's wheedling worked because that's really our God-ordained role in Creation: people fix things. Then I've heard Muslim Imams tell the exact same story, and all of them have maintained that Abraham learned the heart of Islam's own view of God: that God is perfect and always at least one step ahead of us. It's obvious that we all have a valid way of looking at it, that none of us are particularly interested in learning from each other, and that we'll never be able to agree. The good news is that the reason we all believe what we believe, and can get such totally different ideas out of the same simple story, goes a long way toward explaining both the problem and the solution to today's war in the Middle East.

When I tried to discuss all this with the Orthodox rabbi in Calgary, he stonewalled me. It's not possible to discuss the way our beliefs differ without using examples of what we believe, and it turned out that he wouldn't admit to believing anything at all. One of the things I like about Judaism is that of the three of us, it's the least obsessed with adherence to specific doctrines. Almost a thousand years ago, the famous Jewish scholar Moses Maimonides came up with a list of thirteen basic things that he thought every Jew had to agree to believe in, but even that hasn't completely caught on. But this makes a discussion of the role of belief in religion problematic, and that's forced me into doing more of a "methodological" criticism. Thankfully, I think that's turned out to be the right way to go, regardless. As I wrote in the beginning of this book, the Jewish religion doesn't profess anything very different from anyone else. It's not so much what they say that sets them apart as it is why they say it.

The history of Judaism in Israel hasn't ever been an easy one. Starting with Joseph's captivity and enslavement at the hands of his brothers, through the Egyptian captivity and down the ages until today, the Jewish people and Israel have been struck by catastrophe after catastrophe, invasion after invasion, and war upon war—despite the Covenant of Abraham and its promises of both greatness and blessing. It's been a rough four thousand years. They've spent most of the time trying to survive, but they've also felt compelled to understand what's been going on.

The modern Jewish scholar Gershom Scholem is credited with the observation that Judaism has evolved through three distinct stages. In the first, "Primitive" phase of the religion, God was perceived as being part of the cosmos. Primitive societies see divinity in every aspect of their lives and in the world around them. Primitive religions are by nature polytheistic and inclusive, since the only way to affect change is by acknowledging the existence of a deity and then petitioning it, and that often means following the animistic practice of worshiping everything, a practice that Moses changed when he brought the Ten Commandments. Scholem's perspective helps explain why worshiping the golden calf seemed so natural to so many of the Israelites while they were waiting for him to come down from Mount Sinai. Before Moses, even though they were God's people, they'd been living in Egypt among a people with many other Gods and didn't really know Him. With Moses, God became singular, separate, and jealous. That ushered in Scholem's "Creative" stage.

In the Creative stage, the God of Israel became both all-powerful and all-just. Through Moses, God had let the Israelites know that He was more powerful than anything and in control of everything. That meant that God became "removed" from His creation as well, no longer living in the thunder and lightning but above and beyond it and, above all else, in control. God also became more distant from the believers and more difficult to grasp and comprehend.

After that came a stage that Scholem called the "Mystical." According to him, we're still in it today. He described the Mystical stage as the process of God's subjects finding a way back to a deep and intimate relationship with the Creator, where God moves from being "El Melekh Ram"—The Mighty King—toward becoming "Abba-Father" or even "Yedidi"—My Dearest Friend. According to Scholem, the Jewish perception of God above has moved full circle back to God among us. God has become a personal deity once again.

I have a profound appreciation for the religion of Judaism. The insights of their prophets have influenced the path of almost every religion we currently have, and its men and women have been an inspiration to people everywhere, believers and nonbelievers alike. Unfortunately, all those stages and all the effort that Jewish rabbis and scholars have put into understanding, influencing, and occasionally trying to manipulate our Creator may have been a big part of the problem, if all God's wanted from us is simple obedience. All three of Scholem's phases of religious philosophy make different assumptions about the nature of God. Based on those assumptions, the things you'd do if you wanted to manipulate Him are obvious and distinct. The history of Judaism in general and Israel in particular show how much of an impact each of the assumptions and their related errors has had on the Children of Israel when they made them.

The problem with primitivism is that it assumes God is easy to manipulate, partly because being part of everything makes a God easily accessible, but also because there are often so many different gods to choose from. The Old Testament record of Israel's early history is the story of the battle between that belief system and true monotheism. It's striking how, from Moses to King Solomon, as monotheism gained the upper hand in the hearts of its people, Israel's lot improved. It's also striking how quickly it went downhill again when that changed. By the year 740 B.C.E., Israel was divided into two kingdoms, with near anarchy in the north and animism in the Temple of Jerusalem. Rather than worshiping only one God when they wanted to change something like crop fertility, the outcome of a battle, or how often it rained, Israel had returned to the primitive practice of playing different gods off each other. Their prophets were deeply disapproving and warned of impending catastrophe. The Book of Isaiah begins with Isaiah 1:2–3 in which God admonishes the Southern Kingdom:

> Hear, O heavens! Listen, O earth! For the Lord has spoken: "I reared children and brought them up, but they have rebelled against me. The ox knows his master, and the donkey his owner's manger, but Israel does not know, my people do not understand."

Both Hosea and Amos backed him up in the north with comments like those found in Hosea 1:9, when Hosea's son by the prostitute Gomer was born, and Amos 3:1–2:

> "Call him Lo-Ammi (Not My People), for you are not my people, and I am not your God."

> Hear this word the Lord has spoken against you, O people of Israel—against the whole family I brought up out of Egypt:

"You only have I chosen of all the families of the earth; therefore I will punish you for your sins."

Jeremiah was even more critical, but it took the Babylonian captivity to convince Jews to return to the God of Abraham and the Laws of Moses.

Next, the Jews decided to put God on a pedestal. In Scholem's Creative phase, the scholars of Judaism had to find a way to reconcile the majesty of God with the (perceived) mediocrity of the material universe. Israel had been invaded by Babylon and the Jews forced to leave their homeland, and after they were allowed to return and rebuild the Temple, the Greeks and then the Romans invaded Israel yet again! They decided these invasions would be easier to explain if God wasn't directly involved in their day-to-day affairs, so they relied on potentially unreliable intermediaries instead: angels, spirits, or the Jews themselves. God became less accessible, His relative absence was to blame for the Jews' problems, and the Jews were therefore responsible for fixing them. Kenneth Hanson's book *Kabbalah: The Untold Story of the Mystic Tradition* records how Judaism went from a religion where every Jew could call on the name of God when he needed Him to one where the High Priest could say God's name only once a year, on Yom Kippur. The Romans' sacking and razing the Temple brought an end to that conceit, but during those days, Rabbi Akiva made his pronouncement on the reasons for poverty, and the Israelites first began their work organizing and collating the arcane methods of manipulating Creation with potions and amulets that eventually resulted in the Kabbalah, a Jewish mystical system recently popularized by Madonna. This book's second section demonstrates how, despite Jesus' attempts to guide the Jews back to the Covenant, all their creative mysticism only confused everyone so much that it gave us the Christian Trinity!

Judaism has had more than its fair share of holy men. Almost everyone knows about Jesus, but few non-Jews are aware that there have been many others, too. One of them, Rabbi Hanina ben Dosa, was asked to help the son of the great Rabbi Gamaliel, who was ill, in a story that will sound familiar to many Christians. Gamaliel sent two of his students to make the request. When Hanina saw them coming, he went to his upper room to pray. A while later he came down and told the students, "Go, the fever has left him." When the students returned and told Gamaliel what had happened, they were all amazed to realize that the moment of Hanina's comment coincided exactly with the moment that Gamaliel's son's fever broke.

Another famous miracle worker was called Khoni the Circle Drawer because he was once asked by the people to bring rain; in response, he drew a circle in the sand and told God that he wouldn't leave until God granted their plea. God did. Khoni is a famous Jewish folk hero, but the way he interacted with the Jewish establishment illustrates the problem with Scholem's Mystical stage. The Talmud's Ta'anit 23a recounts that when Khoni met the High Priest Simeon after the rain incident, the High Priest Simeon told him, "Were you not Khoni, I would have you excommunicated, but what am I to do with you, who can coax the Almighty to do his will, like a son coaxes favors from his father!" Simeon had assumed that God paid particular attention to Khoni's requests because he was special in an arcane or even inappropriate fashion. Because that assumption led Khoni's fellows to try to control God by controlling Khoni, the miracle worker's story has a tragic ending. The historian Josephus records that, when approached by two warring Jewish factions who each asked him to intervene on their behalf, Khoni prayed to God: "Lord of the Universe, as the besieged and the besieger both belong to Thy people, I beseech thee not to answer the prayers of either!" Josephus concludes, "He was thereupon stoned to death".

Jewish men and women throughout history have worked hard to make the world a better place, just like God told them to. Tragically, throughout that same history, Jewish theologians tasked with the guidance of the Jewish people have found ways to blame God when things haven't worked out the way they expected, and that has influenced us all, too. They've assumed that He wasn't as powerful as He said He was (the Primitive stage), that He wasn't paying enough attention to them (the Creative stage), or that He played favorites (the Mystical stage). Muslim scholars have taken a different approach and inevitably made their own very human errors, but the difference between the Muslim and Jewish scholarly perspective is important for all of us—it really comes down to a question of what we're supposed to do when we think things go wrong.

It's hard to understand the twists and turns of fate, even if you accept that there's a divine Will behind it all. When we're asked to wait and suffer in faith, believers struggle with the temptation to conclude that God doesn't care or that He isn't really there. As the oldest of the three faiths of Abraham, Judaism has had to face this trial longer than the rest of us, almost from the very beginning. Even immediately after Moses led the Israelites out of Egypt through the parted waters of the Red Sea, Numbers 11:1 records:

Now the people complained about their hardships in the hearing of the Lord, and when he heard them his anger was aroused. Then fire from the Lord burned among them and consumed some of the outskirts of the camp. When the people cried out to Moses, he prayed to the Lord and the fire died down.

Despite manna from heaven, Numbers 11:4–6 tells us:

The rabble with them began to crave other food, and again the Israelites started wailing and said, "If only we had meat to eat! We remember the fish we ate in Egypt at no cost—also the cucumbers, melons, leeks, onions and garlic. But now we have lost our appetite; we never see anything but this manna!"

It even started to wear Moses down. Numbers 11:21–23 recounts:

But Moses said, "Here I am among six hundred thousand men on foot, and you say, 'I will give them meat to eat for a whole month!' Would they have enough if flocks and herds were slaughtered for them? Would they have enough if all the fish in the sea were caught for them?"

Finally, Numbers 11:31–33 completes the tale:

Now a wind went out from the Lord and drove quail in from the sea. It brought them down all around the camp to about three feet above the ground, as far as a day's walk in any direction. All that day and night and all the next day the people went out and gathered quail. No one gathered less than ten homers (about sixty bushels). Then they spread them out all around the camp. But while the meat was still between their teeth and before it could be consumed, the anger of the Lord burned against the people, and He struck them with a severe plague. Therefore the place was named Kibroth Hattaavah, because there they buried the people who had craved other food.

Non-Muslims are often offended by what the Quran says about Jews and Christians because many of them think that they're three different religions. Few remember that the Jewish tribes of Arabia initially recognized Muhammad as a Prophet that God had sent to them and only denied it later when they decided that they didn't like what Muhammad said. The Old Testament is an honest witness to how often the Children of Israel didn't like what the other prophets said either. Much of God's revelation through Muhammad is addressed directly to the Children of Israel, and censuring God garners Jews the strongest criticism of them in the Quran. Al-Maeda 5:64–65 is unequivocal:

> The Jews say: "Allah's hand is tied up." Be their hands tied up and be they accursed for the blasphemy they utter. Nay, both His hands are widely outstretched: He giveth and spendeth of His bounty as He pleaseth. But the revelation that cometh to thee from Allah increaseth in most of them their obstinate rebellion and blasphemy. Amongst them we have placed enmity and hatred till the Day of Judgment. Every time they kindle the fire of war, Allah doth extinguish it; but they ever strive to do mischief on earth. And Allah loveth not those who do mischief.

It's an awfully vehement condemnation. Some Muslims generalize and use this verse to justify their own dismissal of Jews and Judaism, but truthfully, the Quran only condemns the idea that God isn't completely in control. To a Muslim, that sort of thing is obvious blasphemy and dangerous theology. If God can be judged or criticized by His creation, then His judgment becomes subordinate to our own. If God is really all-knowing, all seeing, and all-powerful, as all three of our religions claim, then acting as if God is subordinate to His creation will always result in catastrophe.

Few words describe today's Holy Land better than *catastrophe*. It is the primary source of conflict driving strife between Muslims, Christians, and Jews throughout the world today, and it's become difficult to see any path leading from the way we are to the way we should be. Everyone knows that the situation is awful, and Muslims, Christians, and Jews have all got our own ideas regarding what needs to change, but if we want to avoid making it even worse, the first question to ask is how to be sure we're right.

If everything is actually going according to some as yet inconceivable plan, we still need to know how we should respond when events take a turn for the worse. Alternatively, if it turns out that we really are supposed to fix things, we still need to know how to make them better. It's really become a question of submission versus intervention: how can we know what to do, and how far are we supposed to go? Rather than keeping our religions in a permanent state of conflict, the first real step on the path to peace may be finding the point where submission and intervention come together, learning to walk together on the path that Abraham first trod with his sons, Israel and Ishmael.

With only a few notable exceptions, the Muslims of the world have condemned the slaughter, abuse, and genocide that have plagued the Jewish race throughout history. We've managed to live together on the same planet successfully for over a thousand years, and for most of that time, many Muslims have even done their best to help Jews find a little security in what's frequently been an otherwise unfriendly existence. Israel, on the other hand, is another matter. Even though the vast majority of Jews claim that God has given them the responsibility of demonstrating His hospitality and loving-kindness there, Muslims around the world are united in their conviction that they haven't done a very good job of it, particularly for the last sixty years. Prior to 1948, Palestine was a vibrant and diverse place to live, marred by unrest and interreligious violence, some of which was done in the name of Israel. When the United Nations decided to create a Jewish homeland, few Palestinians understood why they were expected to give up their ancestral homes to pay the price for Europe's Holocaust, but they were frankly terrified to learn that some of the most radical Zionists were going to be in charge! Since those days, Palestinians have been gradually and inexorably herded into progressively smaller and less attractive compounds, and they've seen this herding justified to the rest of the world only by the fact that they've resisted at all.

Men claiming to represent every side of the profoundly complicated conflict there have committed crimes against humanity, but the worst crime of all might be that their evils could have been prevented by any one of us. If God's instructions regarding the way He expects us to conduct ourselves in His Holy land had been hidden, or if they were particularly hard to understand or impossible to deliver on, then our failures might at least have been a little easier to explain. Honestly, though, God's perspective on His Covenant with Abraham, with ample commentary, examples, and illustrations drawn from the lives of our prophets and our myriad holy men and women, has been laid out in plain sight in all our holy books all along.

For some reason, the nature of God's expectations when He chose to set the Children of Abraham apart in the first place has never been the subject of much curiosity on any of our parts. To guide their flocks, most rabbis have focused on Moses and the Law he brought, even though both the choice and God's reasons for it preceded both of them. Few of the rest of us have looked at it very closely either. In the story of Lot and Abraham, it's God's dialogue with Himself that's the most interesting part of the story; it's there that God reveals what the Jews' role as His "Chosen People" really is. That, in turn, explains what's actually gone wrong with Israel today, and it finally shows how we're really supposed to fix it. In the story of Abraham, Lot, and Sodom and Gomorrah, Genesis 18:17–19 explains exactly why Abraham and his children were set apart in the first place and what God has always expected from all of us in return.

- **Judaism wasn't created just to set Jews apart from the rest of us.**

- **Islam wasn't revealed to condemn Jews or Judaism.**

- **By working together instead of tearing the world apart, we can show everyone how to live together in peace.**

CHAPTER 21

....

THE COVENANT

In the end, finding the path to lasting peace is going to come down to living up to the deal God made with Abraham in the beginning. That Covenant is often said to be "unconditional" because it seems to be described that way the first time it's mentioned. Genesis 12:1–3 says:

> YHWH said to Avram, "Go you forth from your land, from your kindred, from your father's house, to the land that I will let you see. I will make a great nation of you and will give you blessing and will make your name great. BE A BLESSING! I will bless those who bless you, and he who curses you, I will damn. All the clans of the soil will find blessing through you!"

It all sounds like the deal that's too good to be true, which makes it hard to explain why things have gone the way they have without concluding that God promised more than He could deliver. On the other hand, God's internal dialogue six chapters later argues convincingly that from His perspective, the Covenant wasn't meant to be unconditional at all. God is quoted in Genesis 18:17–19, as we saw in the last chapter:

> Then the Lord said, "Shall I hide from Abraham what I am about to do? Abraham will surely become a great and powerful nation, and all nations on earth will be blessed through him. For I have chosen him so that he will direct his children and his household after him to keep the way of

the Lord by doing what is right and just, so that the Lord will
bring about for Abraham what he has promised him."

God is saying quite clearly that when He made His promises to Abraham,
God knew exactly what He was going to get in return.

What can we say about the Covenant? Christianity has interpreted
it in its fashion, claiming that the blessing that came through Abraham
was Jesus, because that's the only way they think they can make it work
for them. Alternatively, Muslims claim that the blessing *is* the religion of
Abraham, because that's Islam. Finally, most Jews seem to believe that the
mighty nation that God promised is the blessing, because that's obviously
what they'd prefer. However we feel about it and whatever we make of it,
we should look more closely at how the deal was written. The Covenant of
Abraham is the sole justification that any of our religions have for existence!
We all claim to be Abraham's "children and his household after him," and
we all claim to be the vehicle through which God's blessing will come to
the rest of the world.

Because Abraham commanded his children and household to live their
lives according to God's Way, the world will someday be a better place for
everyone, them included. The Children of Abraham who choose to live
God's Way will be the blessing for all of us, and the Israel that God intends for
them depends on their living the Way of the Lord. The Covenant described
in Genesis says that God's Israel will be the inevitable consequence of the
people there treating each other properly. That sounds very different from
the Middle East today, and it makes the Covenant—if rightly observed—
the best thing that ever happened to either Israel or Palestine.

Most Muslims seem to think that the clearest path to justice for the
Muslims and Christians of Palestine is to claim that the promises of the
Covenant are a figment of the Jewish imagination. If Abraham's Covenant
were really just something that the Jews had made up on their own, it would
likely have been worded in such a way as to provide them with greater
justification than it does for the power and authority they seem to currently
be striving for in Israel. Instead, Abraham's Covenant with his God demands
a different sort of relationship entirely. The Covenant requires that they do
"what is right and just" to activate God's blessings, and that makes the word
that is translated as "what is right and just" into perhaps the most important
word in the Hebrew language. Although *tzedakah* does mean those things,
it also means much, much more. The root of the Hebrew word (which

can be approximated in the Latin alphabet only as *tzade dalet qof*) means "righteousness," "justice," and "charity," but the character of the virtues it describes is so profoundly archetypal that some Hebrew scholars even say that real tzedakah is something more akin to brotherly love.

Tzedakah in modern Judaism has come to mean little more than giving money to the poor, but that's really only the poorest meaning of the word. The real charity of tzedakah is the charity that comes from sharing all of God's blessings—not because they're yours to give or keep, but because they came from God, and the greatest blessing comes from giving them to others just as they were first given to you. The justice of tzedakah isn't one that's imposed on the weak by the strong. Tzedakah justice comes about when all of us are treated as equals, by God and by each other, because that's how God meant it to be. Tzedakah justice is about responsibility, not power. Tzedakah righteousness comes about when charity and justice are practiced the way they're meant to be. There's no question that Israel by tzedakah will be different from what we have there today, but no believing Jew, Muslim, or Christian should doubt that it will happen someday. According to our holy books, God chose the Jews for the sake of all of us. We should be sure, no matter who we are, that Israel will someday step up and show the world the true Way of the Lord.

According to the Covenant, instead of showing that God has somehow withdrawn from Creation, the last four thousand years of our history in the Middle East and throughout the rest of the world has actually made an unfortunate lot of sense. Without tzedakah, nothing good was supposed to happen in the first place. When you look at Jewish history from that perspective, it tells a very different story, one that's much less sympathetic than the one we generally hear in the West. The Egyptian debacle, the fall of the first Temple and the second, and the hardships of the Diaspora all came about because they failed to follow the dictates of justice and charity. As the Children of Abraham have branched out and dispersed across the face of the earth, whenever we've taken the opportunities God has given us to show kindness and love, we have prospered, and when we haven't, tragedy has resulted. Whenever the people of Israel have lived by tzedakah, the extent to which they've really followed it has determined their safety and security. When tzedakah fails, disaster has always followed.

Today, Orthodox Judaism commends the 613 Mitzvot, or Commandments. Only six of them, less than one percent, say anything about the treatment of strangers. They command Jews to:

Love the stranger
Not wrong the stranger in speech
Not wrong the stranger in buying or selling
Not intermarry
Exact strangers' debts from them
Lend them money at interest

It's an interesting list, but it has much more to do with trade than it has to do with tzedakah. The Covenant, on the other hand, has nothing to do with trade at all! In the Old Testament, again and again, Jews are commanded to treat non-Jews as equals. Exodus 22:21 tells them:

"Do not mistreat an alien or oppress him, for you were aliens in Egypt."

Leviticus 19:33–34 expands on this:

"When an alien lives with you in your land, do not mistreat him. The alien living with you must be treated as one of your native-born. Love him as yourself, for you were aliens in Egypt. I am the Lord your God."

Finally, Leviticus 24:22 confirms:

"You are to have the same law for the alien and the native-born. I am the Lord your God."

Tragically, modern Judaism omits or ignores almost all of those commands. Ever since the early days of the Talmud in the critical juncture between Israel's Creative and Mystical phases, Jewish scholars have agreed that the word *Ger*, which my NIV Bible translates as "alien" and other versions translate as "sojourner" or "stranger," only means "convert to Judaism." That decision was convenient: at the time, most of the aliens, sojourners, and strangers were foreign invaders! It helped Jews to deal with the invasions by maintaining a different set of laws governing their interactions with non-Jews, but it's hard to justify given the way the word appears in the rest of the book. *Ger* was also used to describe the Children of Israel when they lived in Egypt, and they certainly didn't all convert while they were there! A similar change has occurred with the word *goy*, which really just means "nation." Even though *goy* has come to mean "Gentile" or "non-Jew" instead, one of the first times this word is used in the Torah is in God's promise to make Abraham a mighty nation. In fact, far from restricting the grace of YHWH to only one group of believers, both 1 Kings 8:41–43 and Isaiah 56:7 confirm that Jerusalem, its Temple, and its God were meant for everyone:

> As for the foreigner who does not belong to your people Israel but has come from a distant land because of your name—for men will hear of your great name and your mighty hand and your outstretched arm—when he comes and prays toward this temple, then hear from heaven, your dwelling place, and do whatever the foreigner asks of you, so that all the peoples of the earth may know your name and fear you, as do your own people Israel, and may know that this house I have built bears your Name.

> And foreigners who bind themselves to the Lord to serve him, to love the name of the Lord, and to worship him, all who keep the Sabbath without desecrating it and who hold fast to my covenant—these will I bring to my holy mountain and give them joy in my house of prayer. Their burnt offerings and sacrifices will be accepted on my altar; for my house will be called a house of prayer for all nations.

The Covenant of Abraham and the Laws of Moses weren't merely intended to make Jews different and to set them apart from the rest of us. The commands were also designed to make sure that everyone in the Holy Land was treated the same. According to God's commands, Israel was never supposed to become a happy homeland to just one people. It's supposed to be a land where everyone lives together in peace.

One command, from God by way of Ezekiel, could bring peace to the entire region if we all followed it. In Ezekiel 47:21–23, God commands Israel to treat Palestinians as family:

> "You are to distribute this land among yourselves according to the tribes of Israel. You are to allot it as an inheritance

for yourselves and for the aliens who have settled among you and who have children. You are to consider them as native-born Israelites; along with you they are to be allotted an inheritance among the tribes of Israel. In whatever tribe the alien settles, there you are to give him his inheritance," declares the Sovereign Lord.

Try for a moment to imagine a Middle East where Jewish Israel recognized Christian and Muslim Palestinians as coinheritors. The impact that it would have on the rest of the world and on the three religions of the Children of Abraham is unimaginable. And yet, in Ezekiel, God declares to Jews, Christians, and Muslims that we are all the same.

We're the same in other ways as well, because the Covenant and our failure to abide by its terms also helps explain the currently frustrated state of Islam. Ishmael was Abraham's child, too; that means that none of us have lived up to *our* responsibilities. Jewish stewardship of the Holy Land isn't even supposed to be an issue in Islam. Ezekiel, whom Muslims remember as Dhu al Kifl, is one of our prophets as well. If that's not enough, we even have two Ayat in the Holy Quran that confirm with which people the stewardship for Israel rests: Al-Maeda 5:20–21 and Al-Isra 17:104. They both say virtually the same thing.

> Remember Moses said to his people; "O my People! Call in remembrance the favor of Allah unto you, when he produced prophets among you, made you kings, and gave you what he had not given to any other among the peoples. O my people, enter the Holy Land which Allah hath assigned unto you, and turn not back ignominiously, for then will ye be overthrown to your own ruin."

> And We said thereafter to the Children of Israel, "Dwell securely in the land of Promise": But when the second of the warnings came to pass, We gathered you together in a mingled crowd.

The way politics have bedeviled Islam for the last thousand years, it shouldn't be a surprise that they've contributed to our troubles with Judaism. Evidence of our own perfidy can be seen in the way that these Ayat have been translated and taught. Religious translation and education can both be political tools; it can be hard to resist the temptation to tweak the meaning of a verse you don't like. These two Ayat are an excellent example of that sort of misrepresentation, as their current interpretations and translations consistently weaken the meaning of the words.

Most Muslims are convinced that God assigned the Holy Land to the Children of Israel, implying that the situation could change. If something is given, it can be taken back. If something is assigned to one person, it can always be assigned to someone else. But the Arabic word that's translated as "assigned"—*KatabAllahu*—actually means something more akin to "destined" or "God-ordained." KatabAllahu doesn't mean that the land was merely assigned to the Jews; it says that the responsibility for Israel is and always will be theirs. Likewise, the second Ayah describes the land as more than just the land of promise. It describes the Jewish people living there upon their return (after the second warning has come to pass) with the connotation of a people who have triumphantly come to, or have finally and ultimately achieved, their promised and forever secure homeland. Finally, the first Ayah implies that if Judaism ever does abandon Israel, it will be destroyed. The second Ayah confirms that the fates of Israel and the Jewish people are linked, and it clearly states that Muslims will be intermingled with Jews in Israel when we're all finally there to stay.

The Middle East today illustrates the way all of our religions have let us down. Islam proclaims the unity of God, faith, and religion, but Muslims have interpreted that ideal in terms of our own leadership, politics, and control. Unable to accept that Muslims might not be the ones God intended to be in charge everywhere, we've ignored the words of the Quran and tried to replace them with our own ideas of the way we think things should be. Because Muslims have been convinced that God must want us to run everything, we've so far missed out on what could have been ours if we'd only read the Quran, supported the Jewish return, and reminded the Jews to include Muslims and Christians, too.

Jews, on the other hand, have always known that they were supposed to get Israel, have assumed that the recurrent frustration of their plans is God's fault, and have decided that it's their duty to make it happen. Their real responsibility all along has been only to hold up their side of the bargain. Because they've tried to rely on their own strength instead, they have an unstable and oppressive state that none of them can safely and confidently call their home. The greatest religious paradox in the Middle East today may be that the strongest claim the Jews have to Israel is actually found in the words of the Holy Quran. There, there's no question whom the land really belongs to, but according to the Torah, since Abraham made the Covenant for all his kids, the land could still go either way!

The poor Christians may be the most confused of us all; they honestly don't know what they want in the Holy Land. All three religions know that peace is a good thing. According to Jesus, Christians are supposed to aspire to becoming meek, mild peacemakers. Israel is their Holy Land, just like it is for the rest of us. Given all of that, you'd think that peace in the Holy Land would obviously be the best thing of all for Christians, just like it should be for the Muslims and the Jews. The problem is, what many really want is Armageddon! They think when it happens, they'll finally be able to prove to everyone else that they were right; unfortunately for all of us, that's exactly what many Christians think they have to work towards. Because of some particularly persuasive leaders, in the last few decades many Christians have become convinced that the Book of Revelation says that before Jesus can come back, they need Jews living in Israel surrounded by an angry horde waiting to pounce. Given that, the foreign policy of the United States and Britain—the two countries that claim to be following Christianity the closest—makes a whole lot of sense.

The reason there's no peace in the Middle East and the war there is spreading to threaten the peace of the rest of the world is simple. We've all been paying lip service to peace and love, but our religions are making us work counter to that purpose. Christians are actually striving toward the war to end all wars, despite Jesus' message of peace, goodwill, and love. Instead of submitting to God, Muslims have been trying to make everyone else submit to us instead. The Jews know they're supposed to trust God, but instead, they've decided to trust themselves. What we believe has made us all do the opposite of what we're supposed to, and instead of the showpiece of God's goodness that it's meant to be, we've made the Middle East an illustration of how our beliefs, doctrines, politics, impatience, and disrespect for God have put us where we all are today.

The solution that all our holy books offer is simple if we'd all take the time to read them. Tzedakah is one of the most important words in Hebrew because of what it means. In Hebrew, a *tzadik* is a righteous man, or even "the" righteous man, because tzedakah fulfills the Abrahamic Covenant. Likewise, the same word in Arabic—*sadaqa*—is one of the most important words in the Quran because it means virtually the same thing. In Islam, *sadaqa* means "truth" and "truthfulness," "faithfulness" and "trustworthiness." It also refers to one who is sincere and worthy of praise. It means "charity," "justice," and the confirmation of truths that have been spoken before. Both words in both languages mean the fulfillment of all of our responsibilities to God.

If any of us truly are the people we believe we are, then we will eventually have to accept that we are all members of the same family. The real message of the Torah, the Gospel, and the Quran is that we are all the Children of Abraham; that makes us all family to each other, too. Families don't always get along, and the battles between brothers can sometimes be the bloodiest of them all, but that sort of thing never pleases the parents. Children are all different. We all begin differently and grow up along our own paths. We all play different roles, but if we have good parents, the standards by which they judge us, the way they look at us, and the expectations they have of us are always the same—not because of who we are, but because of them.

For the Jews through Isaac who became Israel, for the Arabs through Ishmael his brother, for Christians through adoption, and for all other non-Arab Muslims through our own return to Abraham's simple faith in God, the Covenant still stands. If we're honestly trying to please God, we're all still bound by tzedakah/sadaqa and the simple truth that St. Paul tried so hard to express: that of all the virtues that we may choose to extol and of all we do, think, or feel, only the good we do really matters, because in the end, that's all God will allow to remain. We have all declared ourselves the three religions most aware of what God wants and the best equipped to deliver it because that's what we all want to believe. Despite that, somehow we've all managed to completely miss the point; according to the words spoken by every one of our prophets to every one of us, love (for God and for each other) is all God's ever wanted from any of us, all along.

- **The Covenant of justice and brotherhood speaks to all the Children of Abraham.**

- **Both *tzedakah* and *sadaqa* mean "love," "charity," "kindness," and "fulfilling all our promises to God."**

- **All God ever wanted was for us to treat everyone else well, whether we agree with them or not.**

CHAPTER 22

....

ISLAMIC ZIONISM

So why did Muslims, Christians, and Jews start fighting over the Holy Land in the first place? For what it's worth, I blame Hitler. Despite an eons-long history of squabbling over land, water, and personal honor, interspersed with rare but regrettable atrocities committed by every side, the last sixty years of strife is without historical precedent. Neither is there any religious basis for this conflict: as I've maintained throughout this entire book, when you examine our three faiths closely and objectively it becomes clear that Christians following Jesus, Jews following Judaism, and Muslims following Islam remains the best hope for us all. However, most Muslims blame Israeli "Zionists" for all their problems, and most Jews blame "Radical Islam." Meanwhile, more than a few Christians continue to hope that the battles between the two of us can bring about a happy ending, at least for them.

One thing is certain: any ending short of one side's extermination will require every side participating in an open and honest conversation, together reviewing a surprisingly short but still painful history with open eyes, and looking to the future instead of the past. Furthermore, lasting peace in the Middle East will require bridge building by our leaders and a strong incentive to move across that bridge in the rank-and-file amongst us all. Perhaps in this "Age of Change" initiated by President Obama—a Christian with a Muslim middle name and an Israeli chief of staff—that dialogue might finally have a chance to begin.

Many years ago a friend who specialized in the care of the critically ill told me his approach to ethical decision making. I've since found it applicable to many different situations. He told me, "David, rational people—given the same information—will always come to the same conclusion." He continued, "If rational people disagree, your only job as an ethicist is to ensure that they have the same facts. Once you've done that, you'll find your work is already done." He then observed, "On the other hand, I've noticed that when someone seems irrational, it's often because they're not aware of their own preconceptions. That renders them unable to express their reasoning clearly either to themselves or to anyone else." He concluded, "When that situation arises, your job becomes helping them to understand themselves."

Is there anything rational about the current conflict between Israel and Palestine? Perhaps the most senseless aspect of the entire affair is how little interest there is in a resolution: both Israelis and Palestinians seem committed to their current path despite all their suffering, and perhaps even because of it. Irrational too is the fact that despite all the evidence to the contrary no one seems willing to admit that their own side bears any real responsibility for what's going on. Israelis, the Israeli Defence Force, the Settlers, Hamas, al-Fatah, enraged Palestinians, angry Muslims, and Jewish and Christian Zionists all claim that their actions are above question, some even claiming that their every deed—even those repugnant to more objective observers around the world—is ordained by God. Finally, in irrational response, instead of defending God from that vile accusation, we, their coreligionists around the world, defend their right to make it.

Just what is Zionism, either Christian or Jewish? The word *Zion* is itself over three thousand years old, and originally referred to a mountain fortress conquered by David and renamed after him. It has come to refer to Jewish Jerusalem and the Jewish Promised Land and to symbolize the aspirations of the entire Jewish people. As such, many people think Jewish Zionism is primarily a religious movement, but when it began it certainly wasn't, and according to many devout Jews it still has little to do with Judaism today. Primarily used to describe the modern-day manifestation of an "Israel-centered" Jewish unity stretching back thousands of years, to many non-Jewish people around the word *Zionism* has become synonymous with racism, racial chauvinism, oppression, and territorial aggression combined. The reason? There are many different "Zionisms," each energized and exemplified by the beliefs and actions of its own powerful founder.

Despite the common non-Jewish misconception that Zionism began as a European response to the religious imperative of a Jewish state in the Holy Land, Theodore Herzl—the man generally credited with "creating" modern-day Zionism—wasn't religious at all. Raised in a middle-class

Hungarian home, Herzl moved to Austria at the age of eighteen and devoted much of his early life to German nationalism. Trained as a lawyer, he found better employment as a journalist, and it was while covering the Dreyfus affair—an unpleasant example of institutional anti-Semitism involving a Jewish French army officer wrongly accused of spying for Germany—that he decided to dedicate the rest of his life to Jewish freedom.

Herzl founded Zionism as a secular political movement, growing out of a long tradition of Jewish European political activism. Long excluded from full participation in European society, Jews were granted legal equality with Gentiles only after the French Revolution, only in western Europe, and often only on paper. Consequently, the main impetus of the majority of Jewish activist organizations was equal rights for Jews in Europe itself, and before Herzl there was surprisingly little interest in a separate Jewish homeland, particularly one in Palestine. In fact, Theodore Herzl's Zionism-founding book, *Der Judenstaat*, "The State of the Jews," contemplated putting the Promised Land in Argentina.

Herzl founded the Zionist Organization dedicated to a Jewish state—that became the World Zionist Organization in 1960—because he came to the conclusion that a *secular* Jewish state was the only possible remedy for anti-Semitism. His views would probably be considered quite strange by today's standards: his own writings make it clear he considered anti-Semitism to be not the outgrowth of an anti-Semite's racism, but a natural consequence of the character of Jews themselves:

> The Jewish question persists wherever Jews live in appreciable numbers. Wherever it does not exist, it is brought in together with Jewish immigrants. We are naturally drawn into those places where we are not persecuted, and our appearance there gives rise to persecution. This is the case, and will inevitably be so, everywhere, even in highly civilized countries—see, for instance, France—so long as the Jewish question is not solved on the political level. The Jews are now carrying the seeds of anti-Semitism into England; they have already introduced it into America.
>
> —*Der Judenstaat (The State of the Jews)*

Anti-Semitism played an obvious and influential role in creating Zionism. Conversely, the relationship between Zionism and Judaism has often been an uneasy one. Nathan Birnbaum—responsible for naming the movement "Zionism" in the first place—actually abandoned it early on, concluding that the state Herzl envisioned was not compatible with his faith. Theodore Herzl honestly considered Judaism to be counterproductive and planned his state along bourgeois European lines, intending to keep faith in Israel a private matter, outside the public sphere. Socialist Labor Zionism, which predominated among Jews in Israel prior to 1948, went even further and was often even actively antireligious, blaming Judaism itself for the fatalistic "Diaspora Mentality." Many religious Jews today still express the same concern that human attempts to "create" a Jewish state in the Holy Land are inherently blasphemous. However, that does not make them "anti-Israel": religious Zionism has made its own accommodations to Zionism, best summed up in the twentieth-century proclamations of Rabbi Dav Kook, who concluded:

> Zionism was not merely a political movement by secular Jews. It was actually a tool of God to promote His divine scheme and to initiate the return of the Jews to their homeland—the land He promised to Abraham, Isaac and Jacob. God wants the children of Israel to return to their home in order to establish a Jewish sovereign state in which Jews could live according to the laws of Torah and Halakha and commit the Mitzvot of Eretz Israel. Moreover, to cultivate the land of Israel was a Mitzvah by itself and it should be carried out. Therefore, settling Israel is an obligation of the religious Jews and helping Zionism is actually following God's will ...
>
> Secular Zionists may think they do it for political, national or socialist reasons, but in fact the actual reason for them coming to resettle in Israel is a religious Jewish spark ("Nitzotz") in their soul, planted by God. Without their knowledge, they are contributing to the divine scheme and actually committing a great Mitzvah.

Secular or not, the vast majority of early Zionists intended to found an open, inclusive, and democratic Israel. Rabbi Kook's vision of a land cultivated in obedience to God was a positive and nonexclusive one. Likewise, despite Herzl's belief that anti-Semitism was a natural consequence of the Jewish racial character, he envisioned a land where Jews and non-Jews would live together in peace. His novel *Altneuland,* "The Old New Land," described a Zion combining the best of Jews and non-Jews alike, and he didn't promote armed assault as a means to that end: His own belief was that non-Jews unwilling to participate in developing the Israel he foresaw could be dealt with in other ways, primarily economic. His solution—while unpleasant by polite standards—would still have been a vast improvement on the Israel we find there today.

> Spirit the penniless population across the frontier by denying it employment... both the process of expropriation and the removal of the poor must be carried out discreetly and circumspectly.
> —from *The Complete Diaries of Theodore Herzl,*
> by Raphael Patai

For a while it looked like his more positive aspirations would come to pass, even after Herzl passed away. Asher Ginsberg, also known as Ahad HaAm, shared the leadership of the World Zionist Organization with Chaim Weizman, and together they energized the Zionist movement with their vision of Jewish settlements, a revived Hebrew language, and an Israel with a Jewish majority sharing the land with the native population in peace. After paying a visit to Palestine, Ginsberg/HaAm wrote:

> Abroad we are accustomed to believe that Israel is almost empty; nothing is grown here and that whoever wishes to buy land could come here and buy what his heart desires. In reality, the situation is not like this. Throughout the country it is difficult to find cultivable land which is not already cultivated.

Like Herzl, Ginsberg was not religious, but he revered his religion regardless. Although he partook of Herzl's political Zionism he viewed it as only a means to an end, that end being nothing less than a revitalized Judaism throughout the world. In his own response to anti-Semitism— often called "Cultural Zionism"—he concluded that Jews and Judaism must return to their roots, culturally, linguistically, and geographically. However, unlike Herzl—whom he considered naïve—Ginsberg realized that any attempt to impose a "Jewish" state would automatically create conflict with any native population already there.

One of his most notable disciples was Martin Buber, the Jewish-German philosopher and author of *Ich und Du* ("I and Thou"), still considered one of the seminal works on the dialogical nature of existence. For a time Buber even edited the weekly Zionist publication *Die Welt,* until he left it to dedicate himself to his own writing. He remained active in Cultural Zionist causes, particularly adult Jewish education. He established the Jewish National Commission to promote the rights of Jews in Eastern Europe, became editor of *Der Jude,* a monthly Jewish magazine, and cofounded Rosenzweig's House of Jewish Learning before being named Honorary Professor of the University of Frankfurt in 1930.

When Adolf Hitler was named German Chancellor in 1933, Martin Buber resigned in protest and moved to Jerusalem. There, he received a professorship at the Hebrew University and became active in Zionist causes in the Holy Land. He helped found an organization called Brit Shalom, "The Covenant of Peace," to promote a culturally combined Arab-Jewish Israel, committed to the ideal that both would eventually live together in peace. Politically, he was a member of Ichud, a group promoting a binational solution to Palestine's many problems. In 1946, he even published *Paths to Utopia,* describing his hopes for a society of diverse individuals growing together in communities created by ongoing intercultural dialogue.

Unfortunately, in addition to the inclusive "western European" Zionism there was a different sort at play as well. Among the founders of Israel, one man alone bears the brunt of responsibility for introducing the world to the violence that has come to characterize Zionism's darker side. In the complex history of Israel, Vladimir Jabotinsky's legacy is perhaps the most complicated of all. "Revisionist" Zionist leader, founder of the Jewish Self-Defense Organization of Odessa and the British-declared terrorist group Irgun in the Holy Land, by his own admission Jabotinsky, known as Ze'ev, "Wolf," was raised without the moderating influence of either Jewish faith or tradition. Unlike the philosophies of Herzl, Kook, Ginsberg, and Buber, Jabotinsky's Zionism was forged in the crucible of Eastern Europe, where anti-Jewish violence was both open and common. Even there his violent response to anti-Semitic pogroms throughout Russia made him a controversial figure, and he carried that reputation with him to Palestine. Despite that, however, he helped write a draft of the Israeli constitution that recognized the rights of Arabs as equals, and he promoted the idea of a shared Arab-Israeli cabinet. Though eventually barred from Palestine by the British, he was a decorated officer in the British Army, for which he established the Jewish Legion in the Middle East theater. His zeal for Israel was evident through his life—his MBE was granted in recognition of his heading the first company to cross the River Jordan into Palestine—but he died an exile in Britain, and his bones were barred from an Israeli burial by the Israelis themselves.

Raised as he was with little faith and in violent times, given his inclinations—and despite his occasionally more egalitarian tendencies—Jabotinsky harbored no illusions about the eventual inevitability of armed conflict with the Palestinian people, writing in his book:

> A voluntary reconciliation with the Arabs is out of the question either now or in the future. If you wish to colonize a land in which people are already living, you must provide a garrison for the land, or find some rich man or benefactor who will provide a garrison on your behalf. Or else—or else, give up your colonization, for without an armed force which will render physically impossible any attempt to destroy or prevent this colonization, colonization is impossible, not difficult, not dangerous, but IMPOSSIBLE! Zionism is a colonization adventure and therefore it stands or falls by the question of armed force. It is important... to speak Hebrew, but, unfortunately, it is even more important to be able to shoot—or else I am through with playing at colonizing.
>
> Zionist colonization must either be terminated or carried out against the wishes of the native population. This colonization can, therefore, be continued and make progress only under the protection of a power independent of the native population—an iron wall, which will be in a position to resist the pressure to the native population. This is our policy towards the Arabs.
>
> —*The Iron Wall,* Vladimir Jabotinsky, 1923

Zionist Israel was born of many fathers, but David Ben-Gurion was the man who pulled all those threads together in the country that became the Israel of today. Raised in Poland while it was still part of the Russian Empire, he began his own Zionist quest as a member of Paole Zion, an organization that combined Marxism with Zionism to form Labor Zionism, the dominant Zionism in Israel when it was founded and arguably still the most influential form in Israel today. Arrested twice during the Russian revolution of 1905, Ben-Gurion moved to Palestine in 1906 to escape further persecution. He worked, lived, and fought on behalf of Jews and Judaism in Palestine as a fruit picker by day and a soldier by night, until the Ottomans expelled him for his political activities. Settling in New York City, he then found an opportunity to return to Palestine with the British Army as part of Jabotinsky's Jewish Legion to drive the Ottomans out in return.

A singularly skilled politician, Ben-Gurion soon surpassed Jabotinsky and all other potential Jewish leaders in Palestine, eventually becoming chairman, in 1935, of the executive committee of the Jewish Agency for Palestine—the governing organization for Jews in Palestine from 1923 until 1948, when it became the provisional government of Israel. As leader of the Jewish people in what was to become Israel, at a time when it was primarily a nation of Arabs administered by the British, he walked a complex road: on one hand enforcing restraint when faced with Arab attacks on Jewish civilians while still approving of Irgun's anti-British terrorism; on the other promoting Labor Zionism's antireligious agenda and yet brokering a working relationship with the Orthodox Agudat Israel party by promising them a Friday Shabbat and autonomy in religious affairs. Although he split with Jabotinsky over Jabotinsky's opposition to the partitioning of Israel from Palestine, his own statements make plain his real plans for the countryside:

> We must expel the Arabs, and take their places.
> —from a letter to his son Aron, October 5, 1937

> The compulsory transfer of the Palestinian Arabs from the valleys of the proposed Jewish state could give us something which we never had, even when we stood on our own during the days of the first and second Temples ... We are given an opportunity which we never dared to dream of in our wildest imaginings. This is MORE than a state, government and sovereignty—this is a national consolidation in a free homeland ... With compulsory transfer we would have a vast area [for settlement] ... I support compulsory transfer. I don't see anything immoral in it.
> —from *Righteous Victims: A History of the Zionist Arab Conflict, 1881–2001,* by Benny Morris

We must do everything to insure they (the Palestinians) never do return ... The old will die and the young will forget.
> —from his diary, July 18, 1948, *Ben-Gurion: the Armed Prophet,* by Michael Bar Zohar

If I were an Arab leader, I would never sign an agreement with Israel. It is normal; we have taken their country. It is true God promised it to us, but how could that interest them? Our God is not theirs. There has been anti-Semitism, the Nazis, Hitler, Auschwitz, but was that their fault? They see but one thing: we have come and we have stolen their country. Why would they accept that?
> —quoted by Nahum Goldmann in *Le Paradoxe Juif* (*The Jewish Paradox*)

We walked outside, Ben-Gurion accompanying us. Allon repeated his question, "What is to be done with the Palestinian population?" Ben-Gurion waved his hand in a gesture which said "Drive them out."
> —Yitzhak Rabin, leaked censored version of Rabin memoirs, published in *The New York Times*, October 23, 1979

Those statements make it plain that the disintegration of Palestine the world has witnessed over the last sixty years resulted from a plan laid almost a century ago. That plan was not a *fait accompli*: there were many Zionists—including the movement's founders—whose more moderate perspectives would certainly have made Israel a different place than it has become over the last sixty years. Tragically, Zionist politics, uneasy Arab-Jewish realities, and then the Holocaust rendered thoughts of a Jewish homeland not completely under Jewish control inconceivable to many, if not all, Jews in Israel and around the world. The confrontational Zionism born of Eastern Europe's violent anti-Semitism moved to the forefront despite the work of moderates like Martin Buber, who warned David Ben-Gurion in 1949:

> We will have to face the reality that Israel is neither innocent, nor redemptive. And that in its creation and expansion we as Jews, have caused what we historically have suffered; a refugee population in Diaspora.

Unfortunately for all, Buber's perspective proved to have little influence. *The Jewish Newsletter* from June 2, 1958, reported that Buber lamented to a New York Jewish audience:

> When we (the followers of Prophetic Judaism) returned to Palestine ... the majority of Jewish people preferred to learn from Hitler than from us.

Hence my conviction that the war between Semitic Israelis and Semitic Palestinians is the last great evil that Hitler left us and the fullest possible realization of Hitler's anti-Semitism made manifest in the world today.

That said, I don't think many Muslims would be comfortable with how much Hitler had to do with Radical Islam either. The common misperception that Radical Islamists have roots stretching back to the beginning of Islam—a perception that has been carefully nurtured by the Radical Islamists themselves—is no truer of them than the common misperception that Zionism is deeply rooted in Judaism. There is also no foundation for the claim of the Radical Islamists that conflict is inevitable. Osama bin Laden and Hamas may both claim:

> It is the Muslims who are the inheritors of Moses.
> —Osama bin Laden, *Letter to the American People*

> The Islamic Resistance Movement believes that the land of Palestine is an Islamic *Waqf* consecrated for future Muslim generations until Judgment Day. It, or any part of it, should not be squandered: it, or any part of it, should not be given up.
> —Hamas Charter

But few Muslims thought this was so until Hamas and bin Laden came along. Most of us take our inheritance from Abraham. It's instructive to note that Osama was trying to claim the status as the inheritors of Moses' legacy for Muslims in the context of the Middle East, because it serves as confirmation that he too was aware of the importance of Al-Maeda 5:20–21. According to that passage, in direct contradiction to Hamas's Charter, although Israel is an Islamic *Waqf*—a word that means "endowment"—it is an endowment for the Jews too.

Traditionally Muslims have protected the Jews' right to live in Israel, and likewise for centuries the safest place for Jews outside it to openly practice their religion was in Muslim lands. When Jerusalem first fell to a Muslim army, returning the seventy Jewish families who had been forced to leave by the Christian patriarch and then cleaning up the Old Jewish Temple site—which had been turned into a refuse dump—were among the first things Caliph Umar did. When the Crusaders attacked Jerusalem in 1099, it was a combined army of Muslims and Jews that defended the city, and when that defense failed, both Muslims and Jews were slaughtered together. Then, it wasn't until Saladin defeated the Crusaders in 1187 that Jews began to return to Jerusalem once again. Afterwards, Muslims presided over seven hundred years of peaceful coexistence. Richard Satloff's *Among the Righteous* documents the proud history of Arabs who resisted Nazi Germany and protected Jews throughout Europe and Africa during the Second World War. He describes the Grand Mosque of Paris as "a virtual Grand Central Station for the Underground Railroad of Jews in France" and records that the predominately Muslim nation of Albania ended the war with more Jews than it began because of the collective efforts of its citizenry.

Most Radical Islamists today chart their history from Muhammad ibn Abd-al-Wahab, the cleric who came to prominence with the Saudis in Arabia—but the movement's real beginnings were much later, in the 1920s. Rather than beginning Radical Islam's anti-Semitism, Muhammad ibn Abd-al-Wahab was not even particularly anti-Jewish. The primary thrust of his own reformist efforts was twofold. he condemned anything except pure monotheism, which he called *Tawhid*, and he was against *Taqleed*, a Sunni practice that he felt had become nothing but uninformed and blind emulation of the earliest Muslims. Neither of these imperatives would have brought him into conflict with Jews or Judaism—most of his ire was actually reserved for his fellow Muslims. In fact, he would likely have condemned the current anti-Semitic fervor and the attempts to claim an Islamic precedent for it out of hand. Dedicated as he was to contextual interpretation, he would have known that those Quranic Ayat which *can* be interpreted in an anti-Semitic light dealt either with specific instances where Jews failed to follow their own religion adequately—and so constituted a Prophetic call to return to their own monotheism—or else the political maneuverings of Jewish tribes of Medina, whose machinations against Muhammad after accepting him as Medina's head of State constituted treason in wartime. Their crimes were what they did, not what they believed.

Historically, the different status suffered by Jews relative to Muslims has been an inconstant feature of a malleable and inconstant political environment: Muhammad had many Jewish friends and even a Jewish wife whom he would have been required to treat the same as the rest. It is a matter of accepted Muslim dogma that at its outset Islam protected Jewish rights, taxed them equivalently—the *Jizyah* tax on non-Muslims was meant to compensate for their exemption from military service—and gave them equivalent though different status as well. While it is an unfortunate matter of historical truth that those initiatives were not always maintained, not every tale bears close scrutiny. One noteworthy example is the fate of the Banu Qurayza, a Jewish tribe of Medina who intrigued against Muhammad when Islam first began. The story of six hundred men beheaded and the remaining women and children enslaved—all done in accordance with the Jewish rules of conquest set out in Deuteronomy, and imposed by a judge of the Banu Qurayza's own choosing—was first recorded by ibn Ishaq, author of a biography of Muhammad titled *Sirat Rasul Allah,* "The Life of God's Messenger." However, ibn Ishaq was condemned as a liar by his contemporary, the much more respected Islamic jurist Imam Malik, for transmitting such false and anti-Jewish tales, which according to Malik had their origin with the descendents of the Banu Qurayza themselves. There is no history of such a punishment—which would have been absolutely contrary to Islam's principle of every individual suffering for his or her own misdeeds—being exacted in Islamic courts: something which would have certainly happened were the story true as told. In fact, the vast majority of purportedly valid anti-Semitic Hadiths currently in circulation come from either his collection or that of al-Tabari—which al-Tabari based upon ibn Ishaq's work. As a scholar dedicated to valid Hadiths who condemned innovation wherever he thought he found it, Abd-al-Wahab would have condemned emulating ibn Ishaq's innovative anti-Semitism in no uncertain terms at all.

Martin Goodman's *Oxford Handbook of Jewish Studies* concedes that most Arab anti-Semitism in the modern world arose in the nineteenth century against the backdrop of conflicting Jewish and Arab nationalism.

As such, it has always been primarily political in both origin and motivation, and the same can be said about all the various and often warring factions that make up Radical Islam today. There are many: internationally we find al Qaeda and the Muslim Brotherhood, in Afghanistan the Taliban, and in Algeria the Groupe Islamique Armé and the Islamic Salvation Front; around the world the list goes on. Each group has a different charter, and at times they even find themselves at war with each other, but they share a common political origin: beginning as a force of rebellion against the status quo, with their Islam—frequently misrepresented and abused—serving as a rallying point rather than their reason for being. Only as Palestinian nationalism developed in opposition to Jewish nationalist aspirations did their Islam develop its current anti-Semitic flavoring, and only as Israel ramped up its anti-Palestinian activities has the Muslim world come to share their point of view. My wife was raised as a devout Muslim in Pakistan in the '70s, and she doesn't recall learning anything about Jews, Judaism, or Israel until arriving in Canada in her teens.

Palestine's version of Radical Islam was instigated by the political opportunism of the then Grand Mufti of Jerusalem, Haj Amin Muhammad al-Husseini. A member of the powerful al-Husseini family of Jerusalem and Judea, al-Husseini came from a long line of Jerusalem mayors and muftis and seemed destined for a multicultural political career. Most of his initial education came at the hands of Turkish educators, French Catholic missionaries, and the Alliance Israelite Universelle's anti-Zionist Jewish director, Albert Antebi. With his formal Islamic education limited to a few months' stay at Cairo's Al-Azhar University under Rashid Rida, he certainly seemed bent on a more secular life than he eventually settled into, choosing to finish his schooling at the secular Ottoman School of Administration in Istanbul.

Al-Husseini's politics followed an eclectic course as well. He began the First World War with the 47th brigade of the Ottoman army. However, while on leave in Jerusalem he was captured by the British and chose to fight alongside them instead. In fact, dispatches sent at that time by Captain C. D. Brunton noted that al-Husseini was particularly cooperative and pro-English. Employed as a recruiter, he enlisted Palestinian men to participate in the Arab revolt of 1916—an attempt by Sherif Faisal bin al-Hussein bin Ali al-Hashemi (whom most today remember as the role Sir Alec Guinness played in the movie *Lawrence of Arabia*) to overthrow the Turks and create a separate Arab state from Syria to Yemen. He supported Faisal's bid to become King of Greater Syria, joined the Syrian "Arab Club," and became a columnist for the Syrian newspaper *Suriyya al-Janubiyya*. However, despite his support for Faisal—a signatory to the Faisal-Weizmann Agreement recognizing the Balfour Declaration and promising Arab support for a Jewish homeland—he became more active in opposing the growth of Palestine's Jewish population as well, breaking faith with and undermining King Faisal when Faisal needed his support the most.

Whether al-Husseini played *some* role in the violent riots that broke out upon the Balfour Declaration's implementation in 1920 is not disputed. However, the reasons why were a significant source of controversy at the time. The Palin report—the outcome of a British Foreign Office investigation into the causes of Palestinian violence—blamed both Jews and Muslims and the British sentenced both Ze'ev Jabotinsky and al-Husseini to prison terms, which both of them escaped—al-Husseini by fleeing to Transjordan. Palin reported that Chaim Weizmann and Lieutenant Colonel Meinertzhagen both claimed that al-Husseini was acting on the instructions of Field Marshal Allenby's chief of staff to demonstrate Arab resistance to a Jewish homeland, but those charges were never proven and Meinertzhagen was dismissed. Whatever his reasons, those riots and the central part al-Husseini played proved pivotal in his own life and in deciding the destiny of the Middle East and Palestine.

Despite the help Faisal gave the British in the First World War, they proved a poor ally to his plans as well. In Europe, the British and French signed the Sykes-Picot agreement, ceding control of Syria and Lebanon to French forces, and Faisal's ambitions were promptly dashed by their subsequent invasion of Syria. Without Faisal's support, nationalistic political maneuvering in the area took a new and purely Palestinian turn, which al-Husseini seemed particularly suited to. His skills in the art of *Realpolitik* are evidenced by the fashion in which he orchestrated his return to power: pardoned by the British to allow his appointment by British High Commissioner Herbert Samuel to the exalted posts of *Grand Mufti* and President of the *Supreme* Muslim Council—two positions that were actually *created* by the British and given to him despite his receiving fewer Palestinian votes than the other three candidates, in the expectation that he would play a moderating role—his actions over the ensuing years became progressively disruptive and anti-British instead.

As Palestine's Muslim leader, al-Husseini undertook the restoration of the Muslim holy sites on Temple Mount in Jerusalem, a controversial decision with profound religious and political overtones that proved to be of pivotal consequence. Whatever his intent, the restoration led to increasingly acrimonious conflicts with the growing Jewish population. Governed as it was by Ottoman law delivered by British courts and argued by Jewish and Muslim lawyers, the situation became progressively inflamed until it came to a head in 1929. On August 15, a strongly nationalistic Israeli celebration was held at the site on Tisha B'av, the holiday commemorating the original destruction of the Temple. The following day, after celebrating Mawlid al-Nabi, the Prophet Muhammad's birthday, Muslim crowds destroyed Jewish property there, without, however, hurting those Jews present at the time. Unfortunately, a day later a Jewish boy was stabbed to death while playing football, and a Muslim youth was badly wounded in a brawl. On August 21, mourners in the funeral procession of the Jewish boy attempted unsuccessfully to break into the Arab Quarter, and on August 23 three Arabs were murdered on Jewish land. Although al-Husseini gave a speech—at the request of the British—calling for calm, in reply a large crowd of Arabs gathered and launched a series of mob attacks that were met by strong Jewish resistance. In all, 136 Arabs and 135 Jews died.

Who exactly deserves the most blame for those riots remains contested, but however they occurred, they marked the end of any hope for peaceful coexistence. The ensuing years were filled with behind-the-scenes mobilizations of both Muslim and Jewish clandestine organizations. There is no question that al-Husseini played an important role in the anti-British Arab revolt of 1936–1939, and those years contained the beginning of his flirtation with Fascism as well. Klaus Gensicke's *The Mufti and the Holocaust* recounts that the pro-Zionist German Consul-General Heinrich Wolff sent a telegraph to Berlin in 1933 reporting that al-Husseini had assured him that Palestinian Muslims were enthusiastic Fascists, looked forward to spreading Fascism through the region, and requested German aid in dealing with their Jewish concerns. Wolff reported that the Muslims' naïveté was such that they failed to recognize the link between German Jewish policy and their own problems, and that they had no understanding of Nazism's goals or their own role within the movement.

Whether real or feigned, al-Husseini's enthusiasm resulted in little support and less action from Europe's Fascists—Germany and Italy were both actively avoiding engagement with England and the United States—but it thrust him and the Palestinians into the arms of the Axis in the run-up to the Second World War. In July of 1936, al-Husseini told

Italy's consul general that Mussolini's backing would allow him to take a greater role in the region, and subsequently guerrillas under his control were responsible for most of the early attacks on Jewish Israelis. That led the British to give more support to the Israeli side in response—despite their initial inclination to the contrary—for the sake of maintaining order. The British army helped train a number of pivotal Jewish militias, David Ben-Gurion's hand held the Jews of Israel back during this crucial period, and although al-Husseini's avowed purpose was merely the end of Jewish immigration, he led the Palestinians to become increasingly at odds with the British governing forces as well.

After the assassination of Acting District Commissioner Lewis Yelland Andrews, al-Husseini was deposed as president of the Muslim Council, the Arab Higher Committee was declared illegal, warrants were issued for his arrest, and the final chapter of his long, strange, and unpleasant political career began. Escaping to Lebanon and then Iraq, he continued to lead anti-British and anti-Zionist efforts in Palestine with less and less effectiveness, all the while seeking support from the French and the Americans with less and less success. His anti-Semitism became increasingly strident and indiscriminate, attacking Jew and Muslim alike and costing him popular support. Hillel Cohen's *Army of Shadows: Palestinian Collaboration with Zionism, 1917–1948* records how opposition to him grew to the extent that many Palestinian Arabs refused to fight beside him:

> Al-Husseini defined all competing nationalistic views and actions as treasonous. Patronizing a Jewish doctor, employing a Jewish worker or being employed by a Jew—all became illegitimate. Thus, Husseini's uncompromising maximalist positions, alongside his camp's unwillingness to tolerate the views of its opponents, paradoxically ended up expanding the definition of traitor and collaborator. When Abd al-Qader appeared in the village of Surif, in the Hebron district, to speak before the village elders, there were some who said to him: "You murdered eighty mukhtars, and you should be fought before we kill the Jews." Abd al-Qader replied that he killed traitors. He was told: "You are a criminal, and your uncle (Amin Muhammad al-Husseini) is a criminal and you are all an assembly of traitors."

Isolated, al-Husseini was soon forced to flee to Iraq, then to Iran, and then to Italy, barely steps ahead of the Allies, all the while issuing *Fatwas* declaring Holy War against them and requests that Berlin bomb Tel Aviv. Presenting himself to Benito Mussolini as the head of a secret Arab nationalist organization, he met with Adolf Hitler on November 28, 1941, but his move to Berlin did little to further his ambitions. Though he was frequently present at official events and well known to Hitler's inner circle, there is little evidence that his agenda against Israel had any influence. He was quite successful, though, in providing an excuse for the Nazis to pursue their own agenda. For instance, he prevented the exchange of a significant number of Jewish prisoners for German prisoners of war—even repulsively blocking the release of Jewish children—and he recruited many Muslims to the Nazi cause. But he was ultimately unsuccessful in his bid for a special force to attack Jews in Palestine, and his attempt to poison the water system in Tel Aviv failed. Arrested and sentenced by the Yugoslavians as a war criminal in the war's aftermath, his only role in the Holocaust was to serve as an indirect confirmation of the death toll, recalling in his memoirs his sense of shock when told by Himmler that Germany had successfully exterminated three million Jews prior to the summer of 1943.

In retrospect, al-Husseini's greatest victims were the Palestinians themselves. When he and the British broke faith with King Faisal's dream of a peaceful transition from Middle Eastern colonialism, he played into the hands of Jabotinsky and Ben-Gurion, ending both Faisal and Weizmann's hopes for a peacefully shared Arab Jewish self rule. He then chose the losing side in the Second World War and—just as his pre-war maneuvers drove the British into the arms of Israel—his post-war actions drove the rest of the Arab world away. From exile in Egypt he continued his efforts to shape Palestine's destiny behind him. While helping organize the Holy War Army, he demanded that the Arab states set him up in a provisional Palestinian government. Although he received some support from other Arab nations, who likely viewed it as an opportunity to withdraw from Palestine and block the ambitions of King Abdullah of Transjordan at one blow, that only caused Abdullah to withdraw his Arab Legion from their role in the fray. That decision precipitated a Palestinian collapse for which all the players share the blame, but the political situation was such that al-Husseini and his ambitions for Palestine were perceived as primarily responsible. As a final insult, although there is little evidence that he played any role in the

Holocaust, al-Husseini's flirtation with the Nazis has allowed sixty years of Zionist historians to justify the disproportionate price Palestinian Arabs have paid for Hitler's extermination of the Jews.

So what about the—almost entirely North American—phenomenon of militant Christian Zionism? Even though Hitler can't be blamed for it, anti-Semitism and the Holocaust have had far more to do with its development than most Christians appreciate. Likewise, politics have influenced recent North American perceptions and behavior more than most are willing to admit as well. In November of 2001—two months after the 9/11 attack on the World Trade Center—an ABC poll showed that only 14 percent of Americans thought Islam encouraged violence. Since then, that number has climbed to almost 50. According to the Pew Forum, over 70 percent of Americans now think of Muslim Americans as "different from other Americans." But while differences do exist, their nature may be surprising: although a 2006 University of Maryland poll confirmed that 24 percent of non-Muslim Americans thought intentional armed military attacks on civilians could be justified, a poll done by the Pew Forum found only 8 percent of American Muslims felt the same.

Despite that, the predominant North American belief is completely the opposite: that Islam encourages its adherents to be *more* violent rather than less. In a decade that has seen Muslim nation after Muslim nation invaded and decimated by Western armies despite repeated Muslim pleas to negotiate peace in Palestine and elsewhere—and during which the death toll among Muslims has climbed into the hundreds of thousands, while combined Western losses have been less than even one-tenth of that—the percentage of Americans who say *Islam* encourages violence has steadily climbed, reaching over 70 percent (according to Gallup) among America's conservative Republican—primarily Christian—"base." Today, less than one-quarter of evangelical Christians admit to a "favorable" opinion of Muslims, although fewer than one in ten actually knows a Muslim. Canada's experience mirrors that of the U.S., with a 2006 Environics poll and a 2008 Leger marketing poll both reporting that over one-third of Canadians have an "unfavorable" opinion of Muslims, with that number climbing to over one-half among those reporting no contact. What has happened to North America's "compassionate conservative" Christianity?

At the turn of the twentieth century, just as the political movement of Zionism was taking shape in Europe and the seeds of Radical Islam were being sown in the Middle East, an American named Cyrus Scofield completed an annotated version of the King James Bible promoting a system of biblical interpretation called Dispensationalism, and with it the idea that the Second Coming of Jesus could not take place until certain other events occurred. These included the rebirth of a Jewish state in Israel and the rebuilding of the Jewish Temple in Jerusalem. As that century progressed, the list of necessary preconditions came to include the destruction of Jerusalem's Muslim temples as well. The final event would be the battle of Armageddon, prophesied in the Bible's Revelation.

Christian leaders expounding that school of biblical exegesis have strongly influenced the beliefs of Christian Americans. A 2002 CNN/ Harris Interactive poll found that 20 percent of Americans believe Armageddon will occur within their lifetimes, and a 2003 CBS *60 Minutes* investigative news article entitled "Zion's Christian Soldiers" revealed the extent to which even radical dispensationalist interpretations have taken hold. According to Jerry Falwell—who claimed to represent 70 million evangelical Christians—and other leaders of the Christian Right as well, many of America's Christians now believe that their own happy ending requires the eradication of Palestine's Muslims and the death of Christian conversion of Israel's Jews. Frankly, I don't know how you can be more anti-Semitic than that.

Just like Jewish Zionism and Radical Islam, Christian Zionism has struggled to create the appearance of deep historical and theological roots. However, Christian advocacy for a Jewish presence in the Holy Land remains a new phenomenon, found prior to the eighteenth century only among a few scholars, Puritans, and members of the Plymouth Brethren Church. In Europe, there has actually been a long tradition of the opposite point of view because of the "Curse of Eusebius", an early fourth-century Christian Bishop of Caesarea, who had declared that Jews were forever barred from rebuilding in Jerusalem because of their sins. It was not until the nineteenth century that the idea began to develop any sizeable mainstream following, with a popular and largely secular European movement titled "Restoration of Jews to the Holy Land."

When it began, European Restorationism was primarily intended to address European political concerns, although it did have a religious component as well. As the Ottoman Empire weakened and Egypt entered an expansionist phase under Muhammad Ali, Western interests aligned behind the stabilizing influence of a Jewish state in Palestine being promoted by the seventh Earl of Shaftesbury, Anthony Ashley-Cooper.

Concurrently, among the European citizenry at large, growing interest in a convenient solution to the plight of Eastern European Jewry came together with the quaint expectation that Jews who returned to the Holy Land would convert, rebuild the Temple and prepare for the Second Coming of Christ. This notion prompted four ministers from the Church of Scotland to travel through Palestine inquiring into the region's readiness for Jesus' return. It was one of these four, Alexander Keith, in his travelogue *The Land of Israel According to the Covenant with Abraham, with Isaac and with Jacob,* who actually coined the popular phrase:

> A land without a people, for a people without a land.

Keith makes it sound as if moving Europe's Jews to Palestine was an immediate imperative. How he missed all the other people already living there is hard to explain; British bureaucratic record keeping—the key to their empire's effective administration—paints a vastly different picture of the land as a vibrant and productive place, but Keith's description proved popular regardless.

Michael Makovsky's book *Churchill's Promised Land: Zionism and Statecraft* recounts the complex interplay between sympathy for Jewish suffering in Eastern Europe played out with the NIMBY—Not In My Back Yard—principle and even outright anti-Jewish anti-Semitism in the rest of the "civilized" world. Putting a new Jewish state down where the old one had been was no doubt easier to contemplate without having to consider the fate of other inhabitants, but it is worth noting that Restorationism was not explicitly anti-Palestinian. Since it had its popular beginnings at a time when there was as yet no theological or political basis for either racist or anti-Islamic sentiment, the posture of Restorationism towards Palestinians has generally been one of benign neglect. However, there is no question that Europe's political leaders were much more aware than the general public of the potential impact such an undertaking would have on the indigenous people, and had still little sympathy for the locals' concerns. Winston Churchill's personal views were particularly reprehensible. Testifying before the Peel Commission, he explained:

> The indigenous population has no more right to Palestine than a dog in a manger has the final right to the manger, even though he may have lain there for a very long time ...

No wrong has been done to these people by the fact that
a stronger race, a higher grade race, or at any rate, a more
worldly-wise race, to put it that way, has come in and taken
their place.

Shocking as it is to hear "master race" arguments from Churchill's
lips, his attitudes no doubt reflect an attitude that would underlie many
decisions made by European leaders in the crucial years between the First
and Second World Wars.

Originally the organized Christian church and church doctrine played
only a minor and indirect role in Christian Zionist advocacy, because few
Christians thought that a Jewish presence in the Holy Land had anything
in it for *them*. Up until the beginning of the last century, Christian
eschatology—the study of the "end-times" in prophecy—had moved from
the early Christian certainty that Jesus would return at once, through the
Catholic view of "amillennialism" (with every moment being equally likely
to mark his return), through the many different Protestant interpretations.
All of these views share one important characteristic: none of them give
prophetic guidance or encouragement regarding how Christians might try
to "speed the day." That situation began to change when Plymouth Brethren
Preacher John Nelson Darby first began explaining the relationship
between God and Creation in terms of a series of chronologically ordered
"dispensations." According to Darby, human history began with the
dispensation of Innocence to Adam and Eve, followed by Conscience
through sin, then Government, Patriarchy, and Mosaic Law. Jesus was the
vector through which God dispensed grace, and the final dispensation we
await is the Millennial Kingdom, to be ushered in by the Middle Eastern
events espoused by the Scofield Bible.

If true, Darby's thesis meant Christians had a profoundly important
vested interest in the demographics of the Holy Land, because Jews
living there were the necessary victims of Armageddon, ushering in the
end of the world. Not surprisingly, those predictions weren't universally
popular—particularly on the other side of the planet—and for the first
half of the twentieth century, Dispensationalism mostly puttered along
in the background of American Christianity, slowly gaining a foothold
primarily in the evangelical hellfire-and-brimstone market, but with little
interest shown anywhere else. It is an understatement to say that when
Israel was founded in 1948, in North America Dispensationalism and

Christian Zionism went mainstream: according to a 2006 Zogby poll, over one-third of Americans currently "believe" in Christian Zionism. With its compelling storyline—that a clock had begun counting down towards the return of Jesus—this perspective gained instant credibility in explaining why Christians should care a great deal about events in the Middle East, and their doomsday clock has been ticking steadily louder ever since.

Even after 1948, neither Dispensationalism nor Christian Zionism became immediately racist or Islamophobic, but the seeds were sown. Regardless of how they got there or what they did to stay, the presence of Jews in the Holy Land was defined as Good in an absolute sense by members of both groups, and those who opposed it—no matter their reasons or the righteousness of their claims—were just as absolutely defined as Bad. To make matters worse, the Scofield Bible was, inexplicably, revised by the Oxford Press as well: while early editions had noted that Allah was the Arabic Christian name for God and that Abraham's natural posterity should include the people of Israel *and* Ishmael, both those comments have been absent from all editions since 1967. Soon, as dispensationalist exegesis came to disinherit the progeny of Ishmael, so too did the Christian Zionists, eventually adding the destruction of Islam's Holy sites in Jerusalem to the steps leading up to Jesus' Second Coming, and even at times supporting the racial cleansing of Israel—buoyed up by the preposterous and implicitly genocidal claim that there is no such thing as a "Palestinian"—as well. To make such a preposterous claim, one has to willfully ignore the fact that there have been non-Jewish Arab Muslims and Arab Christians living peacefully, lawfully, safely, and productively in what is now called Israel for over a thousand years.

However popular Christian Zionism has proved in North America, the reaction among Christians living elsewhere—and particularly in the Middle East—has been mixed at best: since few dispensationalists believe that peace can be attained without divine intervention because of Jesus' prediction of "wars and rumors of wars" in Matthew 24:6, and since they often view Middle Eastern peacemakers with profound suspicion because of Daniel 9:27's prediction that the Antichrist would be such a man, Middle Eastern peace is an issue that has come to profoundly divide the Christian world.

The Jerusalem Declaration of Middle Eastern Christian leaders made in August of 2006 presents a very different Christian point of view from that which most North American Christians are familiar:

THE JERUSALEM DECLARATION

"Blessed are the peacemakers for they shall be called the children of God." —Matthew 5:9

Christian Zionism is a modern theological and political movement that embraces the most extreme ideological positions of Zionism, thereby becoming detrimental to a just peace within Palestine and Israel. The Christian Zionist programme provides a worldview where the Gospel is identified with the ideology of empire, colonialism and militarism. In its extreme form, it places an emphasis on apocalyptic events leading to the end of history rather than living Christ's love and justice today.

We categorically reject Christian Zionist doctrines as false teaching that corrupts the biblical message of love, justice and reconciliation.

We further reject the contemporary alliance of Christian Zionist leaders and organizations with elements in the governments of Israel and the United States that are presently imposing their unilateral pre-emptive borders and domination over Palestine. This inevitably leads to unending cycles of violence that undermine the security of all peoples of the Middle East and the rest of the world.

We reject the teachings of Christian Zionism that facilitate and support these policies as they advance racial exclusivity and perpetual war rather than the gospel of universal love, redemption and reconciliation taught by Jesus Christ. Rather than condemn the world to the doom of Armageddon we call upon everyone to liberate themselves from the ideologies of militarism and occupation. Instead, let them pursue the healing of the nations!

We call upon Christians in Churches on every continent to pray for the Palestinian and Israeli people, both of whom are suffering as victims of occupation and militarism. These discriminative actions are turning Palestine into impoverished ghettos surrounded by exclusive Israeli settlements. The establishment of the illegal settlements and the construction of the Separation Wall on confiscated Palestinian land undermines the viability of a Palestinian state as well as peace and security in the entire region.

We call upon all Churches that remain silent, to break their silence and speak for reconciliation with justice in the Holy Land.

Therefore, we commit ourselves to the following principles as an alternative way:

We affirm that all people are created in the image of God. In turn they are called to honor the dignity of every human being and to respect their inalienable rights.

We affirm that Israelis and Palestinians are capable of living together within peace, justice and security.

We affirm that Palestinians are one people, both Muslim and Christian. We reject all attempts to subvert and fragment their unity.

We call upon all people to reject the narrow world view of Christian Zionism and other ideologies that privilege one people at the expense of others.

We are committed to non-violent resistance as the most effective means to end the illegal occupation in order to attain a just and lasting peace.

With urgency we warn that Christian Zionism and its alliances are justifying colonization, apartheid and empire-building.

God demands that justice be done. No enduring peace, security or reconciliation is possible without the foundation of justice. The demands of justice will not disappear. The struggle for justice must be pursued diligently and persistently but non-violently.

"What does the Lord require of you, to act justly, to love mercy, and to walk humbly with your God." —Micah 6:8

This is where we take our stand. We stand for justice. We can do no other. Justice alone guarantees a peace that will lead to reconciliation with a life of security and prosperity for all the peoples of our Land. By standing on the side of justice, we open ourselves to the work of peace—and working for peace makes us children of God.

"God was reconciling the world to himself in Christ, not counting men's sins against them. And he has committed to us the message of reconciliation."—2 Corinthians 5:19

His Beatitude Patriarch Michel Sabbah—Latin Patriarchate, Jerusalem

Archbishop Swerios Malki Mourad—Syrian Orthodox Patriarchate, Jerusalem

Bishop Riah Abu El-Assal—Episcopal Church of Jerusalem and the Middle East

Bishop Munib Younan—Evangelical Lutheran Church in Jordan and the Holy Land

No matter how confused the issues surrounding Israel and Palestine have become, some things have remained very clear: one is that each side thinks it is behaving in a manner that is rational and correct, and another is that every one of our faiths gives succor to belligerent leaders whose expectations exclude any hope for the happy and willing participation of those who aren't their followers. In reply, I think we all know that Jesus, Muhammad, and Moses—and for that matter the Buddha and the Dalai Lama—would all agree that for it to be real, peace has to be shared. If believers honestly think God is smarter than we are, then wouldn't it make sense that when mixing religion with politics we agree to put religion first? The express purpose of each of our faiths is to help us individually do what God wants us to do, all acknowledging that His plan—which we may or may not properly perceive—is superior to any we can develop ourselves. Since the express purpose of politics is to find ways to manipulate other people to do what *we* want, it just doesn't seem a good idea to do it the other way around.

When faith begins, everyone believes their religion is going to help them be good. Inevitably, when leaders subvert that faith and use their religious platforms to manipulate followers for their own purposes, everyone suffers. The situation becomes even worse when those leaders try to manipulate or misrepresent another group's religious teachings for their own aggrandizement, because they then subvert more than just their own: when Jerry Falwell said that Muhammad was a terrorist, as he did on the CBS television program *60 Minutes*, or John Hagee declares that "those who live by the Quran have a scriptural mandate to kill Christians and Jews ... it teaches that very clearly," as he did on National Public Radio's *Fresh Air*, or when Benny Hinn spews, "This is not a war between Jews and Arabs, this is a war between God and the Devil," as he did on NBC's *Dateline*—they either stupidly and arrogantly, or else purposefully and dishonestly, confound their own followers, but they also lend their unwitting support to al Qaeda and every other terrorist organization striving to subvert the faith of credulous Muslims. When over a billion people believe Muhammad is the finest example of the best a believer can aspire to, it is profoundly counterproductive for Falwell, Hagee, and Hinn to claim he did the exact opposite of what he actually did do, particularly when it's also the opposite of what they say *they* want Muslims to do. It's hard not to conclude that instead of serving God and God's plan for peace as they claim, they have craved conflict and the power, influence, and consequent wealth it brings them—all along.

God has told us all repeatedly that he wants us to live in peace, and there is no question that for it to be true, peace *must* be shared. As a Muslim revert—God's servant David raised at the feet of dispensationalist preachers—I cannot help but see a consensus view, but I'm sure Falwell, Hagee, and Hinn have never even considered whether the present Palestinian experience *is* the apocalyptic suffering of God's people predicted in the Bible. This book began by demonstrating that a heritage of destructive self-righteousness is something Muslims, Christians, and Jews *all* share. I hope the second and third parts of the book make sufficiently clear both the inappropriateness of allowing current doctrinal differences between Christian and Islamic beliefs about Jesus to condemn either side, and how inappropriate is so much of the dogmatic development that Christianity and Islam have undergone. Finally, I fervently hope this portion adequately proves that there is a pathway to peace that can be found in *all* our prophetic guidance. Conflict is not the God-ordained step towards Christ's Second Coming, or a reborn Israel, or a righteously Islamic world that so many of us have come to believe: not when that belief causes believers to do so much evil themselves. I read Revelation 14's description of Israel as a woman held up by the moon crowned with twelve stars, and I see this image proclaiming Israel and Islam separate but working together. Wouldn't that be better than what we have there today?

One state or two, shared, divided, or segregated, it is not my purpose to kibitz for any particular solution to the ongoing nationalist struggles between Jews and Palestinians; but I will speak to the methods many are using to seek their own resolution. Although the religion of Judaism does not require that an individual claim a personal relationship with God, the

Hassidic philosopher Martin Buber was speaking profoundly from his faith when he pointed out that our lives are a series of interactive dialogues, and that considering one's existence similarly is the only way in which one can properly interact with God as well. With an insight at ease with the Bhagavad Gita's doctrine of detachment and the Buddha's Four Noble Truths as well as the overwhelming submission to God shown by both Jesus and Muhammad, Buber pointed out that any attempts to control the content or outcome of a dialogue transform that relationship's partner into a mere object and put an end to the holistic nature each dialogue contained when it began.

Christianity and Islam both proclaim that individual Creator-Created relationship as their ultimate goal, and all three faiths proclaim that every person on earth shares the potential for a positive and ongoing relationship with God. Assuming that to be true, does it not follow that our faith is best used to guide believers personally and individually to make good choices rather than to guide or coerce others to fulfill our own political conceptions of the way things should be? There are only two reasons to follow any religion: either to use your faith to remake yourself into something better for everything, or to use the faith of others to remake everything into something that is better for you. *All* of us who choose one of those two paths are on the same side as the rest who make the same choice, no matter what their religion. Religion informed by politics, particularly racially charged politics, leads to one confrontational set of decisions, but politics informed by faith—in honest submission to the God who made us all different for reasons of His own—leads to a decidedly different path than the one so many of us are currently on.

I call that path Islamic Zionism. The fact that it sounds like an oxymoron is itself proof of how far we have strayed, because in a very limited sense, it simply means submitting to what each of our religions has actually told us regarding the eventual and appropriate demographic makeup of Israel/Zion, without imposing racist or chauvinist interpretations to arrive at a distorted understanding of what God "really" meant. In a slightly broader interpretation—with Zion, the Holy City of God, serving as a symbol of God's ultimate cosmopolitan purpose—it means everyone doing the good things that all our religions tell us to do while avoiding excuses to do the bad they all condemn, ultimately trusting God to ensure the outcomes He has promised us will all come to pass. In a truly universal sense Islamic Zionism is an allegory for faith itself, because each of our founders originally told us the very same thing while they were here, espousing slightly different versions of the same Golden Rule: that none of us truly have faith until we crave for others that which we crave for ourselves. In the Middle East, that means Jews and Muslims wanting the *other* side to live in peace, and Christians craving a happy ending for more than just themselves.

Islamic Zionism: wouldn't *that* be a better testament to the grace, glory and goodness of God?

- **Up until a little more than eighty years ago, Muslims, Christians, and Jews lived together pretty well in the Holy Land.**

- **Since then, racism and nationalist politics have had more influence on Jews, Christians, and Muslims than *any* of us should be comfortable with.**

- **If *we* made politics, and believe *God* made us, shouldn't faith guide our politics instead of the other way around?**

The Torah told me:

God wants us to learn to get along.

Our religions are all trying to tell us how.

PART V

FAITH:
THE SOLUTION

CHAPTER 23

....

FAITH ON THE
OPEN MARKET

The gulf between our three creeds' commandments and what we their followers are actually doing obviously begs the question: how did we manage to get so far off track in the first place? Despite providing clear guidance and excellent examples, it seems each of our religions serves to illustrate a different way that we can arrive at the same sad place, opposite to where we're supposed to be. When I first started writing what finally ended up as this book more than ten years ago—before things *really* began to unravel—I built it around my own personal struggle to find God's path to peace in Christianity, what I learned when studying the Quran and the Bible together, and why I came to the conclusion that Islam is presently the better guide to following Jesus and Muhammad into the service of God. However, as our world's situation has worsened—and it's become obvious seekers can lose their way on any path—the book has grown, and now I hope it's become more about the importance of walking with your eyes wide open wherever you are.

My first book, *Choosing Faith,* ended up being popular in the Muslim community as an evangelical tool and became paradoxically popular as a Bible study guide for a few courageous Christians. However, it also provoked arguments and even some scuffling between Campus-Crusade-for-Christ types and their Muslim Student Association counterparts. When I heard about their fights I realized that I hadn't succeeded in writing the book I'd wanted to. It was supposed to bring people together and help them realize how much they had in common. It was supposed to be about the importance of fidelity. I'm certainly not the first person to share the brilliant realization that Christians aren't doing what Christ said they should, but I didn't mean it to sound like a criticism of individual Christians: my intent was to point out exactly where what Christianity taught had been manipulated into a different message than Jesus intended. Instead of blaming him or his followers, I faulted Christianity's vast and confusing body of texts and interpretations—some of which even seem designed to obfuscate matters—and so I did what was primarily a textual criticism. I assumed that way I'd manage to avoid offending individual Christians, but it didn't work out quite as I expected.

Faced with unexpected controversy, I tracked down some of the angriest Christians I could find and learned they all had one complaint in common. They weren't upset about the fact that I had done a textual criticism; they didn't even question whether I had done a good job of it. Their problem was that I hadn't done the same with Islam. They said that it wasn't fair! At first I dismissed their comments, because there's really no basis for a *textual* criticism of Islam. Muslims have literally only one version of the Quran, and its internal content checks are quite unassailable—among other things, I think that the base-19 calculations are probably true. But when I thought a little longer about what they had said, I realized that they had a point. I couldn't really rebut their observation that individual Muslims weren't any better than individual Christians. Since both religions bill themselves as exemplary guidebooks to peace with God and creation, and since their followers seemed equally likely to go astray regardless, the unavoidable conclusion was that a lot of Muslims weren't doing what the Quran told them to do either. With that stipulated, I realized I hadn't actually gotten to the heart of the problem at all and needed to try again. Also, I think the last ten years of world history have given us ample proof that any book attempting to deal with the conflicts between Muslims, Islam, Christianity and Christians has to include Jews and Judaism too.

In this book, instead of doing a textual criticism of only Christianity I've managed to do one that includes Judaism and Islam—despite the invariability of their base texts—because the *text* of any religion isn't really made up of its literal prophetic revelations anyway. Believers all have to follow what they think that revelation means to them. Even if you speak the language, someone still has to translate that message in a fashion that makes sense to you in your life today. In every religion, that shared understanding of God's intent has been generated through an ongoing process of debate and consensus, with waves of change radiating out from points of doctrinal conflict and uncertainty that are of necessity exquisitely responsive to the religious realities on the ground. When it looks like some point of dogma isn't sustainable in a particular situation—for example, religious injunctions against murder faced with potential genocide at the hands of a numerically superior force—sometimes the dogma doesn't survive.

Given human diversity, the variety of experiences we encounter, the individual way we experience God, and the common assumption that God experiences us as individuals as well, why *do* we care so much about the way other believers interpret God's commands? We rarely disagree about the importance of those commands or—within our own faith groups at least—about Whom they came from. However, it's obvious that prioritizing and interpreting those instructions in our individual lives requires some wiggle room: honestly, when you look at all the changes that all our religions have gone through in the last thousand years, it's surprising we manage to find any consensus within them at all, let alone between them. None of our founders placed much emphasis on using anything but the most basic religious beliefs as criteria for membership, yet exclusivity based on dogmatic agreement has become vitally important to many of us all the same.

I prefaced this book with the observations that everyone believes something, and that even those of us who don't believe *in* anything at all outside ourselves still believe that we're right. Frankly, that's inevitable: why would anyone belong to a religion that they thought was false? Doctrinal "drift" seems inevitable as well. In this book I've given quite a few examples of how the process of change has affected the revelations of Islam, Christianity, and Judaism, because I'm trying to deal with the problem it creates in the context of what I think is the greatest conflict facing our world today, but the differences between all our diverse members actually make a surprising amount of sense when you know the history behind them. I've focused on Islam, Christianity, and Judaism for myriad reasons, but they are really only the most current examples of a flaw that's plagued our religions for as long as we've had them. At their core, virtually every one has always said the same things: that compared to our Creator we're more alike than we are different, and that living, learning, and trying to become better people makes us all better for everyone—including that Creator—to have around. How can such inclusive messages of hope become so divisive and make us do so much harm?

Religions can seem so very powerful. They've been around for longer than recorded history, and the influence they've had throughout that history is unquestionable: they've left behind more artifacts, temples, codes, stones, books, scrolls, and schools than anything else, and they've left their mark on everything. Big as they are, it's easy to believe that we're powerless by comparison. It's hard to remember—even though it's something that most are quite explicit about—that they are made up of people driven by the same things: we all just want to be happy, and most of us want a place to belong. In fact, when you think about it, religions are even like individual people in a lot of ways. They're almost alive! They consume things (like time, energy, and people), they create (sometimes), and they generate waste. They're born out of us from seeds we believe were planted by God, and they grow much like we and our families do—once a community of faith attains a certain size and complexity, new ones spring up around it, slightly different, but always retaining a identity-defining attachment to the source from which they came.

Whenever a new one starts off, the process is quite simple. Religions inevitably have to begin with a person and his or her message. Whether or not you're a believer, it's obvious that there must be something about what that first believer says or does—something unique in how his or her message is presented—that makes it seem more attractive than the alternatives. If that weren't so, the person wouldn't be able to attract any followers. People choose to follow a prophet when they decide that God has chosen the person first, but successful religions aren't a cult of personality: those only last as long as their leader does. It's not actually the prophets themselves that matter even when they're alive; if it were, few of us would expect that their specialness could be disseminated to the rest. The real seed is the message, which first attracts a prophet's followers, who then become believers, led and taught by the prophet who delivered the messages in the first place. Inevitably, from the moment they're born, religions have a structure: the message of the prophet, giving a body of shared beliefs, and practices following from what that prophet did. They also start with a hierarchy, which creates an industry dedicated to its maintenance. Finally, there's suddenly a ready-made community for everyone to belong to, all of them dedicated to the same initial common purpose: learning to please God.

Religions mature quite quickly. The newly born religious community starts off unified because all the people are there for the same reason: they believe that their prophet can help them improve their relationship with

God. The group is cohesive because the purpose, practices, and structure of the community are apparent and accepted by everyone. The leadership is obvious: the prophet is right there! The beliefs are those of the prophet, and the entire community already believes that they're on the right track: that's why they joined in the first place. However, other matters often become more important as religions age, spread, and grow. While they may not be the reasons people joined, a religion's community, industry, and hierarchy are frequently the reasons why they stay. We like communities; they give us all a place to be and surround us with people who—often—agree with us. We like hierarchies; they make us feel safe by defining our place and give some of us a path to promotion. We appreciate the industry of religion because, frankly, it often gives believers a job. The more religions grow, the more of those benefits they have to offer, and that's great up to a point. The problem is, those communities with their hierarchies and industries live and grow alongside our faiths—serving as vehicles for the message after the prophet is gone—but then just like that prophet, they eventually fade and die: sooner or later every one of them always has.

Most believers pretend great confidence it won't ever happen to theirs, but our faith communities all share that same existential anxiety, made more menacing by the simple fact that when one dies everybody suffers, and those most dependent suffer the worst of all. To further complicate matters, how to deal with that potential demise isn't an area where most religions give much guidance, perhaps because prophets don't have to worry about community longevity. Communities literally create themselves around them; prophets belong because everyone else joins them! The rest of us aren't quite so lucky.

As members of any religion, we have an immediate, powerful vested interest in our own community doing well, surviving, and growing that is directly proportionate to our level of participation. Why some succeed and others fail is open to debate; almost everyone who belongs to one assumes that his or her religion has God on its side. However, as soon as you have more than one religion being openly practiced in the same place it becomes obvious that what's going on is actually a popularity contest. Religious competition wasn't a problem when we were all more isolated from each other. It became a problem only when we stopped living in small, isolated groups and started interacting more. Since then, the natural tendency amongst believers has been to shop around, with that individual tendency being inversely related to their level of commitment. Some movement between religions is inevitable: given alternatives, people will always go for the choice that seems to be better for them, and *better* is a complex and very personal calculation. The trouble is, religious competition is a zero-sum game: when one group gains a member by anything but birth it means some other group has shrunk.

There's an old Sufi parable describing how different religions could actually live together quite well if we were more willing to accept the fact that most of them are trying to do the same thing in different ways, and more willing to trust God to work it all out in the end. If you picture all of humanity as standing around in a great circle, with God in the center above us, then the middle of the circle is where we're closest to everyone, God included. Sufis believe that God created us all with a yearning to seek that closeness; in doing so, we inevitably draw close to each other, despite the fact that we may be headed in what seem to be opposite directions, depending on where we start from. Eventually, according to Sufis, with God's help we all end up in exactly the same place; different religions just come in from different directions.

I like Sufis, but you have to admit that their perspective doesn't lend itself very well to religious marketing. Furthermore, the industrial and hierarchical aspects of our faith communities can't possibly benefit from believers coming together. There's a reason that the most divisive and unpleasant comments come from those of us who have the most to gain from our differences in terms of personal power, wealth, and influence, whether they're mullahs, preachers, rabbis, presidents, popes, prime ministers, kings, or dictators. Whenever a religion becomes a source of income or power, it becomes a business. When that happens, religion immediately stops being about helping us to control ourselves and becomes about them controlling as many of us as possible—maximizing market share. The members to whom market share matters the most are those who have the most to lose if others leave, but the members most likely to leave are actually those to whom it matters the least. Tragically, that means that among those involved in any religion's leadership, instead of being defined by the message that started it off, their own religion immediately begins to be defined by membership size and their own influence over it, and the extent to which they can turn independent believers into followers who perceive themselves to be different from everyone else.

Faced with those pressures, any religion is going to try and make itself as palatable as possible and make the rest look less so. But have any of you noticed how many claim their members are supposed to rule the world? Christopher Hitchens' *God Is Not Great* does an exemplary job recounting the history of that particular conceit: it's an obviously potent growth strategy, and an excellent advertising ploy to boot, but it would be easier to believe if the prediction were not precisely as common as its failure to come true—at least so far. Most call the belief "manifest destiny" and claim it for their own group alone, and yet manifest destiny is an explanation, philosophy, or phenomenon that has been consecutively associated with Israel, Islam, the Royal Houses of Europe, the British Empire, and the United States for as long as they've been around. It's linked to the history of the Holy Grail, the caliphate, the Hidden Imam, the Knights Templar, and the idea that Jesus' blood runs in the veins of the ruling families of Europe and the United States. Some invoke it to claim that Jews have been conspiring to take control of the entire world; others use it to make the same charge against the Vatican. Lately al Qaeda has tried to claim it back for themselves. Conspiracies abound. According to some accounts, the British monarchs are descended from the lost tribes of Israel or the ancient rulers of Troy. According to others, the Masons have been manipulating world history behind the scenes to bring about a golden age of democracy for the last thousand years—unless you'd rather believe that we've all been conquered by the Bush family, acting for the Lizard Kings of Mars: I always thought George W. and Dick Cheney both looked a little reptilian. True or not, the theories all make for pretty entertaining reading.

Basically, manifest destiny is any explanation that says that a particular race or group of people have a God-given responsibility to rule over everybody else. The reason it's been associated with so many groups is that it's pretty much universal. I doubt that there's ever been a religious organization that has found itself in a position of authority whose members haven't assured themselves that God meant them to be there, and meant them to stay. Likewise, among those of us on the opposite end of the stick, there are probably few who haven't looked to some prophesied future in order to reassure ourselves that God has something better in store for us someday. Manifest destiny is a strange sort of construction. It sounds good if you're a member of the group that's "destined" because it gives a certain moral basis to that point of view. At the same time, if you're not one of the chosen, it's an insult that can be used to impugn the moral authority of the same group from the outside. In my experience, exhortations based on it have rarely been used to encourage anything that turns out to be a good idea, but invoking it always seems to make a course of action a lot easier to sell. Above all, it makes an excellent sales pitch for a religion, particularly when times are good. Unfortunately, it also makes for hard feelings and worse when those times turn bad.

Europe and North America have been Christian for a long time, and they've enjoyed around five hundred years' worth of political and economic dominance. That period has also seen the development of modern representational democracy and capitalism. It's not surprising that all these phenomena have become associated with each other. In the 1800s, the United States found itself endowed with vast reserves of industry, energy, and people, as well as a bunch of territory to the west inhabited by Native Americans and administered by Mexico and Spain. U.S. leaders wanted to spread out and needed to sell the expansion to everyone else. They took the idea of manifest destiny and gave it an American flavor by linking its religious impetus with the ideals of freedom, democracy, and commerce. They did such a good job that the concept has pretty much resided in America ever since. That's primarily how success, wealth, power, and world domination actually got so bound up with the Gospel of Jesus in the first place.

Since then, the leaders of the First World have had gradually increasing success using manifest destiny to explain to their citizens why they should defend their wealth, despite what Jesus said. However, that's become complicated by the simple fact that—as other countries' resources have been transplanted to Europe and America—people from other parts of the globe have inevitably moved in along with them, and that means there's been a gradual mixing of races and religions, with a dilution of the privilege that some had been claiming was a gift reserved by God solely for the members of their religions. According to Pope Benedict XVI (in an interview he gave to the French newspaper *Le Figaro* while he was still Cardinal Ratzinger), the growing strength of Islam in Europe threatens the West's historical purity. At the same time, the political and economic dominance (as well as the relative safety) of the First World has come under attack from the outside. For the first time in over a generation, war has been brought to the shores of the United States, a nation whose destiny is the destiny of Christianity—at least in the hearts and minds of its citizens.

In the United States, Christianity, democracy, and capitalism have become so inextricably linked that an attack on one or two becomes an attack on all three. To an outsider, the violence and bloodshed that were unleashed in return for the attack on the World Trade Center on September 11, 2001, may seem a little disproportionate. Two entire countries were laid to waste, with their civilizations pushed back into the Stone Age, and tens of thousands of entirely innocent children, women, and men were killed. When George W. Bush called for his great crusade, the only reason that it didn't sound unreasonable to many Americans was because they knew that they were doing more than just protecting themselves. Most of them have been taught that they have a God-given responsibility to lead the rest of the world from the day they're born. That means they were really fighting for the rest of us, too. By everything they believe is true about God, themselves, and everyone else, it's supposed to be their destiny.

Muslims know what it's like to lose our place in the world because we once had a manifest destiny, too. To the Muslim mind, the centuries following the revelation of the Quran to Muhammad were a golden time. We saw our empire grow, and with it our economic, religious, and political influence. It was actually a pretty good time in the history of the world, and it's worth noting that Muslims, Christians, and Jews lived together in relative harmony. Our time in the sun came to a crashing end in 1492 when we lost the Andalusia region in Spain to Christian kings of the north and the Spanish Inquisition (is it really just a coincidence that that's about the same time we stopped even trying to make Ijtihad   Muslims trying their individual hardest to do what they believe is best—work?), and we started to lose the rest of the empire. We've been in retreat ever since. Just like most Americans, most Muslims are raised believing that's not the way it's supposed to be. We know that God will eventually return things to their proper order. Until then, some of us assume that we're supposed to try to make it so ourselves! Our own once and future manifest destiny is the main unspoken justification for Islamic terrorism. It's simple: we're supposed to be in charge, and anyone who says otherwise is automatically an enemy of both Islam and God, fit only to be destroyed.

Judaism (both the people and the religion) has taken a lot of heat for manifest destiny through the years, and some people even claim that Jews invented it. That's not true; what manifest destiny says about "us," God, and "everyone else" has likely been the same everywhere since the dawn of the self-serving rationalization. However, Jews may deserve at least some of the blame for introducing the basic logical contradiction that's made the idea so dangerous. Although the idea that they possess a "manifest destiny" is something most peoples seem to have believed at one time or another, for much of history they've generally done so in a relatively passive way. People in power have used it to explain why they are where they are, and their slaves and servants have used it to explain why things won't stay that way forever. Only a fraction of us have actually taken our manifest destiny as a justification for *creating* that destiny for ourselves; for the most part we've left the actual manifesting up to God. Jews were among the first to develop a theologically logical way to justify personally looking after such matters themselves in their "Creative" phase, but since then the rest of us have picked it up pretty well. Our mistake should be obvious. If our destiny really is being shepherded by God, the Omniscient, Omnipotent, and Omnipresent Creator of the universe, why do we need to do anything—particularly break the rules He gave us—to put ourselves where He wants us to be?

Muslims, Christians, and Jews have so much in common. We all believe that God is everywhere, sees everything, and can do anything. We all claim that God is on our side. Despite that, our histories are full of stories of manipulation and conspiracy, recording the injuries unjustly visited upon us by our enemy of choice, juxtaposed with stories of our own glorious battles, pogroms, purges, and bloodbaths. We all hear—lately, it seems, almost on a daily basis—explanations from every side that all say basically the same thing: "It's the other guys' fault," and, "We really are better than them." If our side does something wrong, it's "regrettable" but obviously the work of elements that don't represent our own superior values, or else it's someone else's contrivance, part of a conspiracy to make us look bad. However, if someone else from another group does something wrong, that's all the proof of our own superiority we need! In the end, "they" are always the ones who start it, or else we only did it because we knew they were just about to. No matter how abhorrent our group's actions against another, "we're" always doing it for "their" own good, or else for the good of the ones who are more like "us." No matter our background or pedigree, we are all sure that, when it's all over and we're finally in control, everyone will be better off. It must be reassuring to know you're always on the side of the good guys.

One conclusion you can draw from the way all of us behave is that nobody ever wants to think that they're bad, and another is that our religious and political leaders have always tended to agree we're wonderful no matter what we're doing, as long as it works for them. Whatever the objective reality, independent of the judgment of history, in times of conflict, every one of our clans, tribes, states, and countries has characterized itself as right and its opponents as wrong, and wherever possible used religion to do so. And that's given believers permission to do things that we know we really shouldn't do. The more passionate the disagreement, the more extreme the rhetoric: my way becomes "right" and gradually morphs into "absolutely good" and approved by God Most High, while the other side's "wrong" becomes "absolute evil." Every time it's happened, our sanctification and our opponent's demonization has been justified by our beliefs and our religions, while our unquestionable right to believe what we want has been the most basic belief of them all. It's an excellent growth strategy, and the only problem I can find with the process is that it is the *absolute opposite* of what Moses, Jesus, and Muhammad tried to do while they were here.

Arrogant exclusivity was *never* part of *any* of our revelations when they began. Moses' last sermon to the Israelites made explicit the fact that God's Covenant included alien non-Jews, in Deuteronomy 28:1–15[emphasis added]:

> These are the terms of the covenant the LORD commanded Moses to make with the Israelites in Moab, in addition to the covenant he had made with them at Horeb. Moses summoned all the Israelites and said to them: Your eyes have seen all that the LORD did in Egypt to Pharaoh, to all his officials and to all his land. With your own eyes you saw those great trials, those miraculous signs and great wonders. But to this day the LORD has not given you a mind that understands or eyes that see or ears that hear. During the forty years that I led you through the desert, your clothes did not wear out, nor did the sandals on your feet. You ate no bread and drank no wine or other fermented drink. I did this so that you might know that I am the LORD your God. When you reached this place, Sihon king of Heshbon and Og king of Bashan came out to fight against us, but we defeated them. We took their land and gave it as an inheritance to the Reubenites, the Gadites and the half-tribe of Manasseh. Carefully follow the terms of this covenant, so that you may prosper in everything you do. **All of you are standing today in the presence of the LORD your God—your leaders and chief men, your elders and officials, and all the other men of Israel, together with**

> your children and your wives, and the aliens living in your
> camps who chop your wood and carry your water. You are
> standing here in order to enter into a covenant with the
> LORD your God, a covenant the LORD is making with you
> this day and sealing with an oath, to confirm you this day
> as his people, that he may be your God as he promised you
> and as he swore to your fathers, Abraham, Isaac and Jacob.
> I am making this covenant, with its oath, not only with you
> who are standing here with us today in the presence of the
> LORD our God but also with those who are not here today.

I know many of my Muslim brothers and sisters are going to be offended by the phrase "who chop your wood and carry your water," but the Torah *is* an Israeli text, and the verse doesn't say that's the only reason for the aliens to be there. Throughout Israel's history Judaism's prophets have done their best to remind Jews to remain inclusive: the abominably inappropriate nature and consequences of the Talmudic decision to change the word *Ger* to exclude non-Jews is one I've dealt with in other chapters, but Deuteronomy further confirms the inclusive intent of Moses too.

Jesus' Sermon on the Mount, the parable of the Good Samaritan, and his passing comment that he had other sheep elsewhere proclaim his inclusive intent as well. That and the high standard he set for his own followers are both confirmed in Matthew 5:43–48.

> You have heard that it was said, "Love your neighbor and hate
> your enemy." But I tell you, love your enemies and pray for
> those who persecute you, that you may be children of your
> Father in heaven. He causes his sun to rise on the evil and the
> good, and sends rain on the righteous and the unrighteous.
> If you love those who love you, what reward will you get?
> Are not even the tax collectors doing that? And if you greet
> only your own people, what are you doing more than others?
> Do not even pagans do that? Be perfect, therefore, as your
> heavenly Father is perfect.

Finally, although the idea of Islam's supremacy seems as much an ingrained part of our religion as any other today, that's not how we began either. Al-Maeda 5:3 tells us:

"Today I have perfected your religion and completed my favour upon you, and I was satisfied that Islam be your religion."

But though the common interpretation is that Allah was declaring Islam's superiority, that's just another example of an occasion where most Muslims are ignorant of the history of an important verse. According to Caliph Umar, it was revealed on the Day of Arafah, during Muhammad's farewell Hajj, at which he delivered his final sermon declaring:

> O People! Listen to my words, for I do not know whether we shall ever meet again and perform Hajj after this year. O Ye people! Allah says, O people We created you from one male and one female and made you into tribes and nations, so as to be known to one another. Verily in the sight of Allah, the most honoured amongst you is the one who is most God-fearing. There is no superiority for an Arab over a non-Arab and for a non-Arab over an Arab, nor for the white over the black nor for the black over the white except in God-consciousness.
>
> All mankind is the progeny of Adam and Adam was fashioned out of clay. Behold; every claim of privilege, whether that of blood or property, is under my heels except that of the custody of the Ka'bah and supplying of water to the pilgrims, O people of Quraish, don't appear (on the Day of Judgment) with the burden of this world around your necks, whereas other people may appear (before the Lord) with the rewards of the hereafter. In that case I shall avail you naught against Allah.

The day Muhammad's Islam was declared "perfected" by God was the day he proclaimed the equality of men and women regardless of race, creed, or gender. In fact, since Muslim dating began with the Hegira when Muhammad moved from Mecca to Medina—because they had all asked him to come and show them how to live diversely together in peace—the founding act of Islam was to create a functioning, multicultural, and multi-religious society. Personally, I think that was the "completion" that Islam brought to the Prophetic tradition. When the people of Medina made Muhammad their Head of State, he created a constitution confirming the freedom and equality of all Medina's citizens regardless of race, creed, or gender, and that was the practice under the first caliphs of Islam as well. There was no intent on the part of any of our founders to impose Islam on the rest of the world: Despite all the attention paid to the penalties suffered by three Jewish tribes—the Banu Nadir, Banu Qurayza, and Banu Qaynuqa— for their acts of treason, there were seventeen other Jewish tribes who lived under Islamic rule in Medina as Jews in peace. When Muslims took control of Jerusalem, Caliph Umar walked up to the gates alone and accepted the terms the people of Jerusalem were willing to live under without caveat, because they confirmed freedom of speech, assembly, and religion, and the equality of all under God and under the law there as well. Perhaps the best proof of Islam's multicultural beginnings is that as it spread and brought the Banu Nadir and Banu Qaynuqa under Muslim rule once again, those Jewish tribes took the opportunity to become fully integrated participants in the longest lasting and most successful multicultural and multireligious society the world has known so far.

It makes perfect sense to claim you're good and everyone else is bad when you're marketing your religion—at least from the perspective of the people doing the labeling—but what happens when you turn it around? Has anybody ever admitted that they went to war because of greed before it was too late to do anything about it? Does anybody ever think they're evil? Did Adolf Hitler—arguably the most evil man in the history of humankind— think he was bad? Did his mother? Did Charles Manson think he killed too many people? Lenin? Mao Tse-tung? The indisputable truth has to be that everybody can't be right, and our wars can't be good-versus-evil if neither side thinks they're the bad guys. That sort of objectivity is a place where our religions could offer some help, but only if they were willing to tell us things we didn't want to hear. That doesn't seem to be what religions do anymore. It wouldn't be good marketing.

The sad truth that all the Children of Abraham might do well to face is that none of our religions are functioning the way they're supposed to. Instead of helping us individually become better people today than we were the day before, we've turned them into advertising tools more suited to the manipulation of mobs. I think every believer—no matter his or her background—could agree that our founders would have had done just fine living in a multicultural world, if only because instead of arguing over who was better they would have worked for the benefit of all and let their actions speak for themselves. Every one of them was focused on the product they delivered—a path to peace, self-improvement, and service to God and God's creation—rather than market share. It is only our own anxious self-interest and willful misrepresentation of their intent that has unmade so much of the good work our Prophets tried to do. Despite our current practice, their intent was solely that we should better see our own faults in order to improve ourselves rather than study the failings and weaknesses of others in order to augment our hegemony.

Believers have made a mess of the world, no question; but it doesn't have to stay that way. The best thing about owning your mistakes is that it means you can actually do something to rectify them. Becoming wealthy, comfortable, and powerful might not have been the best thing that could have happened to Christianity—Jesus' warning about the dangers of Mammon certainly makes sense looking back from this end of history— but at least they're in a good position to change things. I know that Jesus would have recommended showing everyone else more kindness, patience, generosity, forgiveness, and love. Likewise, although there isn't a lot of reason for Muslims to be proud of what we've done to the religion of Islam, the Quran is actually quite encouraging about what simple changes are necessary to make it what it once was. Once we remember how to love each other—and everyone else—the way the first Muslims did in the beginning of Muhammad's Islam, we might be more pleasant to have around. Last, it seems that neither the people nor the religion of Judaism are quite ready to bring about God's Tzedakah Israel based on justice, kindness, and brotherhood just yet. It is encouraging, however, that all three of our religions confirm that they will choose to live the way of the Lord eventually. Personally, I hope that they decide to do it soon.

- **Religions are supposed to tell us what we need to know, not what we want to hear.**

- **We need to know how become what we are supposed to become, and how to do what we are supposed to do.**

- **We'd rather hear how to make people do what we want them to do instead.**

CHAPTER 24

....

BELIEF AS BRIBERY

It turns out that our religious business models are behind most of the other reasons we're not getting along too. Marketing faith to a multicultural world isn't an easy task, and might even be fundamentally impossible without subverting the entire reason for religion in the first place. Since they all offer basically the same thing at the same price—a better relationship with the Creator of the Universe in return for belonging to them and believing in what they say—how do you go about proving yours is better than the rest?

When there was only one faith to choose, the promise of heaven in return for our commitment—particularly when coupled with the threat of hellfire in return for noncompliance—probably seemed more compelling, but as more and more people have begun to realize that all faiths make the same promise in return for believing in so many different things, for many of us I know those inducements have started to ring hollow. I think many believers would also admit that at times, the absence of an immediate reward in return for pleasing Someone as purportedly powerful as the Creator of the Universe can be a tough pill to swallow.

However—at least for Islam, Judaism, and Christianity—faith is not really supposed to be about immediate rewards at all. Even though Jewish texts do profess that sufficient obedience will make one prosper, no prophet ever promised it would happen right away. Jesus' message was all about doing good things for others even if it made life worse for you, and Caliph Ali—Muhammad's son-in-law and one of his favorite people—once declared:

> "Islam in fear of hell is the Islam of a slave, and Islam in the hope of Heaven is that of a merchant. The best Islam is Islam for the sake of God's Glory alone."

While few of us are capable of that sort of altruistic commitment full-time, the ethical superiority of *doing* what's right for the *sake* of what's right is recognized by everyone, whether we're religious or not. However, how do you sell an ideal like altruism?

Thankfully it's often not necessary to do so. For those believers drawn to their religion by the promise of becoming better—infused with the faith that God will help them get there—it's even an uncomfortable idea to consider: those are the ones among us who might have a chance of measuring up to Caliph Ali's or Jesus' high standards. However, in the arena of competitive religion every soul is an asset worth fighting for, every gain is a victory, and every loss a defeat. Beyond the promise of future glory, which is a hard sell when all other religions make that claim too, the only way that our faiths can make themselves more marketable—to those less inclined to altruism and more interested in results right now—is by giving people something they want, right now.

Religions becoming more responsive to what their members desire may sound like a good idea, but it doesn't work out very well if the things we desire are the problem. Most of us will happily acknowledge that we're not as good as we wish we were, and most believers will admit that they hope their religion will help control their worst impulses. If those impulses end up controlling the religion instead, it can turn a religion on its head! Although the basic principle isn't a bad one—providing enough rewards in this life to keep us coming back is a wonderful idea—it only works if we want *good* things. Sadly, what some people want is often far from pretty, and when we manipulate our faiths to grant those desires, it's bad for everyone: religious self-abuse—I know that's an old Catholic code-phrase for masturbation—lies behind most of what we find abhorrent in each other's beliefs and behavior.

Currently, I think the most troubling example has to be gender discrimination in Islam. That's not to say that it isn't a problem in other faiths as well: squabbling between our sexes has been going on for about as long as we've had them, everyone's always trying to gain some sort of an advantage, and religion has often been one of the vehicles we've used. Frankly, the effort men have put into mangling our religions for the sake of our sex lives should embarrass everyone. It has plagued us all at different times and in different places, but there's little question that today the most obvious examples can be found within those who claim to be following Muhammad. The damage that those men have done to Islam, and what that in turn has done to the relationship between Muslim men and women and their image around the world, isn't one I think we'll ever be able to live down.

It's ironic, but the reason Muslim men have become such self-indulgent faith abusers might be that gender equality was a big part of Islam's original message. When and where Muhammad grew up, people didn't treat women very well. Fathers exposed female children on hillsides, claiming that it was a test to see whether God really wanted them to survive. Husbands beat their wives and generally treated women as property. Those few women who actually owned property often had to find a man to manage it for them and then try to find a way to manage the man: Khadijah, Muhammad's first and favorite wife, was such a woman, and the honorable way Muhammad fulfilled her trust was the reason she asked him to marry her in the first place. Those were dark and sexist times, and in response a significant portion of the Quran condemned those practices, clarifying that as far as God is concerned, despite our physical differences women and men start off equal in essence, to be differentiated by what we do, not by what we are.

Back then, no matter who they were or where they were from, women were generally assumed to be inferior creations, doomed to subservience and a secondary relationship to God. In direct contradiction of that status quo, Muhammad received Al-Ahzab 33:35 and Al-Mumtahina 60:12:

> For Muslim men and women, for believing men and women, for devout men and women, for true men and women, for men and women who are patient and constant, for men and women who humble themselves, for men and women who give in Charity, for men and women who fast (and deny themselves), for men and women who guard their chastity, and for men and women who engage much in Allah's praise, for them has Allah prepared forgiveness and great reward.

> O Prophet! When believing women come to thee to take the oath of fealty to thee, that they will not associate in worship any other thing whatever with Allah, that they will not steal, that they will not commit adultery (or fornication), that they will not kill their children, that they will not utter slander,

intentionally forging falsehood, and that they will not disobey thee in any just matter, then do thou receive their fealty, and pray to Allah for the forgiveness (of their sins): for Allah is Oft-Forgiving, Most Merciful.

That world-changing paradigm shift is commemorated in the name of the Surah itself: *Al-Mumtahina* means "She who is to be examined," an obvious reference to the fact that God was dealing with women directly. Muhammad even granted the status of Imam—the highest rank in the religion below *him*—to a woman named Um-Waraqah bint Abdullah, giving her the right to lead Muslim prayers for the men and women around her because of her knowledge and wisdom, and even providing her with a male *Mu-addin*, "a caller to prayer," to invite those within earshot to join them. Early Islamic jurists, including al-Mozin, Abu Thawr, and even al-Tabari, concluded that because of that precedent any sufficiently trained woman could lead mixed congregations, and although that opinion has become more controversial since then, the precedent remains.

Likewise, it was in direct contradiction to many men's assumption of women's inferiority in their personal relationships that Muhammad was given An-Nisa 4:19 and Al-Tawbah 9:71:

O ye who believe! Ye are forbidden to inherit women against their will. Nor should ye treat them with harshness, that ye may take away part of the dower ye have given them, except where they have been guilty of open lewdness; on the contrary live with them on a footing of kindness and equity. If ye take a dislike to them it may be that ye dislike a thing, and Allah brings about through it a great deal of good.

The believing men and women are associates and helpers of each other. They (collaborate) to promote all that is beneficial and discourage all that is evil; to establish prayers and give alms, and to obey Allah and his Messenger. Those are the people whom Allah would grant mercy. Indeed Allah is Mighty and Wise.

And it was specifically to protect women from being treated like chattel in their marriages that Muhammad proclaimed:

A matron should not be given in marriage except after consulting her; and a virgin should not be given in marriage except after her permission. (Bukhari Volume 7, Book 62, Number 67)

Consequently, Bukhari further recorded that when Khansa bint Khidam al-Ansariya's father gave her in marriage to a man she didn't want, she went to Muhammad and he declared that her marriage was invalid because of it, at her request.

There is no question that gender roles were a major and contentious issue in the early Muslim community. One cause was the difference between the attitudes towards women in Mecca as compared to Medina. Another Hadith from Bukhari records that Caliph Umar recalled:

We, the people of Quraysh, used to have authority over women, but when we came to live with the Ansar, we noticed that the Ansari women had the upper hand over their men, so our women started acquiring the habits of the Ansari women. Once I shouted at my wife and she paid me back in my coin and I disliked that she should answer me back. She said, "Why do you take it ill that I retort upon you? By Allah, the wives of the Prophet retort upon him, and some of them may not speak with him for the whole day till night." (Bukhari Volume 3, Book 43, Number 648)

Although that story is frequently touted as proof that Umar was sexist, the truth is that although he started off that way he learned from Muhammad's example and became a better man for it. When Umar became caliph, al-Jauzi recalled:

Umar forbade the people from paying excessive dowries and addressed them saying: "Don't fix the dowries for women over forty ounces. If ever that is exceeded I shall deposit the excess amount in the public treasury." As he descended from the pulpit, a flat-nosed lady stood up from among the women in audience, and said: "It is not within your right." Umar asked: "Why should this not be of my right?" she replied: "Because Allah has proclaimed: 'even if you had given one of them (wives) a whole treasure for dowry take not the least bit back. Would you take it by false claim and a manifest sin'" (Al-Nisa 20). When he heard this, Umar said: "The woman is right and the man (Umar) is wrong. It seems that all people have deeper insight and wisdom than Umar." Then he returned to the pulpit and declared: "O people, I had restricted the giving of more than four hundred dirhams in dowry. Whosoever of you wishes to give in dowry as much as he likes and finds satisfaction in so doing may do so."

So, however much Umar didn't like it when his wife put him in his place, and regardless of his earlier inclinations—he had even beaten his sister when she became Muslim before he did—when he was put in charge of the entire Islamic empire and an old woman called him out, he backed down and told everyone that he was the one who was wrong. Islam's perspective of gender equality under God changed even him! For a long time, that perspective gave us a better world for everyone, but it obviously wouldn't have been very popular among people who preferred things the way they were. Tragically, over time their jaundiced point of view has crept back into the way Muslims practice our Islam.

Although women are second-class citizens in many Muslim countries today, it is despite Islam, not because of it. Popular masculine reinterpretation of the Quran has happened time and time again over the last thousand years, particularly regarding Ayat about women. One of modern Islam's leading scholars, Dr. Hassan al-Turabi, opened and closed his seminal work, *On the Position of Women in Islam and in Islamic Society,* with the observations:

> Muslims who advance conservative views on female affairs are normally very literal in their understanding of texts; but they tendentiously opt for an understanding that suits their prejudice.

> Islamists are worthy of the leadership of the movement of women's liberation from the traditional quagmire of historical Islam, and that of their resurgence towards the heights of ideal Islam. They should not leave their society at the mercy of the advocates of westernization who exploit the urgency of reform to deform society and lead it astray. The teachings of their own

religion call upon Islamists to be the right-guided leaders for
the salvation of men and women, emancipating them from
the shackles of history and convention, and steering their life
clear of the aberrations of mutative change.

However, in many places around the world, Quranic Ayat recommending
that women cover themselves in public to protect them from harassment
are still presented as if to say women *should* be harassed if they show
themselves, and others that recommended the Prophet Muhammad's wives
be treated differently to set them apart now require women to be virtually
cloistered so that they'll all be treated the same. Today, many Muslim men
think that Islam requires we oppress women, and a disgustingly large
proportion of our most popular and influential Imams and mullahs seem
quite happy to agree. How did it happen?

Here's the problem with using consensus—scholarly or otherwise—as
an interpretive religious guide. A million people can't make two and two
equal five, but they can almost convince themselves it does regardless, if
they say it loud and often enough. With sufficient motivation, mobs can
convince themselves of just about anything, even to the point of believing
a religion says the opposite of what it does say. There is no better example
of what I'm talking about than sex. Men have *always* struggled with the
urge to control women. There is no question that those of us whose faith
helps us control that impulse sometimes lose out in the short run, even if
we gain something more important in the end. However, religious leaders
who find ways to use religion as a means to having your cake and eating it
too—or in this case possessing the purported right to abuse one's wife and
still keep God happy—have never been short of followers. Inevitably with
those followers has come more power and wealth for those leaders willing
to pander. It's a self-sustaining circle: there have always been leaders willing
to lead us where we want to go and scholars willing to teach us what we
want to hear because that's what we've paid them to do.

The tactics are laughably transparent: if you want a book to say
something it doesn't, try and read between the lines. Over the centuries,
Muslim men have become masters of the craft. For example, in some
business transactions the code of Islamic law called Shariah recommends
that two witnesses participate, and, in the event that a man and a woman
end up sharing the responsibility, that another woman should participate
as well because of Al-Baqara 2:282, the "verse of debt":

> And call upon two of your men to act as witnesses; and if
> two men are not available, then a man and two women from
> among such as are acceptable to you as witnesses, so that if one
> of them should make a mistake, the other could remind her.

This Ayah has received a lot of attention over the years and a lot of people (Muslim and not) have traditionally interpreted it as if it implies that women aren't very reliable. That's not what it says at all. The second woman is there to prevent the *man* from taking unfair advantage of the situation and to ensure that if the primary witness requires assistance with her memory—a situation that arises among witnesses giving testimony even today—the authority remains in the hands of women regardless. For a true and scholarly interpretation, I don't think anyone can say it better than Dr. Taha Jaber al-Alwani, one time Chairman of the Fiqh Council of North America and President of the School of Islamic and Social Sciences in Herndon, Virginia.

> The objective is to end the traditional perception of women
> by including them "among such as are acceptable to you as
> witnesses," and to bring about their acceptance as full partners
> in society by means of this practical recognition. At the time
> of revelation, the question of numbers was irrelevant, as it was
> the equality of women that the Quran sought to emphasize.
> Even the matter of witnessing served merely as a means to
> an end or as a practical way of establishing the concept of
> gender equality ...
> Witnessing (shahadah) and legal authority (wilayah)
> are two totally separate matters. This point is one that was
> ignored by many jurists in their discussions of why a woman's
> testimony is equal to only half that of a man.
> To summarize, there is no difference between men and
> women in terms of their abilities, their propensity to forget,
> in the possibility of their colluding to present false witness,
> or in their ability to speak either the truth or fabrication.
> Moreover, the objectives of the Quran do not include
> anything that would indicate otherwise. Therefore, there
> is no evidence to suggest that there is anything other than
> equality between the sexes.

If reading between the lines doesn't work, willfully misunderstanding the meaning of a word can be even more effective. That might be the reason why the Arabic root *Dzaraba* is one of the most broadly interpreted words in the entire language. It can mean "set forth," "coin," "avoid," "cover," "compare," or even "heal." The one thing the meanings all have in common is the idea of action done for a higher purpose. For example, the word originally meant "strike" or "beat" as well, in the context of "striking a match," "beating a new path," or "striking a coin," and that's where the problem lies. A form of the word is used in a verse (An-Nisa 4:34) about how men should deal with marital conflict, and currently, the most popular English translation, by Yusuf Ali, declares the following:

> Men are the protectors and maintainers of women, because Allah has given one more (strength) than the other, and because they support them from their means. Therefore the righteous women are devoutly obedient, and guard in (the husband's) absence what Allah would have them guard. As to those women on whose part ye fear disloyalty and ill-conduct, admonish them (first), (next) refuse to share their beds, (and last) beat them (lightly): but if they return to obedience, seek not against them means (of annoyance): For Allah is Most High, Great (above you all).

Another translation by Muhammad Pickthal goes even further:

> Men are in charge of women, because Allah hath made the one of them to excel the other, and because they spend of their property (for the support of women). So good women are the obedient, guarding in secret that which Allah hath guarded. As for those from whom ye fear rebellion, admonish them and banish them to beds apart, and scourge them. Then if they obey you, seek not a way against them. Lo! Allah is ever High, Exalted, Great.

Did God really—after going to all the trouble of declaring men and women different but equal—turn around and tell Muslim men, "Oh, but you can beat your wife, if you choose"?

The Arabic of the Quran is complex and conveys its intent more like poetry than prose. Context, word choice, and the interactions between them exert a profound influence on the meaning of any passage. That makes translation of the Quran difficult and sometimes unreliable, but if deciphering written Arabic is too much of a struggle, then translations are all you have. Even if you're fluent in Arabic, it's still much easier to let others study it for you; it's always been less work swimming with the tide. For over a thousand years, most of those who've studied and interpreted the Quran have been men. Since the people they worked for were men as well, it was actually inevitable that many popular interpretations would be misogynistic, as noted by Dr. Hassan al-Turabi. When Islam was revealed through Muhammad, it literally changed the world within a generation. Since then, every generation that followed has changed the message a little bit back.

An-Nisa 34 is a good example of the result. Today, a variety of different scholars from a number of faiths and backgrounds agree that this verse says God created men superior to women. Non-Muslims even use it to try and discredit the Quran, claiming that the verse is sexist. If that were true, it would have to contradict every other Ayah where the Quran proclaims that from God's perspective men and women are equals—but it doesn't. Yusuf Ali's notes and commentary admit that An-Nisa 34 can also be read "and protect their husbands' interests in his absence as Allah has protected them." However, the reality is likely even more egalitarian. The word for "man" that An-Nisa 34 uses—*ar-Rijaalu*—evokes the lowly rank of the "foot soldier." Clearly, rather than honoring us, God has entrusted Muslim men with the duty to serve Him as *Qawwamoonas al an-Nisa,* a phrase that means "providers for and protectors of women." The verse also explains that that's not because we're superior, but only because God has promised to bless us with the resources necessary to the task. The closest English equivalent to the verb that's used in the verse (*Faddala*) is probably "graced."

Finally, in their gratitude for God's providence, Muslim women give their devout obedience to God, not their husbands. Yusuf Ali agrees that the Quran is quite clear what men get in return. Although *Qawama* implies family leadership, it doesn't mean "power and authority." In Islam, power and authority belong only to God. *Qawama* is about responsibility, and that means God gave us this passage to free women, not to subjugate them, by defining our relationship as a reciprocal one in which we each serve Allah by serving each other as equals under Him in different ways.

The way we currently interpret the rest of the verse seems to indicate that this is one of those times that even the most devout Sunnis will choose to ignore the Sunnah (practices) of the Prophet if it serves their purposes to do so. Muhammad told his followers that the best of them were those who were kindest to their spouses. He predicted that if a man lived as a tyrant in his house, Allah would only resurrect him from the waist up! In all his life, he struck one of his wives only once, when he tapped his beloved Aisha with his toothbrush. When this verse was revealed, there was no need for a verse giving men permission to beat their wives: they all thought they had that right already. It's striking that Muhammad, in his last sermon summing up his ministry, when he reviewed the rights that men and women had from each other and the manner in which he expected Muslim men to deal with marital conflict, left out any mention of "beating." Muhammad and Islam never gave that right to men, because they actually took it away instead.

There are other words that the Quran could have used to approve physical violence in marital conflict if that were God's intention. There was only one word—*idribhunna,* derived from *Dzaraba,* whose meaning in the Quran varies depending on the context, but which always implies an action undertaken for a *higher* purpose"—that could address a man's potential to engage in physical violence and put it in the context of his choice to honor his overarching responsibility to his wife and family for the sake of his eternal soul. God's choosing *idribhunna* makes a Muslim man's actions subject to the best interests of his marriage. No marriage is served by domestic violence, and while he was alive Muhammad brought domestic violence to an end. The words of the Quran, the Sunnah of Muhammad, and his commands to his Companions make it clear that even when a man is faced with the end of all his happiness, faced with tragedy and dishonor, God has given him the responsibility to ensure that anything he does serves a higher purpose than his anger and pain. That Ayah then ends with the stark warning that God is watching everything we do, and should "strike" fear into every married Muslim man's heart. However, despite that, and despite the fact that Dzaraba could also be telling us to "strike" a faithless wife out of our lives or to "strike" out on a new path ourselves, or even to "heal" the relationship in some other way, many of us have chosen to believe those religious scholars who tell us that it means we're allowed to beat our wives, as long as we don't leave visible bruises. At the rate those Muslim men are going, exposing girl babies on hillsides again isn't all that far away from them in this life, and a legless reincarnation waits for many in the next.

Tragically, many Muslim fathers have already fallen into the trap of sacrificing their daughters to something even worse. Cozying up to wife beaters is bad enough, but when did our leaders decide to pander to pedophiles? Some Muslim scholars have even made Muhammad vulnerable to that accusation, leveled by no less of an Islamic authority than Jerry Falwell in an interview on CNN's *Crossfire*. While there is no question whether Muhammad's wife Aisha was younger than he, their relationship's purpose was not to make it possible for Muslim men to marry children. Despite Falwell's claim of scholarly consensus that she was only nine, Aisha's age at the time of her marriage is an area of profound historical uncertainty. Although Sahih Bukhari records that she recalled being six when betrothed and nine when her marriage was consummated, he also records her reporting that Al-Qamar, the fifty-fourth Surah, was revealed while she was old enough to remember it. Since it was given in Mecca five years before her betrothal and more than nine years before her marriage, that observation would put her age at more than nine, unless she could remember events from the moment she was born. Furthermore, since her sister Asma, ten years older, was 100 when she died, and since it is a matter of record that Asma died more than seventy-two years after Aisha's wedding, a calculation based on those numbers puts her age at the time of her consummation at greater than seventeen!

Who pays the price when our faith leaders make false claims? When religions makes themselves more marketable by offering credulous believers a thing they want at the expense of someone else, it isn't religions that pay the price—ever. Even if it turns out there isn't any God after all, the amount of suffering that has been inflicted in the name of faith for the sake of sometimes perverse or tyrannical human desires makes the word *appalling* seem a poor, pale descriptive adjective. On the other hand, if it turns out believers are right and there *has* been a God watching us all along, the eternal consequences for what we have done will be make *dreadful* seem a pale description as well. "I was only following orders" has never been an acceptable excuse in any court of just law, particularly in a court whose judge knows the heart of the accused and knows how easy it would have been for the defendant to check those claims out for himself or herself.

Why are we here? No matter what our faith background is, that's one question every one of us struggles with. Life is certainly less complicated if there is no God behind it: however, the philosophy you'll come to from that perspective isn't a pretty one. Nihilistic hedonism has driven many to an early and guilt-ridden grave, realizing that any joy they received only came their way because it didn't go to someone else. The t-shirt philosophy "He who dies with the most toys wins" can't really be true either, no matter where you sit on the divine question. If there is no God and no life after this one, then there was no contest to win in the first place. If God gives us only this life alone, then death brings nothing but an end. With an afterlife but no deity or judgment, then having to surrender everything you've amassed sounds like more of a punishment than a prize! Why are we here, if there is a God?

I think the answer might actually be found in all that human diversity that otherwise seems to be the root of so many of our problems. Given the fact that we *are* so different, with so many different creeds, races, and colors, and two very different gender forms shared and sometimes enjoyed by all, what could God have been thinking? Al-Hujraat 49:12 proclaims:

> O mankind! We created you from a single (pair) of a male and a female, and made you into nations and tribes, that ye may know each other not that ye may despise each other. Verily the most honored of you in the sight of Allah is (he who is) the most righteous of you. And Allah has full knowledge and is well acquainted (with all things).

Could it really be that simple? The greatest and most important work of my life, and my greatest source of joy and fulfillment, is my children, who are here only because my wife and I are *not* the same. Could all the differences between all our cultures, societies, and races be meant to serve a higher purpose as well? Is God's prime command really "Vive la différence?" Seeing how badly humanity's many attempts to make people around the world more the same are going, it might be worth a try.

- Religions sometimes sell themselves by offering us something we want, but at someone else's expense.

- Before taking that advantage, believers should likely confirm those claims for themselves.

- Religions aren't the ones who pay for those mistakes, either in the short term or the long.

....

CHAPTER 25

FREUD ON FAITH

A re any of us having fun anymore? I don't think so. Even though a few of us have contrived to give ourselves a pretty good time, it's been hard on the majority, and we've managed to give both God and religion a bad name. We've also made it easy for a succession of secular philosophers to mock us for our hypocrisy. For the most part they've concluded that if religion can be used by some of us to control the rest, then manipulation has got to be its only function. Karl Marx even claimed that religion was the "opiate of the masses." It's hard to disagree with him; using belief to manipulate the masses even worked for him for a while! Religion and ideology have always been two of the best tools with which to influence people. I wonder, though—instead of claiming that that's proof that religion is a merely human contrivance, should we see it as the best single proof for the existence of God?

We really are inexplicable creatures. Part of the difficulty we have figuring out what we're supposed to do with our time on this earth is that so much of what we find ourselves doing is impossible to explain, even to ourselves! One of the most influential twentieth-century secular philosophers, Sigmund Freud, based his entire theory of our psychological construction (with its libido-driven Id) on the universal evidence of the impact that the quest for pleasure has on us, and the manner in which it can be used to explain even the most bizarre behaviors. Called the "pleasure principle," this idea basically hypothesizes that we all have inborn drives that motivate us, consciously and unconsciously, to try to return to conscious/explicit or unconscious/implicit memories of pleasure. If something feels good or makes us happy, Freud claimed, there's a part of us that can't help trying to have that something again.

His conclusions about the many-faceted nature of awareness and personality, our susceptibility to motivations that we may or may not be aware of, and the base nature of the rewards that drive us remain virtually unchallenged even today, whether you're a Freudian or not.

Freud developed the idea of the Ego—our conscious self interacting with the world around us—and came up with the "reality principle" to explain the way we behave when we choose not to do something pleasurable, either because that pleasure appears unobtainable or else because the consequences of seeking it are sufficiently severe. That led him to postulate the Superego, our Ego supervisor, whose influence explained why we would sometimes choose to forego an obvious and immediate reward for the sake of some future goal that we think might be even better. What he couldn't find a way to explain was why it was that sometimes, in the interest of things completely separate from ourselves (like countries, religions, or philosophies), some of us would choose to act in a fashion that had no hope of ever resulting in any sort of fun. He had particular difficulty explaining how, in some situations, we could do things that could result only in suffering for ourselves and everyone else, too.

Many members of Freud's generation ended up traumatized by World War I, and as a psychiatrist, Freud had to help his patients deal with it. Few Europeans were prepared for that sort of thing. Before the war's onset, Europe had been going through what was perhaps its most pleasant and civilized period ever, a time that we now call the Edwardian Era. In the late nineteenth and early twentieth centuries, social, intellectual, and economic evolution in Europe had resulted in what many felt was a golden age. The middle class had become wealthy enough to begin to enjoy their leisure, and with extra time on their hands, both they and the aristocracy began to break down barriers between countries, classes, and individuals. Ultimately, that process triggered the assassination of Archduke Ferdinand, but before that, it gave everyone a heady sense that they might have finally put the worst of the past behind them. Many hoped that civilization (and the "civilized" pleasures it promised) would help everyone to be happy and give them all a good reason to learn to live peacefully. Instead, it gave them a war that was so big and destructive, they called it the Great War—until an even bigger one came along.

World War I forced everyone living through it to realize that civilization is sometimes only skin deep and that even the most outwardly civilized people could still end up doing horrible things to each other. Freud realized that despite his pleasure principle, he had to consider another drive, one that could make apparently normal and civilized people do things that couldn't possibly result in any sort of pleasant outcome. In the war and its aftermath, he saw how horrendous we could be to each other and how little justification we needed to do awful and destructive things. To help his patients come to terms with it, he knew he needed to explain it, too.

Freud realized that the worst atrocities were committed by men acting completely contrary to their own needs and pleasures—even to the point of death—in the interests of an agenda completely divorced from their own selves. He needed to try to understand why, instead of seeking pleasure the way he thought they were supposed to, men would willingly die and take as many other men with them as they could in the name of something or someone else. He realized that such actions would extinguish the Id, home of our pleasure-seeking drive—either symbolically, by ignoring its imperatives, or in reality, by killing the entire person it lived within, body and all. He'd already concluded that all our actions were energized by an attempt to return to a pleasant state of being. He recognized the apparently universal nature of the need to submerge our selves and our priorities into something bigger than ourselves. Moreover, he concluded that it had to be a personally destructive process, motivated by a different sort of drive altogether. To explain why this would be allowed by the pleasure-seeking Id, he hypothesized something that he called the "death drive," later termed "Thanatos" by his students. Experiments with protozoan reproductive strategies—some of which were admittedly lethal for individual paramecia—suggested that this drive sought to return a person's Id to a purportedly pleasant state of nonexistence!

Most people today agree that Freud didn't believe in God. When he invented the death drive, I think he demonstrated his antireligious bias and created his most controversial hypothesis to support it. It also seems to me that he missed the point. The drive he described that motivates us to link our lives to something outside of ourselves has never been powered by an attempt to cease to exist. Rather than looking for an end to everything, the people acting under the influence of Thanatos are seeking what they believe to be the greatest pleasure of all. That's why it's able to overwhelm the other pleasure drives. The joy people receive when joining themselves to something they believe is more important than even their own lives is a profound one, and it doesn't spring from dark wells like despair or a quest to extinguish the self. When men or women take that path, they're almost always motivated by hope and the sometimes catastrophically mistaken conviction that they're becoming something greater than they were by becoming part of something greater than they are. When you look at it through their eyes, Freud's Thanatos might just be another way of describing faith.

If you examine the monuments that religion has left behind and the vast amount of time and effort that our religions managed to consume, it's obvious that faith has to be driven by something strong, universal, and fundamental, like lust or hunger. When you look at how compliant religion makes us, it's obvious that it has to plug into our psyches somewhere deep, even deeper than we have any ability to perceive or to control. Every pleasure we have is really only pleasant because it satisfies a drive. We have the drives we do because they serve an obvious biological need. The fact that we experience hunger and the way it motivates us makes sense. The compulsion we all have to eat fulfills a physical requirement that can't be safely ignored. The urge to have sex and maintain the species makes sense, too. If it weren't for the addictive pleasure it brings, the energy and time that sex consumes would be a monumental waste! Few of us would do it, and we'd be wiped out within a generation. Both drives justify their existence by the urgency and importance of the need they fill. That realization begs an obvious question, though: what is either faith or Freud's "death drive" for?

People who believe in faith believe that it's something everybody has, whether he or she believes it or not. Most of our religions say faith is a gift from God. Even those who don't believe in faith or God at all seem ready to agree that we all have a compulsion to attach ourselves to things, even to the point of submerging our own individuality. We know that the drive to do so affects virtually everything we do. We know that, based on the evidence it's left behind, faith is one of the most powerful drives that we have. Finally, we know we don't have a good alternate definition for faith. The definitions we do have tend to tell you more about what we think faith does than about what it is. Christianity stresses belief, but not everyone thinks that belief is so important. In Judaism, faith is simply obedience to the commands of God. *Emonah*, the Hebrew word for faith, combines the characteristics of trustworthiness and reliability with the act of placing trust in God and God's commands. Having Emonah simply means that God can count on you to count on God. *Iman,* the Arabic word that's translated as "faith" in English, was defined by the Prophet Muhammad as "the belief of the mind, the confirmation of the heart, and the action of the hands." All those definitions have one thing in common: whatever it is, faith is what drives us to do whatever it takes to get along with God.

If faith really were just another way to describe Freud's death drive, it would explain a lot. For one thing, it would explain why so many otherwise sane men choose to watch their favorite football team play ball rather than playing with their wives instead! The vast majority of the weird things that we all do, whether they're in the name of church, country, mosque, or even some sport that we love, derive from the inexplicable tendency we all have to inexplicable obsessions. So what is the characteristic that the objects of our interest share (apart from their ability to captivate us)? To those of us who are so enthralled, the object seems worthy of our wonder, our commitment, and our time. The fact that we make those attachments isn't something that anyone would question, but the reason we do it is hard to explain from a purely biological perspective.

If we really are nothing more than meat, skin, and bones, then the sort of power that either religious faith or Freud's death drive has over us is hard to justify. The biological drives make sense: they're necessary to maintain both our physical being and the continuity of our species. Faith and the death drive, on the other hand, are about repudiating our animal nature. Unless you honestly believe that everyone subconsciously remembers and longs for the inconceivable joys of the amoeba, there's really no way to justify thinking our Id would yield up its quest for pleasure. Also, a compulsion to transcend the Id only makes sense if there's actually something to transcendence—a state or a place to transcend to—in the first place! That would mean there must be something more: if there isn't, then the power faith wields should arguably be less than that of the biological drives. The fact that it's stronger than they are (based on the way a believer's faith can make her joyfully ignore food, sex, or even her own survival) is a good indication that there's more in store for us than what we see in this life alone. That argues strongly for the existence of an afterlife—and if there's actually one waiting for us when we die, then that makes God more likely too.

Faith, or Freud's Thanatos, might also be a hint that God isn't as dumb as we sometimes want to believe He is. Stop and consider just how unlikely it is that a God as powerful and pervasive as the God of Abraham is believed to be would actually design us and the universe in such a way as to leave important things, like the ending, up to chance. Believers often act as if the unfolding history of creation is an uncertainty. Although we might believe that God had a wonderful result in mind when He made the universe and put us all within it, we're all also very concerned that the plan has gone off the rails. Trying to explain how that would happen is where most of our religions make their greatest leaps of creativity.

Each of our religions claims that it alone is the key to getting things back on track, but that really doesn't make a lot of sense. If God really is as bright as most believers think, then it's likely He's smarter than we are. If God really is as big and all-encompassing as so many of us claim, it's unlikely that things like the eventual successful completion of "the plan," or even our own participation in it, would have been left up to chance or our own conscious volition. Faith/Thanatos is a good indication that they weren't.

The idea that God might have created us all in such a way as to be able to retain control of things actually makes a lot of sense, but it's never been very popular; we like to believe in our independence. The truth is that this idea doesn't have to offend our sensibilities, the love we have for free will, or even our need to believe that we control our own destinies—given the nature of God according to Christianity, Islam, and Judaism. Rather than being a puppet master controlling our actions from behind the scenes, that sort of God could easily have designed our universe in such a fashion that the final result wouldn't require Him manipulating our choices or actions. It may turn out that a happy ending was inevitable all along.

- **Why does religion have the power it does?**

- **The most powerful subconscious drive Freud found last was the one he understood the least.**

- **The crazy things we do when we reach for meaning outside of ourselves may be the best proof there is of God's existence.**

CHAPTER 26

....

FAITH AND PHYSICS

Believing Muslims, Christians, and Jews all agree that God made everything. By "everything," we're supposed to mean "really everything," a concept encompassing all there is of matter, space, and time. To us, before the moment of Creation, there wasn't anything at all except God, and that includes other moments. Believing that God created time means that ideas like "will be," "have been," and "about to be" should be meaningless, but we tend to use them anyway. We've always lived in a universe of cause and effect, and it's colored the way we think about everything, including God. We act as if the beginning, end, and middle of existence are distinct and related to each other by the inevitable sequence of events. If that were true, it would mean that time is more powerful than God, and none of us are supposed to think something like that!

If time is only another part of everything else that's been made, then a time-bound perspective doesn't always have to hold true for anyone, especially not for the Maker. Our universe is vast and infinite in expanse. On the other hand, it seems to have a limited number of dimensions. We directly experience four of them: length, breadth, height, and time. However, according to Dr. Michio Kaku, world-renowned superstring theorist and author of *Hyperspace* and *Parallel Worlds,* most scientists are leaning toward something more like ten or eleven dimensions. Theoretical physicists around the world are hard at work on something they call the "Theory of Everything," a way to explain how the observable universe works, all the way from subatomic particles to supernovae. String theory needs ten dimensions, while another more recent hypothesis called M-theory requires eleven; that's where the debate currently lies.

Interestingly enough, there's some justification for theologians leaning toward multiple dimensions too because of the recurring nature of the seven heavens that are so often tacked onto everything else we see. Depending on whether or not you think of the dimension of height and the sky above us as the first "heaven," if you add the six or seven heavens to the other dimensions we all know and love, you get ten or eleven too. However many there really are, it's likely that there are a finite number of them that encompass everything, and we can represent that number with the letter X. In the same way you (with your three dimensions) can look at a sheet of paper (functionally a two-dimensional surface) and see all of it at once, a God of $X+1$ dimensions would be able to experience the entirety of the universe, from its furthest physical extents to its beginning and its end, simultaneously. According to Dr. Cumran Vafa of Harvard University, there may even be a twelfth dimension that's separate from the rest, and from that perspective, the whole concept of "simultaneous" would just be the inevitable consequence of making time in the first place. If you're standing outside time, everything happens at once anyway. Furthermore, our postulated Omniscient, Omnipresent, and Omnipotent deity wouldn't be limited by intellectual capacity. I can only read one word on a page at a time. God, as God must be (if God "is"), can't be limited like that. God Most High, the Creator of the universe, to have made it all at all, would have to be able to fully perceive everything, everywhere, all the time, all at once.

A universe created by that sort of a deity couldn't be a conglomeration of points, a sequence of events, or a history. The universe of the God of Abraham, as experienced and created by Him, has to be a God-created artifact: a singular, unified, and completed work of art. The implications of that are as big as the universe itself. One thing that we can't ever seem to agree on is the role that God would play in things, whether as a participant or as an observer. However, functionally it shouldn't make any difference if God set things in motion and stepped back or if He was/is/will be interactive. I can at least imagine how to sink a pool ball into the corner pocket after a short series of bounces off of the sides by carefully managing the pool ball's initial spin, speed, and trajectory. If God needed me to die at a specific time in a specific place, and if God needed to place a certain topspin on a specific top quark one femtosecond after the instant of creation to make it happen, then God could have done so too. Furthermore, despite all the free will in the universe, I would die exactly when I had to.

Alternatively, if God wanted to make it happen in a dozen different ways and replay it each time to examine the permutations, no one else would be able to tell the difference. That's why the question of whether God's plan is unfolding as it should has got to be a nonissue. The question presupposes an inevitable sequence of cause and effect that's as binding on God as it is on the rest of us. If the universe that we live in was created, then God isn't bound at all! All of our concerns about the machinations of fate and each other are unnecessary. If we're right about God, then everything that has happened, is happening, and will happen has a place and a reason in the great unfolding. It's inevitable.

Even assuming we're right, we still don't know the purpose of the universe, and may never know, at least not until it's done. On the other hand, God's problems—the inevitable consequences of some of the decisions He made and the tools He used to overcome them—are obvious. They're part of the scientific record, there for everyone to see. The problems built into the structure of the universe are the inevitable consequence of the interaction of matter, space, and time. Even as He was creating them, God would have been limited by those characteristics inherently necessary to their function: matter has to occupy space, space without matter has to be empty, and time's got to pass to be of any use to anyone. God would have needed a good reason to make them the way He did because that left a puzzle that couldn't be ignored. The old question about what happens when an unopposable force comes upon an immovable object has always had an obvious answer: it goes around! I think that you can tell a lot about God by the path He took.

We've begun to realize that there are some awfully complicated physics needed to describe the way time, space, and matter interact. Quantum mechanics explain how a limited bunch of primary "bits" can be assembled in a lot of different ways to make a near infinity of different things, beginning at the level of the very small. It's interesting to note that at that scale, time seems able to move in both directions. So do all of the other functions of quantum space-time. Energy and matter flow into each other, and either one can suddenly spring into existence or disappear out of or into thin air. Everyone lately has been fascinated by the possibilities of "zero point energy," an apparently limitless power source that becomes available if you can tap into the fabric of space-time at the scale of the stitching. In quantum space, causes don't necessarily precede their effects, and events don't occur until they're observed! It's only when you get close to the size of things like us that everything seems to settle down and make sense.

Still assuming God's real, we might finally be in a position to notice what He's been up to. Why make something as complicated as an eleven-dimensional space-time continuum when two or three might have sufficed? When you look at a work of art, you can often discern the values and ideals of the artist, as well as what he or she is trying to get across, from the way the work's been done. I think we can figure out a lot about God just by looking at what's in front of us. Obviously, if there is a God, He's a creative Creator. You can also often discern the nature of an artisan by examining the tools he or she has used to solve problems. Carpenters use hammers. Engineers use process. Comics use their wits. Each uses something that's characteristic of who he or she is to achieve his or her goals. I think it's reasonable to look at God the same way. It all makes me wonder: why would God have chosen to do the things He's done, when there might have been easier ways to do it?

Time has got to be a pretty big conundrum from the perspective of a Creator, once He's put everything in place. The problem with time, in brief, is that matter can be either organized or random, and organized matter is much more complicated than the random variety. That difference means that making and keeping matter organized consumes energy, which is only another, different kind of matter (of the most random sort) in the first place. In a way, you can think of organized matter as being more concentrated because it contains matter, energy, and information joined together; if we're right about our physics, they're all really the same thing. In basic chemistry, when you join solutions of different compounds in different concentrations, they blend together. Everything gets gradually diluted by the rest, like ink in a pool of water. It's no different for organized, complex matter that's mixed in with everything else in the universe; given time, it's going to spread out and get diluted, too. The consequence is that matter and energy, interacting with a universe that includes time flowing in one direction from cause to effect, requires something we call entropy—the inevitable way that matter and energy both tend to become more random, less organized, and less complex as time goes by. That's a problem for a Creator, because entropy is the opposite of creation. Creation is the process of making things more complex and interesting, not less.

It would have been far simpler just to keep Creation the way it was when God first made it. The only reason a creative Creator would have chosen to put up with something as irritating as entropy would be that it gave Him something else He wanted. Whatever the reason, it has to be a good one, because if it weren't, God wouldn't have chosen to put up with it. It would have been a waste of time! It turns out there's really only one thing we know about that uses matter, space, unidirectional time, and quantum mechanics all together at once, and to us it's a very important thing. The fact that it exists at all means that it's got to be supremely important to God too, and that tells us one of the most wonderfully reassuring things that we can learn from the conjunction of science and religion. The only thing that seems to need everything working together exactly the way they do is *our consciousness of it*. That means that the most important thing in the universe, if God Who Made It All really *is*, is us! We should probably all show ourselves more respect.

Neuroscientists, philosophers, theologians, and physicists are all currently coming together in the study of consciousness, realizing that it's something they all have in common, in more ways than one. Like faith, it's something we don't have a good definition for. We know it's important: Descartes' "I think, therefore I am" makes it sound like it's at the heart of our existence, and based on our understanding of the quantum nature of the universe, it seems likely that he was right—it's at the heart of everything else's existence too.

Quantum mechanics is marvelously complicated physics, but thankfully not many of us have to worry about it. At the level of scale that we notice things, it really isn't necessary to understand anything that's going on. The explanations that require that sort of mental exertion are only necessary for questions that few of us will ever ask, dealing with things either much bigger than we can think about or much smaller than we can see. Virtually nothing that happens around us on our level of size needs either quantum functions or quantum explanations—rather than the more limited insights classical "Newtonian" physics provides—to explain the things we see happening, except perhaps that we are capable of being consciously aware that we see them happening at all. Although we still don't know much about the phenomenon of consciousness itself, there are strong indications that it is both directed and required by the very same quantum mechanical laws that explain the way things *really* work. Research into the effects of anesthesia on consciousness demonstrates that consciousness is profoundly influenced by events occurring at the scale of the very small, controlled by quantum mechanical laws. Since one of those laws states that some events don't even occur until they're consciously observed to do so, apparently a role for our consciousness has even been hardwired into the fabric of space-time! The more we learn, the more we're beginning to realize that consciousness looks like a medium-scale manifestation of the same quantum mechanics that govern the universe of the very large and the very small. That means that for some reason, our universe was/is structured in a way that promotes, encourages, and perhaps even requires our own awareness of it.

Perception requires the cause-to-effect movement of time. I've heard conscious awareness described as if it's a mirror looking inward. What that means is that consciousness is nothing more than the one who's doing the seeing actually knowing he's distinct from what he sees. When you watch a dog run across your backyard, consciousness is as simple as knowing that you're seeing it happen at all. For that, a consciousness like ours needs a consecutive event-based script to follow and a place to follow it from: hence matter, space, time, and quantum mechanics, with its mind-boggling complexities. For whatever reason, it's becoming steadily more apparent that we live in a universe that prefers it that way. Rene Descartes was right! The way the universe is constructed means it was all designed to make him think in the first place—and to ensure that he noticed he was doing it, too.

The other interesting thing about the way the quantum universe works is how it all affects the way we feel when we notice it, particularly when we pay attention. Beauty gives us joy, and honestly, there's really no good reason why it should. Just as it is for hunger, sex, and perhaps faith, pleasures are really only pleasant because they make us do something that's important in an existential way, like eating or having kids. The ability to see and appreciate beauty and elegance really doesn't satisfy any existential requirement at all, unless you happen to believe in transcendence. Finding joy in beauty is what drives us to try to create art. It encourages us to study the universe around us for the sheer joy of learning and seeing how it all works. Fulfilling as they might be, neither pursuit is really very useful. Virtually every scientist and artist out there has experienced the same difficulties trying to get funding for either pure research or creation because it's hard to prove how either of them does us any sort of pragmatic good.

Just like most of our battles with each other over religion, the conflict between religion and science has always seemed to me like another example of our arrogance. It's not science and religion that have been in conflict. Their disagreements have always been a product of our current understanding of them, and they've become heated only when we've been convinced, on one or both sides, that we're absolutely right about what we think is going on. Religion is about accepting that things are the way they are for a good reason, which we don't necessarily have to understand; science is about trying to see how that way really is. Hence, there shouldn't be any conflict between them at all. One question that they could try answering together is both existential and observational: why should we be able to notice beauty at all, and why is there so much of it? Science could be a boring, unpleasant process, and scientists could all be the most depressed, unhappy, and cynical people in the world, but they're not. The reason why is because science is never boring, and it's rarely unpleasant. Scientists are among the happiest and most fulfilled people around because they spend most of their time discovering unexpectedly beautiful, wonderful things. Look under a rock: you'll find creatures that are marvelous, diverse, and interesting, doing marvelous and interesting things in many different ways. Look at the rock, and you'll see something beautiful. Look at it more closely, and it gets even better! Nothing is ever the way that we expect it, and few things are ever the same. Look at snowflakes! Nature's solutions to problems are always different and diverse too. The only characteristics shared by everything that struggles on the side of creation and order against entropy and randomness are their diversity and that they're strikingly beautiful and elegant in their forms and functions at the same time as well. Some of us, even those of us who don't think we believe in God, might even call them creative. Whenever scientists haven't thought so, it's always turned out to be because they didn't really understand what was going on in the first place. Whenever theologians have disagreed with scientists, it's always turned out that they thought that they understood too much.

The pitched battle between scientists and theologians over the process of creation is a great example of how unnecessary that sort of controversy is; none of them were on the scene at the time of creation, but they all act as if they were. The fact is that evolution and creation aren't mutually exclusive. If you've made time, you can make as much of it as you need! God didn't have to hurry. On the other hand, there's no reason to assume that not hurrying means He didn't care. There are a lot of examples in the fossil record and everywhere else to confirm that something has been opposing entropy, and using beauty, elegance and diversity to do it. For some reason (a reason that seems to be built into the universe), we're conscious of it all, and that gives us joy—one of the greatest pleasures there is. That joy and our ability to experience beauty then drives us all to try to understand more and better how things work. It also encourages us to try to create beauty ourselves. Can that all just be a coincidence? The idea that the current state of affairs is somehow just a matter of random chance and that the vast amount of diversity and organization that we see in everything around us is somehow itself simply a matter of random reverse-entropic change seems like just a little too much of a stretch (for me). A universe that prefers any sort of consciousness seems profoundly unlikely; that it would prefer a consciousness that can perceive and appreciate its own beauty and elegance seems pretty much impossible without help.

To many people, there seems to be ample evidence to confirm both the existence of God and the idea that God is good. The series of unlikely (but not impossible) coincidences that have resulted in life, intelligence, and self-awareness—a series that makes it so mathematically improbable that my own consciousness, for example, could have had any statistical likelihood of coming into being before the universe itself comes to an end—seems to argue irrefutably for the presence of a guiding hand. The drive that so many of us call faith confirms that that hand is joined to a (figurative) heart and a mind that wants to know us all. All our collected prophetic revelations, with their wisdom, logic, and love; their inexplicable insights into science and nature and ourselves (which we are only now beginning to grasp); and their repetitive, redundant confirmations of God's core message that weaves it's way throughout each of them (despite all our own selfishly motivated efforts to obfuscate the shared nature of their truth) are all that I need to believe in them all together.

The most amazing thing about religion, particularly the religions of Christianity, Islam, and Judaism, is the precise and perfect way that they've all even predicted our current screwups. I can conclude only that whatever else He's been about, our God uses beauty and elegance to solve problems in diverse and creative ways. Beauty, diversity, and elegance permeate our universe, and the three of them working together are the reason why things are the way they are. God made us to experience them joyfully, and that joy encourages the rest of us to try using them, too.

All this means that we shouldn't lose sleep about whether anyone else agrees with us, whatever we choose to believe, because what we believe doesn't matter as much as many of us would like it to. None of us know why we're here. It might be a matter of random chance, it might be the product of conscious design, or it might be anything in between. We really have no way to be sure—even though many of us manage to convince ourselves that we're certain anyway. If it is just a massive coincidence, then there's no reason to even ask the question, let alone fight about the answer. If we're really participating in a process that's been designed to result in a specific result, then the answer probably doesn't matter either. If God was able to make the universe the way we think He did, then he was able to make it so that all events would work out properly in the end even before He started it off in the first place. When you look at everything in that light, it seems obvious that the whole thing was designed to make a happy ending inevitable. To me, "inevitable" is the signature that God left when He was done.

The good news for those of you who don't believe God exists is that that probably doesn't matter either. We still live in the same universe, and the way both it and we are put together won't change just because our understanding does. Inevitable is inevitable: our ability to experience joy in response to things like beauty, elegance, and diversity will give the secular humanists a pretty good chance of having it their way. That is, even though the drive to become better than we are and to transcend ourselves becomes inexplicable if you don't acknowledge a God to build it into us, the effect it has and always will have on us will still persist. If faith turns out to be a collectively unconscious sort of herd instinct, then eventually we'll notice that we're all in the same herd together. Sooner or later we'll have to realize that, at least as far as humanity goes, there's really no such thing as "them." In fact, the only thing that's really holding us back from that happy ending even now is us believers and what we've made of our religions—particularly the religions of Judaism, Christianity, and Islam.

- If God made the universe, He made it from beginning to end, all at once.

- That means that everything that happens is supposed to happen, and everyone who exists is supposed to exist; it doesn't mean that we know why.

- It also means that God made the universe to let us experience joy, beauty, and love.

CHAPTER 27

....

ENDINGS AND BEGINNINGS

Yᴏᴜ'd think we'd know what religion is supposed to be for by now. The English word *religion* comes from the same Latin root as *legislation,* which means that it started out the same as the word we have for *law.* In Hebrew, the word is *Derech Hashem,* meaning "the way of the name." The connotation that it guides and restricts behavior is similar to the Hebrew word for *law· halakhah,* or "the path that one walks." In Islam, the word for religion is *din,* and it also represents the path we take to fulfill our obligations to God. Once upon a time, we all knew that religion was supposed to help us control our individual selves, not give some of us control of others by controlling it instead.

If there really is an eternal life after this one—of greater consequence than our limited time in the here and now—then that explains *why* God gave us faith: to help keep that eternity a priority. If there really is a God in heaven, then the power faith wields over us explains why God gave us religion as well: to keep faith from getting out of hand. It stands to reason He would have made faith the strongest drive we have, and it's obvious that we're all far more willing to believe things than we like to admit. Without some sort of guidance, we'd all have gone off in a billion different directions centuries ago. Couple creative believing with a powerful inborn compulsion to seek out something greater and more meaningful to join ourselves to than this life alone, and you get the potential for chaos. In fact, you get the potential for exactly the sort of disruptive, argumentative religious chaos we seem to be so happily heading for today.

Every drive needs to be governed. If we eat too much, the consequences are obvious, and the same thing goes for too much sex, sex too often, or sex with too many people, no matter how much we all wish it were otherwise. Too much believing, on the other hand, doesn't have an obvious downside until things get out of hand, the way they are today. That's where religions come in. They all try to limit what we believe and guide us toward good behavior. It works pretty well as long as we don't let our beliefs take control of our religion—giving us things we want whether they're actually *good* or not—instead. When that happens, we allow ungoverned self-interest to take control of the strongest and most subliminal drive that we have! Small wonder if that results in catastrophe. Seen that way, instead of being the most important component of faith, belief might actually be the worst thing that ever happened to religion.

Muslims, Christians, and Jews should realize that if we're right, then God's overwhelming majestic greatness and the consequently inevitable nature of His plan for the universe are all the reassurance we need that it'll all end up okay. It all finally comes back to what Gamaliel said almost two thousand years ago: believers should trust God to keep track of the big picture. If God *is* as we believe Him to be, it is inevitable that each one of us has a relationship with Him. If God made everything out of nothing, it follows there is nothing beyond Him. In a way, that means we even live inside God! With God having made time as well, it also follows that everything that happens is supposed to. That then means that every one of us has been specifically taken into account and the moment of creation tweaked to make us exactly as we are. If we exist, it proves we were meant to. That we continue existing further confirms that we are supposed to as well, because otherwise we simply wouldn't. If we believe in an all-powerful Creator God, then every one of us *was* equally created and *is* equally sustained and cherished by that God, whether we believe it or not.

It's obvious what sets the faith of children apart from the faith we have when we're grown. It's not what they believe that makes their faith different, because the "what" has always been imposed by the rest of us. The younger children are, the less likely they are to know or believe anything at all. The younger children are, the more their faith is composed purely of the trust they place in the people who care for them. Despite what we'd all like to believe about believing, if faith has anything to do with trust at all, then belief has to be the opposite of what faith is for.

No matter what our working definition is, faith's function is to increase our capacity to trust, rely on, and ascribe great value to something or someone outside of ourselves, without necessarily knowing or understanding what's going to happen, what's going on, or why. That implicit, almost blind trust is exactly the aspect that is strongest in the faith of children. Their implicit trust allows them to be easily guided and led by those who care for them. By the time we reach adulthood, however, most of us realize that not knowing where we're going makes such trust seem awfully risky. Trying to somehow manage our lives ourselves based on our religion-based beliefs alleviates that risk, but at a cost. These beliefs serve to justify our actions by linking them to specific outcomes, so instead of serving faith, belief can easily become nothing more than an attempt to gain some semblance of control in our relationship with our Creator. That illusion gives belief a certain cachet, but when it manifests, our faith is inevitably degraded. The believer's decision to act out of that degraded and more measured faith rather than out of trust, obedience, gratitude, or love, becomes contaminated with economic calculations of cost vs. benefit and risk vs. reward. That turns belief into an abomination. Once we begin to believe we have that sort of power, we actually start believing we can control our God.

Whatever you believe, it's obvious that religions limit our capacity for believing in our own self-serving rationalizations. With or without God, we all share the tendency to place ourselves at the center of the universe and to believe that "I think, therefore I am" is somehow more important than "I'm okay, you're okay." We're all selfish. Accepting that simple truth—and the fact that it can only ultimately divide us from one another, inevitably and inexorably to our eventual destruction—puts us back on the road to real human unity again.

It's the awe-inspiring, immense, unimaginable, and supremely sovereign nature of God—the fact that we'll never be able to understand, explain, and manipulate Him or even prove whether He exists or not—that may finally break the power of belief and rationalization to divide us. Whatever we believe, none of us have any choice but to live our lives as best we can. If we do believe in a God as big as Muslims, Christians, and Jews believe in, then we honestly have to accept that everyone is here because he or she is supposed to be. If God is in control, that turns our lives from a meaningless series of connected events into a dialogue with the One who Created us. Our lives are a conversation with God. What happens to us is His side of the conversation; our side is the responses that we make. That means that all of us have exactly the same personal ongoing relationship with God Most High that every religious person claims is the pinnacle of human experience—whether we know it or not!

Some think of belief as the great leveler of religions; it's something that everybody can do, no matter how much or how little he or she has. By this point in the book, I hope I've made it clear that the real levelers are our choices and our reasons for making them. Everybody has to make choices, even if we choose not to believe or to do nothing. I choose to believe, and act accordingly. One of the best reasons that I can think of is that believing makes everything that happens to me more meaningful. I think most other believers will agree, but if that's true, then there are some implications we should all consider. If believing in God makes our individual lives more meaningful, it inevitably means that He is also trying to make everyone else's lives more meaningful, too. If every one of us is participating in a dialogue with our Creator, then He has to be leading all those conversations somewhere, with everyone.

There's a lot of pain and suffering out there. Some of us obviously have it a lot better than others. Some of us have virtually no alternatives to choose between in our lives. Many of us seem to have little power to affect our destinies. Most people tend to look at the vast array of human experience as if it's a sign that God plays favorites, but it might not necessarily be, at least not in the way we all think. Our prophets seem to have had a soft spot for the generosity of the ones among us who've had the least to share! If you believe in God, then you probably also believe that there is a purpose driving everything. If each of us—and everything else as well—was truly created by God for a purpose, then we each have God's (at the very least implied) assurance that whatever that purpose is, it's worth all our trouble; because if it weren't worth it, either we as individuals or else the universe as a whole wouldn't have come to exist in the first place. If we assume that's true, then we should all factor in what it might mean if everyone else had the same promise. If we do, then they do, too. The different situations that so many of us either enjoy, accept, or are forced to tolerate in this life have a very different implication if there is a God at the center of everything. Jesus' warning—"Of them who are given much, much is expected"— should probably scare the living bejesus out of anybody blessed with any alternatives and choices whatsoever. It should be particularly frightening for those among us who have been blessed (or tested) with the time for indulging in pastimes like belief. Therefore, those of us with the leisure to take comfort in our beliefs probably shouldn't be so quick to relax.

People without the time, opportunity, capacity, or inclination to believe are no different from the rest of us in the relationships they have with the Creator or the universe. We all move through the events of our days presented with alternatives. Those of us with wealth and leisure obviously find ourselves presented with a broader range of options than those of us without them. However, if we believe in God, then any self-congratulation should stop right there. Those of us who have little or nothing to share but who choose to share anyway, or those of us who are assailed by cruelty or oppression but still choose to show kindness or love, may actually be better off in the long run. The standards are going to have to be a whole lot higher for those who are thought to be the "lucky" ones. If you're a believer in God, you'd be wise to at least consider the possibility that we don't know for sure who's going to end up at the head of the line at the end, no matter how sure you are that it's going to be you.

The primary purpose of this book is to use today's versions of Islam, Christianity, and Judaism to demonstrate how little any of us can rely on the strength of our convictions to confirm the truth of what we believe. We have all fallen into the same morass: although we believe we've been following our holy books, despite what they say many of us have still found ways to believe what we choose and to do what we want. How we treat others is a good example: our faiths all command us to treat others well, but obviously that would put those who *don't* treat others well at an advantage if there wasn't a God over us keeping things fair. Most believers are more comfortable when their religion benefits them directly, and those who don't trust God often strive to ensure that any advantage remains under their control. Some of us choose to believe that belonging to the *right* religion makes us better than the rest and then use that belief to justify doing things we should know are wrong. It's surprisingly easy to find ways to interpret support for that conceit from religious texts if you already know what you want them to say. When that occurs, religious belief becomes a circular process of self-serving self-deception. If there really is a God in heaven, then trusting ourselves with control of what we believe is far riskier than simply trusting Him to keep the outcomes fair! Even if God isn't real, belief is still an awfully unreliable foundation for something as powerful as religion. Two things are certain: despite all our self-righteous self-justifications, none of our faiths can truly be used to justify killing anyone over what we or they believe about God, and none of our religions can be used to excuse murder or mayhem either. At the urging of leaders who want us to do what *they want,* many of us choose to believe otherwise, but I think our revelations have all tried to take that power away from humanity for a very good reason: belief is the problem with religion, not the solution we all want it to be. Rather than promoting our capacity for believing, every one of our religions commends kindness to others, in fidelity to our relationship with our Creator who made us all, as the necessary first step towards the path to enlightenment. Most also say that it's our kindness to others that confirms whether we remain on that path as well.

No matter what we believe, we're really all the same. Everyone wants to make the world a better place, even if some of us only want to make it better for ourselves. Everyone yearns for a happy ending, even if on the journey there some of us are led astray. Everyone struggles with cynicism and selfishness in the battle to hang on to hope and joy. We all *know* that it's better to give than to receive, even if we don't know why. No matter what we believe, we all make choices and use our hopes, expectations, and values to justify them. We all have to choose what to do from the options that are presented to us. Whether we believe in God, destiny, or random chance, we all know that we can't control what those options are. All we can decide is what we make of them and why. It's in our motivation to make those choices that we all take the same leap of faith, some of us for ourselves, but most of us for the sake of something good, whatever we believe it to be. The twists and turns of believing that we make on our way down after we make the leap—the stuff we so often like to focus on—likely don't matter as much as we think; whatever we believe, we're all joined by the certain knowledge that the outcome is out of our hands too. When we begin, we have no choice but to submit to our fate and trust in our own inevitably inadequate expectations and explanations for what that fate will be and why. At the end, we all have to accept that everything eventually comes to rest and that none of us really know what our resting places will be until we arrive.

- **If God exists, He gave us religion to help us learn to control ourselves.**

- **Instead of doing that, we've all learned how to use religion to control everyone else.**

- **No matter what, that's going to be something we regret.**

CHAPTER 28

....

IN CONCLUSION

What do the ideas I've offered in this book mean for each of us, whether we're a Muslim, Christian, or Jew? I think they mean that we should accept that we're going to be together for a while, until we finally reconcile our supposed differences. Since we don't know how long that's going to be, it might be best if we just settle in and try to enjoy the ride. If we're right and we do what our holy books and prophets have told us to do, we'll be on the right track. If we're not, it's because God doesn't exist and we're not going to win anyway! If God does exist, we might as well accept the fact that He knows what's going on, even if we don't. Muslims should remember how God answered the angels when they questioned His decision to create us in the first place, as recorded in Al-Baqara 2:30:

> Behold, thy Lord said to the angels: "I will create a vice-regent on earth." They said: "What! Wilt Thou place therein one who will make mischief therein and shed blood whilst we do celebrate Thy praises and glorify Thy Holy Name?" God said: "I know what ye know not".

We all want to make so much of the fact that we belong to the religions we do, as if membership itself confers some congratulatory award. Instead, it's entirely possible that they were chosen *for* us because of characteristics we lack or lessons we haven't learned, rather than because of any particular virtues we already possess. The paths we take to the places from which we choose to make our personal expressions of faith are the product of many forces, events, and influences outside of our control. We have each been led to where we are by the events of our lives, and if we've been guided by God, as so many of us think, our road here may well have been defined by our deficiencies. That would certainly explain why so many Christians seem so devoid of forgiveness or compassion, despite the way that Jesus stressed these virtues to his followers. It could also be the reason why Muslims often struggle so hard with things as simple as brotherhood and sisterhood, cooperation, diversity, and respect. Finally, I think it's obvious that the characteristic Judaism is supposed to help its people develop is the combined virtue of justice and generosity. As bad as some of us believers are at demonstrating the virtues our religions are trying to instill, it's striking how the best among us always end up serving as inspirational exemplars of those very traits, both for members of our own faiths and for everyone else too, regardless of which path they follow. The one common characteristic that is lacking in those who don't make that grade seems to be a little humility.

Precious as our religions are, I hope that everyone can accept this one truth: that the belief that simply belonging to them and subscribing to what they say automatically makes any of us better than the rest is just something we made up ourselves. All our current bad behavior, and our religions' failure to make us behave better, is the best proof of this that there could be. Muslims were warned we'd lose our way when we stopped loving each other and fell apart. We have. Christians were told that their wealth would drive them away from their path, and it did. Finally, despite God's laying it all out for them in the beginning of the Torah, Jews have chosen to ignore the Covenant in the one place it matters the most—Israel. We have all gone astray.

Our religions all started out simple, compelling, beautiful, and elegant. The holy books we were sent furnished a framework to guide us as we built our lives. Our originators have even shown us by their living example how to knit that structure into the fabric of our existence. Then, instead of following their advice, we've all chosen to create an entire intricate and growing tapestry of explanation, interpretation, and justification that hangs like a curtain between us and everything else. It affects all our perceptions. The thicker we've made our embellishments, the harder it's become for us to see the way things really are.

In an attempt to understand what we're here for, every one of us has created at least some of what we believe ourselves, shaping it in response to our insecurities. The more threatened we've felt, the more that's colored the result. No matter how good a job we've done, you have to admit that none of us will ever be right about everything. Even if we were, it's a mistake to think that those beliefs and explanations, created by ourselves from our own inadequate knowledge and understanding, can somehow take precedence over anything God created—that includes everyone and everything else.

We believe we're different because we want to. We choose to believe that our beliefs give us some sort of an advantage because that makes us feel more in control. But if we're right about God, then that feeling has got to be an illusion. There's no question that we're here to do different things and to play different roles, whether God's there or not. However, no matter what's going on, we're all similar enough to virtually be members of the same family. If nothing else, that probably means we should all try to get along. Parents hate it when their children fight, and no one really cares who's right or who started it. We all particularly hate it when kids try to lord it over the others because they think they're better than the rest.

Last time Jesus was here, he pointed out how foolish we're being when we focus on other people's faults and ignore our own. He talked about it in terms of dealing with the chunk of wood in your own eye before you worry about the speck of dust in your brother's. It's a good image, and if you carry it a little further, it can help explain the difficulty we have fixing our mistakes and show us how friends can help. When you've got something in your eye, it's often hard to see where or what it is. You may know something's wrong, but you can't see it because you're too close. Once you've figured out what the problem is, a little help from a friend willing to pluck it out can make it easier to deal with it, too. We can all help each other, but only if we can trust one another. Lately, we've all been enjoying each other's misfortunes a little too much for any of us to be comfortable accepting assistance. We aren't going to let anyone near our eyes if we think we're going to get them poked for our trouble!

We all have to live our lives and find our own paths. That will never give any of us the right to condemn the rest, especially given how poorly so many of us seem to understand the paths we're actually on. Finding our way would be a lot easier if we'd help each other see where we're going instead of arguing over who's going to get there first or who knows the best way to get there. We confuse "best" with "only." Some of us will certainly strike closer to the mark faster, but there's a simple, universal truth in the Holy Quran's Al-Anaam 6:108 that we should all pay attention to:

> Revile not ye those whom they call upon besides Allah, lest they out of spite revile Allah in their ignorance.

It will always be wrong to condemn others' choices just because they're not the same as yours. That just makes them more likely to do the same to you. If you're right, you've just made them even worse! Any step toward God is a step toward each other. Arguments only drive people apart. A servant of God, standing in a state of perfect submission to God and full acceptance of the world that God has created, would be able to see all the rest of us moving toward him or her. I expect that he or she would have helpful advice for the rest of us too, regardless of where any of us started out. One thing that all our great, well-respected religious mentors have had in common is that they managed to get along surprisingly well with everyone else.

Many of us have learned to distrust religion because most believers don't get along very well at all. We can't help but try to organize ourselves, but in doing so we inevitably develop criteria to keep some people in and the others out. It's difficult to leave room for honest uncertainty and hard to remember that none of us are perfect. Faith is not about being right; if it were, then the smartest of us would be the best at it, and we all know that's never been true! I hope we can all agree that faith is mostly the trust in God that impels us to act the way we think we're supposed to. If we can, that means that anyone who's trying to please our Creator (whatever the person thinks He's called) is a friend and family member, regardless of his or her beliefs. If we believe in faith, we believe that faith comes from God. It's all we have when we're born without even the capacity for belief, decision, or action, and it's all we have when we die. We know it has to be something simple and universal. We may describe it differently, but even if we don't believe in God, we all agree that, when it does anything, faith causes us to try to draw closer to Him. That inevitably drives us closer to each other as well, even if it sometimes seems only to pull us to within striking range.

If nothing else, the last four thousand years of recorded human history make it clear that it is inevitable that societies develop religious beliefs: they always have. It's also inevitable that we'll group ourselves according to those beliefs and that we'll teach them to our children. If we think we're right, how could we do otherwise? Even if we all have an inborn sense of our relationship with God, the difference between right and wrong, and the importance of choosing one over the other, that doesn't mean that's all there is to religion. There has to be a framework—if only because there has always been. No one has ever lived without belief, even if the only belief he or she has had is in him- or herself. Those of us who claim that they don't believe in anything at all are often the most rigid among us! Those of us who worship God are responding to a need we all share, but we all share a need for spiritual companions to talk things over with, too. Religions help fulfill that yearning. It's just that our creativity with them gets us into trouble sometimes.

One of the things that I appreciate about the Holy Quran, as it was originally given, is that it tells us all that everybody was given a prophet to tell him or her about God. That's always made a lot of sense to me because it never seemed fair to assume that only some of us were granted that sort of attention. And it should encourage us to listen more and communicate better. An-Nisa 4:150–152 tells us:

> Those who deny Allah and His Messengers, and (those who) wish to separate Allah from His messengers, saying: "we believe in some but reject others," and (those who) wish to take a course midway—They are in truth (equally) unbelievers; and We have prepared for unbelievers a humiliating punishment. To those who believe in Allah and His Messengers and make no distinction between any of the messengers, we shall soon give their (due) rewards: For Allah is Oft-Forgiving, Most Merciful.

Our history makes it obvious that religions are under continuous pressure to change. Truthfully, the mutative ability of consensual belief is probably the greatest threat they face! Judaism, Christianity, and Islam all prove that even religions that have textbooks need active protection. Anyone can subvert their religion, insert their own message, and manipulate the rest of us if no one remembers what the original revelation was. We believers have our work cut out for us if we want to be of any use to God. We're going to have to find a way to take back the control of our religions from those who have chosen to use the power of belief for their own purposes, and we need to be sure that they never get it back. Guarding our religions from that sort of thing can be difficult. It requires sound judgment and a good reason to make the effort. When we're young and energetic, we don't have the right perspective; when we get older, the right people rarely feel drawn to the work. Unfortunately for all of us, it's obvious that the people who are drawn to it are often those who should be trusted with it the least.

I think the responsibility to watch over all our religions and to guard them from abuse inevitably falls to those of us with children, if only because we're the only ones who really have the right motivation. If we're good parents, we love our kids and we know their hearts. I think we all know in *our* hearts what it is about their faith that makes it special, and I think we all know it's our job to protect them from people who want to abuse their trust and who pretend to know more than they actually do about anything. Instead of fighting or exchanging insults, we can help each other. For the love of our children, and no matter what our religion is, we can promise God and each other that we'll do our best to help everyone struggling to find a path, and that we'll commit to help each other remember what all our books actually say and accomplish what they say we're really here for.

In the same way that a good tool makes our work easier and better, a good religion should make it easier to act well. A bad tool just doesn't do the job as well, if it does it at all. If God is real, it's inevitable that we'll all end up having done what He intended us to do anyway. Some of us will do so well and willingly, whilst others will comply either poorly or without understanding. If God is good, it's inevitable that willing service will be rewarded. As I understand it, in the universe that God created, everything contributes to God's plan. Even the stupid stuff we do will be incapable of making creation deviate from the end that God has intended since the beginning. God would have inevitably known what we would do before the beginning began to be.

When I first began to study Islam to find the flaws I intended to use to win the arguments I was planning to have, I was surprised by how many Muslims had read the Bible. None of them were shocked by what they read, and all of them expressed confusion as to how Christianity had developed into the greedy, destructive, self-satisfied, and hypocritical religion that it's become. Likewise, I know many Christians and Jews who've read the Quran and wonder how it's made us all so hateful and bloodthirsty! We've all struggled with how Judaism, with its history of oppression and abuse, could have become a religion that justifies the oppression and abuse of others. I hope it's obvious what I think the problem is: we must diligently follow what we know is God's Word as it was written, not as others interpret it for us.

In the past, and even now in countries plagued with hunger and suffering, it's easy for those of us able to read God's Word to control the actions of those who can't. Even among the literate, it's easier to give control of one's faith and actions to a charismatic leader than it is to take responsibility oneself; however, it's not a very good idea if you really want to do what God wants. It's an especially bad idea to ascribe to a creed just because everyone else does, when so many of us have the tools to examine what the prophets actually taught. If you're only following the herds of other believers and not seeking what drives them, you'll practice only the cultural and political aspects of a religion. You may never find out that there's something very real over and above everything else. If that happens, you'll miss out on the one thing you're supposed to gain from the whole process.

This is a record of my own journey so far. One thing that I don't want to do is convince anyone to simply replace one religion with another. I hope that this book is useful and interesting to anyone who takes the time to read it, but I believe that everyone has to make his or her own path to peace with God. The first command given to Muhammad was "Iqra." In English that means "Read"! I believe that God has given us all these holy books so that they can all be read, and I encourage everyone to do so, voraciously. Read everything that you can find. If you're Jewish, Christian, or Muslim, you should pay special attention to the Torah, the Bible, and the Quran, but read them for yourselves. Make up your own mind. Pray regularly. Count on the help of God.

Don't make the mistake of trusting anyone to tell you what the holy books you read mean without checking it out for yourself. Even with the best of intentions, sometimes a scholar will begin an argument with a conclusion already in mind and study only to find verses that support it. The temptation to modify something that is "almost perfect" is understandable. There's ample evidence that that's happened repeatedly in Judaism, Christianity, and Islam, and there's little doubt that it's happened in every other religion, too. It's probably even happened to me.

The Prophet Muhammad was told in As-Shura 42:13–15:

> The same religion has He established for you as that which He enjoined on Noah—that which We have sent by inspiration to thee—and that which We enjoined on Abraham, Moses, and Jesus: Namely, that ye should remain steadfast in Religion, and make no divisions therein: To those who worship other things than Allah, hard is the (way) to which thou callest them. Allah chooses to Himself those whom He pleases, and guides to Himself those who turn (to Him).
>
> And they became divided only after knowledge reached them—through selfish envy as between themselves. And had it not been for a Word that went forth before from thy Lord,

(Tending) to a Term appointed, the matter would have been settled between them: But truly those who have inherited the Book after them are in suspicious (disquieting) doubt concerning it.

Now then, for that (reason), call (them to the Faith), and stand steadfast as thou art commanded, nor follow thou their vain desires; but say: "I believe in the Book which Allah has sent down; and I am commanded to judge justly between you. Allah is our Lord and your Lord: For us (is the responsibility for) our deeds, and for you for your deeds. There is no contention between us and you. Allah will bring us together, and to Him is (our) final goal."

Islam is not a rejection of Jesus, of what he said, or of the Bible. Christianity isn't a replacement for Judaism or a condemnation of Muslims. Jews and Judaism have both shown they can accommodate everyone else's ways just fine. We should all try to remember that the message, if it really does come from One God, must in its fundamentals be one as well. None of us are perfect. No one's going to be right about everything. If we're trying to do and believe what's right, then none of us are going to be completely wrong either. If God is good, then no matter who's right or who's wrong, in the end, it is either possible, probable, or inevitable that faith—in all its myriad manifestations—will eventually make us all one as well. Until then, let's try to be kind. Remember, God loves everyone else, too.

- **All of our religions tell us that God put us here to learn to get along.**
- **All of our religions tell us that God's even gone so far as to tell us how.**
- **We should listen.**

GO IN PEACE! SERVE THE LORD!

BIBLIOGRAPHY

Ali, Abdullah Yusuf. *Roman Transliteration of the Holy Quran with Full Arabic Text.* Lahore, Pakistan: Sheikh Muhammad Ashraf Publishers, 1979.

Ali, Abdullah Yusuf. *The Meaning of the Holy Quran: New edition with revised translation and commentary.* Brentwood, MA: Amana Corporation, 1991.

Armstrong, Karen. *A History of God: The 4,000-Year Quest of Judaism, Christianity and Islam.* New York, NY: Ballantine Books, 1993.

Armstrong, Karen. *Muhammad: A Prophet for Our Time.* New York, NY: HarperCollins Publishers, 2006.

Baqi, Fuwad Abdul. *Al-Lu-lu wal Marjan: A Collection of Agreed Upon Ahadith from Al-Bukhari and Muslim: Volumes One and Two.* Riyadh, Saudi Arabia: Dar-us-Salam Publications, 1995.

Buber, Martin. *I and Thou.* New York, NY: Touchstone Publishing, 1970.

Fox, Everett. *The Five Books of Moses.* New York, NY: Schocken Books, 1983.

Ghazali, Abu Hamid Muhammad al-. *The Incoherence of the Philosophers: A parallel English-Arabic text translated, introduced and annotated by Michael E. Marmura.* Provo, UT: Brigham Young University Press, 2000.

Goldschmidt, Arthur. *A Concise History of the Middle East: Third Edition, Revised and Updated.* Boulder, CO: Westview Press Inc., 1988.

Hanson, Kenneth. *Kabbalah: The Untold Story of the Mystic Tradition.* Tulsa, OK: Council Oak Books, 1998.

Herzl, Theodore. *The Jewish State.* New York, NY: Filquarian Publishing LLC, 2006.

Lawson, Todd. *The Crucifixion and the Qur'an.* Oxford, England: Oneworld Publications, 2009.

Makovsky, Michael. *Churchill's Promised Land: Zionism and Statecraft.* New Haven, CT: Yale University Press, 2007.

Metzger, Bruce M., and Michael D. Coogan. *The Oxford Companion to the Bible.* New York, NY: Oxford University Press Inc., 1993.

Miller, Robert J., ed. *The Complete Gospels: Annotated Scholars Version.* Sonoma, CA: Polebridge Press, 1992.

Morris, Benny. *Righteous Victims: A History of the Zionist Arab Conflict, 1881–2001.* New York, NY: Vintage Books, 2001.

New York Bible Society International. The Holy Bible: New International Version. Grand Rapids, MI: Zondervan, 1978.

Omar, Abdul Mannan. *The Dictionary of the Holy Quran (Arabic Words— English Translation).* Hockessin, DE: NOOR Foundation International Inc., 2003.

Oxford University Press: *The Oxford Annotated Apocrypha.* New York, NY: Oxford University Press, 1991.

Pappe, Ilan. *The Ethnic Cleansing of Palestine.* Oxford, England: Oneworld Publications, 2007.

Rafi, Salim bin Muhammad. *Muhammad: The Beloved of Allah.* Riyadh, Saudi Arabia: Dar-us-Salam, 1999.

Satloff, Robert. *Among the Righteous: Lost Stories from the Holocaust's Long Reach into Arab Lands.* New York, NY: Public Affairs Books, 2006.

Saunders, E. P. *The Historical Figure of Jesus.* London, England: Penguin Group, 1993.

Schlaim, Avi. *The Iron Wall: Israel and the Arab World.* New York, NY: Norton and Company, Inc., 2001.

Stacey, Tom. *The Concise Encyclopedia of Islam.* London, England: Stacey International, 1989.

Tessier, Mark. *A History of the Israeli-Palestinian Conflict.* Bloomington, IN: Indiana University Press, 1994.

Yancey, Philip. *The Jesus I Never Knew.* Grand Rapids, MI: Zondervan, 1995.

INDEX

Dr. David Liepert has been active in multifaith relations for many years. He is a member of the Canadian steering committee for the Tony Blair Faith Acts Foundation and is interfaith and media director and spokesperson for the Muslim Council of Calgary and for the Sayeda Khadija Mosque and Community Center in Toronto. The recipient of numerous community awards and a much sought-after speaker, he is also vice president of the Faith of Life Network—an internationally recognized Muslim organization dedicated to helping diverse communities live together.

Dr. Liepert holds degrees and fellowships from the University of Saskatchewan, the University of British Columbia, and Stanford University in California. He converted to the Muslim faith sixteen years ago. An anesthesiologist and specialist in intensive care medicine, David Liepert currently lives with his wife and children in Calgary.